T0235942

Lecture Notes in Artificial Intelligence   12277

Subseries of Lecture Notes in Computer Science

More information about this series at http://www.springer.com/series/1244

Mehwish Alam · Tanya Braun ·
Bruno Yun (Eds.)

Ontologies and Concepts in Mind and Machine

25th International Conference
on Conceptual Structures, ICCS 2020
Bolzano, Italy, September 18–20, 2020
Proceedings

 Springer

Editors
Mehwish Alam ⓘD
FIZ Karlsruhe – Leibniz Institute for
Information Infrastructure
Karlsruhe, Germany

Tanya Braun ⓘD
Institute of Information Systems
University of Lübeck
Lübeck, Germany

Bruno Yun ⓘD
Department of Computing Science
University of Aberdeen
Aberdeen, UK

ISSN 0302-9743   ISSN 1611-3349 (electronic)
Lecture Notes in Artificial Intelligence
ISBN 978-3-030-57854-1   ISBN 978-3-030-57855-8 (eBook)
https://doi.org/10.1007/978-3-030-57855-8

LNCS Sublibrary: SL7 – Artificial Intelligence

This Springer imprint is published by the registered company Springer Nature Switzerland AG
The registered company address is: Gewerbestrasse 11, 6330 Cham, Switzerland

Preface

The 25th edition of the International Conference on Conceptual Structures (ICCS 2020) took place in Bozen-Bolzano, Italy, during 18–20 September, 2020, under the title "Ontologies and Concepts in Mind and Machine." Since 1993, ICCS has been an yearly venue for publishing and discussing new research methods along with their practical applications related to conceptual structures. This year ICCS was one of the 10 different conferences in the Bolzano Summer of Knowledge (BOSK 2020), which spanned over the course of two weeks. Each of these conferences complemented each other on a broad range of disciplines such as Philosophy, Knowledge Representation, Logic, Conceptual Modeling and Ontology Engineering, Medicine, Cognitive Science, and Neuroscience. Due to the global COVID-19 pandemic, the conference was moved to a virtual venue, with tutorials, keynotes, and research presentations taking place online to provide a safe environment for participants from around the world.

The topics of this year's conference range from Formal Concept Analysis to Decision Making, from Machine Learning to Natural Language Processing, all unified by the common underlying notion of conceptual structures. The call asked for regular papers reporting on novel technical contributions, short papers describing ongoing work or applications, and extended abstracts highlighting the visions and open research problems. Overall, 27 submissions were received out of which 24 were accepted for reviewing. The committee decided to accept 10 regular papers, 5 short papers, and 1 extended abstract which corresponds to an acceptance rate of 59%. Each submission received three to four reviews, with 3.625 reviews on average. In total, our Program Committee members, supported by four additional reviewers, delivered 87 reviews. The review process was double-blind, with papers anonymized for the reviewers and reviewer names unknown to the authors. For the first time, we organized a bidding on papers to ensure that reviewers received papers within their field of expertise. The response to the bidding process allowed us to assign each paper to reviewers who had expressed an interest in reviewing a particular paper. The final decision was made after the authors had a chance to reply to the initial reviews via a rebuttal to correct factual errors or answer reviewer questions. We believe this procedure ensured that only high-quality contributions were presented at the conference. We are delighted and proud to announce that this year's program included two tutorials, "Mathematical Similarity Models" by Moritz Schubert and Dominik Endres (Philipps-Universität Marburg, Germany) as well as "FCA and Knowledge Discovery" by Amedeo Napoli (Université de Lorraine, France). Two keynote talks were also held during the conference: "Towards Ordinal Data Science" by Gerd Stumme (University of Kassel, Germany) and "Compositional Conceptual Spaces" by Sebastian Rudolph (TU Dresden, Germany). Note that this volume provides the extended abstracts of all the tutorials and the keynote talks.

As general chair and program chairs, we would like to thank our speakers for their inspiring and insightful talks. Our thanks also go out to the local organization of BOSK who provided support in terms of registration and setting up a virtual conference. We would like to thank the Program Committee members and additional reviewers for their work. Without their substantial voluntary contribution, it would not have been possible to set up such a high-quality conference program. We would also like thank EasyChair for their support in handling submissions and Springer for their support in making these proceedings possible. Our institutions, the Leibniz Institute for Information Infrastructure Karlsruhe, Germany, the University of Lübeck, Germany, and the University of Aberdeen, UK, also provided support for our participation, for which we are grateful. Last but not least, we thank the ICCS Steering Committee for their ongoing support and dedication to ICCS.

July 2020

Mehwish Alam
Tanya Braun
Bruno Yun

Organization

Steering Committee

Madalina Croitoru	University of Montpellier, France
Dominik Endres	Philipps-Universitat Marburg, Germany
Ollivier Haemmerlé	University of Toulouse-Mirail, France
Uta Priss	Ostfalia University, Germany
Sebastian Rudolph	TU Dresden, Germany

Program Committee

Mehwish Alam	Leibniz Institute for Information Infrastructure Karlsruhe, Germany
Bernd Amann	Sorbonne University, France
Moulin Bernard	Laval University, Canada
Tanya Braun	University of Lübeck, Germany
Peggy Cellier	IRISA, INSA Rennes, France
Peter Chapman	Edinburgh Napier University, UK
Dan Corbett	Optimodal Technologies, LLC, USA
Olivier Corby	University of Côte d'Azur, France
Diana Cristea	Babes-Bolyai University, Romania
Madalina Croitoru	University of Montpellier, France
Licong Cui	The University of Texas Health Science Center at Houston, USA
Harry Delugach	University of Alabama, Huntsville, USA
Florent Domenach	Akita International University, Japan
Dominik Endres	University of Marburg, Germany
Jérôme Euzenat	University of Grenoble Alpes, France
Raji Ghawi	TU Munich, Germany
Marcel Gehrke	University of Lübeck, Germany
Ollivier Haemmerlé	University of Toulouse-Mirail, France
Dmitry Ignatov	National Research University Higher School of Economics, Russia
Hamamache Kheddouci	Claude Bernard University Lyon 1, France
Leonard Kwuida	Bern University of Applied Sciences, Switzerland
Jérôme Lang	Paris Dauphine University, France
Natalia Loukachevitch	Moscow State University, Russia
Pierre Marquis	Artois University, France
Philippe Martin	University of La Réunion, France
Franck Michel	University of Côte d'Azur, France
Amedeo Napoli	University of Lorraine, France

Sergei Obiedkov	National Research University Higher School of Economics, Russia
Nir Oren	University of Aberdeen, UK
Nathalie Pernelle	University of Paris-Sud, France
Heather D. Pfeiffer	Akamai Physics, Inc., USA
Simon Polovina	Sheffield Hallam University, UK
Uta Priss	Ostfalia University, Germany
Marie-Christine Rousset	University of Grenoble Alpes, France
Sebastian Rudolph	TU Dresden, Germany
Christian Sacarea	Babes-Bolyai University, Romania
Fatiha Saïs	University of Paris-Saclay, France
Diana Sotropa	Babes-Bolyai University, Romania
Iain Stalker	The University of Manchester, UK
Gerd Stumme	University of Kassel, Germany
Srdjan Vesic	Artois University, France
Serena Villata	CNRS, France
Bruno Yun	University of Aberdeen, UK

Additional Reviewers

Rashmie Abeysinghe	University of Kentucky, USA
Dominik Dürrschnabel	University of Kassel, Germany
Maximilian Stubbemann	University of Kassel, Germany
Fengbo Zheng	University of Kentucky, USA

Abstracts of Keynote Talks

Towards Ordinal Data Science

Gerd Stumme

Knowledge & Data Engineering Group, Department of Electrical Engineering
and Computer Science and Research Center for Information System Design
(ITeG), University of Kassel, Germany
https://www.kde.cs.uni-kassel.de/stumme

Order is a predominant paradigm for perceiving and organizing our physical and social environment, to infer meaning and explanation from observation, and to search and rectify decisions. For instance, we admire the highest mountain on earth, observe pecking order among animals, schedule events in time, and organize our collaborations in hierarchies. The notion of order is deeply embedded in our language, as every adjective gives rise to a comparative (e.g., better, more expensive, more beautiful). Furthermore, specific technical and social processes have been established for dealing with ordinal structures, e.g., scheduling routines for aircraft take-offs, first-in-first out queuing at bus stops, deriving the succession order as depth-first linear extension of the royal family tree, or discussing only the borderline cases in scientific programme committees. These processes, however, are rather task-specific.

In many cases, entities can be ordered through real-valued valuation functions like size or price. This process of quantification has been boosted by different factors, including *i*) the development of scientific measuring instruments since the scientific revolution, *ii*) the claim that the social sciences should use the same numerical methods which had been successful in natural sciences, and *iii*) nowadays by the instant availability of an enormous range of datasets to almost all aspects of science and everyday life. As real numbers constitute an ordered field, i.e., a field equipped with a linear order, the analysis of such data benefits from the existence of the algebraic operators of fields (addition, substraction, multiplication, division, and the existence of 0 and 1) together with total comparability (i.e., every pair of its elements is comparable) —a combination that allows for various measures of tendency (such as mean, variance, and skewness) as well as for a variety of transformations. If more than one real-valued dimension is present, this yields to a real vector space (as Cartesian product of the field of reals), which results in a multitude of additional descriptive measures and metric properties, such as volumes, angles, correlation, covariance. This is the standard setting for the majority of data analysis and machine learning models, and many algorithms (eg *k*-Means clustering, logistic regression, neural networks, support vector machines, to name just a few) have been developed for these tasks.

However, organizing hierarchical relationships by means of numerical values is not always adequate, as this kind of organization presupposes two important conditions: *i*) every pair of entities has to be comparable, and *ii*) the sizes of differences between numerical values are meaningful and thus comparable. In many situations, however, this is not the case: (*i*) does not hold, for instance, in concept hierarchies ('mankind' is neither a subconcept nor a superconcept of 'ocean') nor in organizations (a member of parliament is neither above nor below a secretary of state); and (*ii*) does not hold, for instance, in school grades (In the German school system, is the difference between 1 (very good) and 2 (good) equal to the difference between 4 (sufficient) and 5 (insufficient/fail)?) nor in organisations (In the European Commission, is an advisor closer to a deputy director general than a head of group to a director?).

To address such variations of data types, S. S. Stevens has distinguished four levels of measurement: nominal, ordinal, interval, and ratio.[1] For data on the ratio level (e.g., height), all above-mentioned operations are allowed (division, for instance, provides ratios). Data on the interval level (e.g., temperature measured in Celsius or Fahrenheit) do not have a meaningful zero as point of reference and thus do not allow for ratios, while the comparison of differences is still meaningful. Ordinal data (e.g., the parent relation) only allow for comparisons, and nominal data (e.g., eye color) only for determining equality.

Although there is a large range of preliminary work, Ordinal Data Science is only just emerging as distinct research field. It focusses on the development of data science methods for ordinal data, as they lack the large variety of methods that have been developed for other data types. To this end, we define *ordinal data* as sets of entities ('data points') together with one or more order relations, i.e., binary relations that are reflexive, transitive and anti-reflexive (or variations thereof, such as quasiorders or weak orders). Ordinal data belong thus to the large family of relational data which have received high interest of the computer science community in the last years, due to developments in related fields such as sociology ("relational turn"), genetics or epidemiology, and socio-technical developments such as the rise of online social networks or knowledge graphs. This means that, for the analysis of ordinal data, one can benefit from all kinds of measures and methods for relational data, as for instance centrality measures and clustering algorithms for (social) network data or inductive logic programming or statistical relational learning from the field of relational data mining. The specific structure of ordinal data, however, allows additionally to tap on the rich – but up to date mostly unexploited for data science – toolset of mathematical order theory and lattice theory. In this talk, we present selected first approaches.

---

[1] S. S. Stevens: On the Theory of Scales of Measurement. In: Science 103.2684 (1946), 677. https://doi.org/10.1126/science.103.2684.677. eprint: https://science.sciencemag.org/content/103/2684/677.full.pdf.

Compositional Conceptual Spaces

Sebastian Rudolph🆔

Computational Logic Group, TU Dresden, Germany
sebastian.rudolph@tu-dresden.de

It has often been argued that certain aspects of meaning can or should be represented geometrically, i.e., as conceptual spaces [6]. *Vector space models* (VSMs) have existed for some time in natural language processing (NLP) and recently regained interest under the term *(vector space) embeddings* in the context of deep learning. It was shown that the *principle of distributionality* [4], according to which "a word is characterized by the company it keeps" – implying that words occurring in similar contexts bear similar meanings –, can serve as a powerful and versatile paradigm for automatically obtaining word-to-vector mappings from large natural language corpora.

While distributional VSMs and the techniques for acquiring them (such as word2vec [7]) have shown to perform very well for tasks related to semantic similarity and other relations between singular words, the question how to lift this approach to larger units of language brings about new challenges.

The *principle of compositionality*, going back to Frege [5], states that the meaning of a complex language construct is a function of its constituents' meanings. A significant body of work in computational linguistics deals with the question if and how the principle of compositionality can be applied to geometrical models. For VSMs, a variety of potential vector-composition operations have been proposed and investigated. Many of those, including the most popular ones (vector addition and component-wise multiplication), are commutative and therefore oblivious to the order of words in a given phrase.

Around a decade ago, *compositional matrix space models* (CMSMs) were proposed as a unified framework of compositionality [8]. CMSMs map words to quadratic matrices and use matrix multiplication as the one and only composition operation. Next to certain plausibility arguments in favor of CMSMs, it was shown that they are capable of emulating many of the common vector-based composition functions.

During the past ten years, more results have been obtained regarding the learnability of CMSMs and their feasibility for practical NLP tasks [1–3, 9]. Among others, it has been demonstrated that CMSMs can capture sentiment analysis tasks using matrices of very low dimensionality, correctly modelling word-order sensitive phenomena (like the different intensities in the phrases "not really good" and "really not good"). Moreover, they can be successfully applied to distinguish idiomatic phrases (such as "couch potato") from compositional ones (such as "stomach pain").

This keynote provides an introduction into CMSMs and gives an overview of their theoretical and practical aspects.

Acknowledgements. Over the years, I have collaborated on the subject with several colleagues. I am particularly thankful to Eugenie Giesbrecht, Shima Asaadi, and Dagmar Gromann.

References

1. Asaadi, S.: Compositional Matrix-Space Models: Learning Methods and Evaluation. Ph.D. thesis, TU Dresden (2020)
2. Asaadi, S., Rudolph, S.: On the correspondence between compositional matrix-space models of language and weighted automata. In: Jurish, B., Maletti, A., Würzner, K.M., Springmann, U. (eds.) Proceedings of the SIGFSM Workshop on Statistical NLP and Weighted Automata (StatFSM 2016), pp. 70–74. Association for Computational Linguistics (2016)
3. Asaadi, S., Rudolph, S.: Gradual learning of matrix-space models of language for sentiment analysis. In: Blunsom, P., et al. (eds.) Proceedings of the 2nd Workshop on Representation Learning for NLP (RepL4NLP 2017), pp. 178–185. Association for Computational Linguistics (2017)
4. Firth, J.R.: A synopsis of linguistic theory 1930-55. Studies in linguistic analysis 1952–1959, pp. 1–32 (1957)
5. Frege, G.: Die Grundlagen der Arithmetik: eine logisch-mathematische Untersuchung über den Begriff der Zahl. W. Koebner, Breslau, Germany (1884)
6. Gärdenfors, P.: Conceptual Spaces: the Geometry of Thought. MIT Press, Cambridge (2000)
7. Mikolov, T., Chen, K., Corrado, G., Dean, J.: Efficient estimation of word representations in vector space. In: International Conference on Learning Representations (ICLR 2013) (2013)
8. Rudolph, S., Giesbrecht, E.: Compositional matrix-space models of language. In: Hajic, J., Carberry, S., Clark, S. (eds.) Proceedings of the 48th Annual Meeting of the Association for Computational Linguistics (ACL 2010), pp. 907–916. Association for Computational Linguistics (2010)
9. Yessenalina, A., Cardie, C.: Compositional matrix-space models for sentiment analysis. In: Barzilay, R., Johnson, M. (eds.) Proceedings of the 2011 Conference on Empirical Methods in Natural Language Processing (EMNLP 2011), pp. 172–182. Association for Computational Linguistics (2011)

Tutorial Abstracts

FCA and Knowledge Discovery

Tutorial at ICCS 2020

Amedeo Napoli

Université de Lorraine, CNRS, Inria, LORIA, 54000 Nancy, France
`Amedeo.Napoli@loria.fr`

1 Introduction and Motivation

In this tutorial we will introduce and discuss how FCA [1, 2, 4, 5] and two main extensions, namely Pattern Structures [3, 7] and Relational Concept Analysis (RCA) [9], can be used for knowledge discovery purposes, especially in pattern and rule mining, in data and knowledge processing, data analysis, and classification. Indeed, FCA is aimed at building a concept lattice starting from a binary table where objects are in rows and attributes in columns. But FCA can deal with more complex data. Pattern Structures allow to consider objects with descriptions based on numbers, intervals, sequences, trees and general graphs [3, 6]. RCA was introduced for taking into account relational data and especially relations between objects [9]. These two extensions rely on adapted FCA algorithms and can be efficiently used in real-world applications for knowledge discovery, e.g. text mining and ontology engineering, information retrieval and recommendation, analysis of sequences based on stability, semantic web and classification of Linked Open Data, biclustering, and functional dependencies.

2 Program of the tutorial

The tutorial will be divided in three main parts, including (i) the basics of FCA, (ii) the processing of complex data with Pattern Structures and Relational Concept Analysis, and (iii) a presentation of some applications about the mining of linked data, the discovery of functional dependencies, and some elements about biclustering. A tentative program is given here below.

– Introduction to Formal Concept Analysis (basics and examples): formal context, Galois connections, formal concept, concept lattice, and basic theorem of FCA.
– Reduced notation, conceptual scaling for non binary contexts, implications and association rules in a concept lattice.
– Algorithms for computing formal concepts and the associated concept lattice, complexity of the design process, building and visualizing concept lattices.
– Measures for selecting interesting concepts in the concept lattice [8].
– Basics on Pattern Structures for mining complex data, the example of numerical and interval data, pattern concepts and pattern concept lattice.

- Elements on Relational Concept Analysis, relational context family, relational concepts and relational concept lattice.
- Applications: mining definitions in linked data, mining functional dependencies, biclustering, hybrid Knowledge Discovery.

3   Conclusion

FCA is nowadays gaining more and more importance in knowledge and data processing, especially in knowledge discovery, knowledge representation, data mining and data analysis. Moreover, our experience in the domain shows that FCA can be used with benefits in a wide range of applications, as it also offers very efficient algorithms able to deal with complex and possibly large data.

In addition, interested researchers have the possibility to attend the two main Conferences, International Conference on Concept Lattices and Applications (CLA) and International Conference on Formal Concept Analysis (ICFCA). Moreover, a companion workshop, namely FCA4AI, is regularly organized by Sergei O. Kuznetsov, Amedeo Napoli and Sebastian Rudolph (see http://fca4ai.hse.ru/). This year, we have the eighth edition of the the FCA4AI workshop co-located with the ECAI 2020 Conference at the end of August 2020. The whole series of the proceedings of the seven preceding workshops is available as CEUR proceedings (again see http://fca4ai.hse.ru/).

References

1. Belohlavek, R.: Introduction to Formal Concept Analysis. Research report. Palacky University, Olomouc (2008). http://belohlavek.inf.upol.cz/vyuka/IntroFCA.pdf
2. Claudio Carpineto and Giovanni Romano. Concept Data Analysis: Theory and Applications. Wiley Chichester (2004)
3. Ganter, B., Kuznetsov, S.O.: Pattern structures and their projections. In: Delugach, H.S., Stumme, G. (eds.) ICCS 2001. LNCS, vol 2120, pp. 129–142. Springer, Heidelberg (2001). https://doi.org/10.1007/3-540-44583-8_10
4. Ganter, B., Obiedkov, S.A.: Conceptual Exploration. Springer, Heidelberg (2016). https://doi.org/10.1007/978-3-662-49291-8
5. Ganter, B., Wille, R.: Formal Concept Analysis. Springer, Heidelberg (1999). https://doi.org/10.1007/978-3-642-59830-2
6. Kaytoue, M., Codocedo, V., Buzmakov, A., Baixeries, J., Kuznetsov, S.O., Napoli, A.: Pattern structures and concept lattices for data mining and knowledge processing. In: Bifet, A., et al. (eds.) ECML PKDD 2015. LNCS, vol. 9286, pp. 227–231 (2015). Springer, Cham. https://doi.org/10.1007/978-3-319-23461-8_19
7. Kaytoue, M., Kuznetsov, S.O., Napoli, A., Duplessis, S.: Mining gene expression data with pattern structures in formal concept analysis. Inf. Sci. **181**(10), 1989–2001 (2011)
8. Kuznetsov, S.O., Makhalova, TP.: On interestingness measures of formal concepts. Inf. Sci. 442–443:202–219 (2018)
9. Rouane-Hacene, M., Huchard, M., Napoli, A., Valtchev, P.: Relational concept analysis: mining concept lattices from multi-relational data. Ann. Math. Artif. Intell. **67**(1), 81–108 (2013)

Mathematical Similarity Models in Psychology

Moritz Schubert and Dominik Endres

Philipps University Marburg, Marburg, Germany
{moritz.schubert,dominik.endres}@uni-marburg.de

Similarity assessment is among the most essential functions in human cognition. It is fundamental to imitation learning, it plays an important role in categorization and it is a key mechanism for retrieving contents of memory.

Hence, the description and explanation of human similarity perception is a pertinent goal of mathematical psychology. In the following, we will outline three of the most relevant kinds of mathematical similarity models: Geometric (Sect. 1.1), featural (Sect. 1.2) and structural (Sect. 1.3) models. These models not only differ in their mathematical details, but also in the way they represent objects as cognitive concepts. Finally, we will discuss the assessment of human stimulus representations, a crucial issue for the empirical evaluation of similarity models.

1 Similarity Models

1.1 Geometric Models

Geometric models Shepard (1962) conceptualize similarity as distances, implying that object concepts can usefully be thought of as points in an imaginary multidimensional Euclidean space. As distances, similarity ratings would have to adhere to the metric axioms: 1) *minimality*, i.e. $s(a, b) \geq s(a, a) = 1$, 2) *symmetry*, i.e. $s(a, b) = s(b, a)$ and 3) *triangle inequality*, i.e. $s(a, c) \leq s(a, b) + s(b, c)$, where s is a real number in the range $[0, 1]$ representing a similarity measure and $\{a, b, c\}$ are objects. Intuitively, all of these seem to hold for similarity (e.g. in favor of triangle inequality, if a and b are very similar and b and c are very similar, it stands to reason that a and c are not all that dissimilar).

An advantage of this group of models is that many stimuli can easily be represented as points on one or several dimensions (e.g. colors with the RGB dimensions).

1.2 Featural Models

Tversky (1977) criticized the use of metric axioms for explaining similarity: In confusability tasks participants tend to identify some letters more often as certain distractor letters than as themselves, a finding that is in direct contradiction with minimality. The empirical result that $s(o, p) > s(p, o)$ often holds in cases where o and p belong to the same category, but p is more prototypical for the category than o (e.g. an ellipse is more similar to a circle than a circle is to an ellipse) provides evidence against symmetry. Finally, plausible counter-examples can be brought against the triangle inequality (e.g.

a pineapple is similar to a melon, because they are both exotic fruits, and a melon is similar to a beach ball, because of its shape, but a pineapple is not at all similar to a beach ball).

As an alternative, Tversky (1977) proposed to represent objects as sets of features. His *contrast model* states $s(a, b) > s(c, d)$ whenever $A \cap B \supset C \cap D$, $A - B \subset C - D$ and $B - A \subset D - C$, where the capital letters represent sets of features of the small lettered objects. Tversky ensured that his scale s is totally ordered through the *solvability* axiom, which, given a set of objects, postulates the existence of new objects with specific feature sets to ensure that any two stimuli can be ordered. However, having to invent imaginary stimuli whenever carrying out a similarity comparison seems to be an implausibly inefficient process for the mind.

Another featural model, the GLW model (Geist et al. 1996) offers a solution to this problem by situating similarity ratings in a partial order, i.e. introducing the option of not being able to determine the ranking of two object pairs. This can be interpreted psychologically as the two object pairs being incomparable (e.g. asking whether a parrot is more similar to a bicycle than a toothbrush is to a car seems like an unanswerable question). The GLW model adds one statement to the set of conditions under which $s(a, b) > s(c, d)$: $\overline{A \cup B} \supset \overline{C \cup D}$, where $\overline{A \cup B}$ are all the features under consideration that are neither part of a nor b. This new condition is supposed to account for the context under which the similarity comparison is carried out. However, an empirical evaluation of the GLW model (Schubert and Endres 2018) suggests that the requirement of all four conditions being fulfilled is too strict and that as a result the model makes very few predictions, strongly reducing its usefulness.

1.3 Structural Models

While representing objects as sets of features is a very versatile approach, it is also possible to derive representations based on relations more directly. *Structural models* (e.g. (Falkenhainer et al. 1989)) try to remedy this shortcoming by giving objects structured representations which state the type of relationship between features (e.g. the two features "pillars" and "roof" in the "cathedral" concept might be connected through a "supports" relationship). In this view, the similarity between two stimuli is the degree to which their two structural representations align which each other (e.g. by encompassing the same features and/or the same relationships).

2 Assessment of Stimulus Representation

For a similarity model to explain human similarity perception, it needs to be able to predict human behavior. One way to test this is to feed participants' cognitive representations of objects into a model as input and see whether the similarity ratings output by the model match the ones given by participants. The inherent challenge in this approach is finding a sufficiently accurate representation of the participants' cognitive stimulus representations.

One approach are *latent variable models* (LVMs) that try to extract the latent parameters underlying participants' similarity ratings. For geometric models, a commonly used LVM is the nonmetric *multidimensional scaling* (MDS) approach described by Shepard (1962). In this procedure, the points representing the stimuli are being iteratively rearranged until the inverse ranking of the distances between them corresponds (as closely as possible) to the ranking of the similarity ratings. Since for N stimuli this can trivially be accomplished in $N - 1$ dimensional space, an additional requirement of the solution is that it uses as few dimensions as possible.

One LVM used for featural models is additive clustering (Navarro and Griffiths 2008), a type of clustering that allows an object to belong to multiple clusters. Hence, the clusters can be interpreted as features of the objects. In order to be psychologically useful, the output of LVMs has to be filled with meaning, e.g. the dimensions produced by MDS have to be named. Ideally, this is done by the participants themselves.

An alternative to LVMs is to ask the participants directly about their cognitive concepts. For example, for featural models participants could be asked to type a certain number of words they would use to describe a stimulus. While direct approaches might make fewer assumptions than LVMs, for non-featural models they ask participants to think in unduly abstract ways (e.g. having to arrange objects in a two-dimensional space).

References

Falkenhainer, B., Forbus, K.D., Gentner, D.: The structure-mapping engine: algorithm and examples. Artif. Intell. **41**(1), 1–63 (1989). https://doi.org/10.1016/0004-3702 (89)90077-5

Geist, S., Lengnink, K., Wille, R.: An order-theoretic foundation for similarity measures. In: Lengnink, K. (ed.) Formalisierungen von Ähnlichkeit Aus Sicht Der Formalen Begriffsanalyse, pp. 75–87. Shaker Verlag (1996)

Navarro, D.J., Griffths, T.L.: Latent features in similarity judgments: a nonparametric bayesian approach. Neural Comput. **20**(11), 2597–2628 (2008). https://doi.org/10. 1162/neco.2008.04-07-504

Schubert, M., Endres, D.: Empirically evaluating the similarity model of Geist, Lengnink and Wille. In: Chapman, P., Endres, D., Pernelle, N. (eds.) ICCS 2018. LNCS, vol. 10872, pp. 88–95 (2018). Springer, Cham. https://doi.org/10.1007/978-3-319-91379-7_7

Shepard, R.N.: The analysis of proximities: multidimensional scal-ing with an unknown distance function. I. Psychometrika **27**(2), 125–140 (1962). https://doi.org/10.1007/bf02289630

Tversky, A.: Features of similarity, **84** (4), 327–352 (1977). https://doi.org/10.1037/0033-295x.84.4.327

Contents

Reasoning Models

Knowledge Bases

A Formalism Unifying Defeasible Logics and Repair Semantics for Existential Rules

Abdelraouf Hecham[1], Pierre Bisquert[2(✉)], and Madalina Croitoru[1]

[1] INRIA GraphIK, Université de Montpellier, Montpellier, France
{hecham,croitoru}@lirmm.fr
[2] IATE, INRA, INRIA GraphIK, Montpellier, France
pierre.bisquert@inrae.fr

Abstract. Two prominent ways of handling inconsistency provided by the state of the art are repair semantics and Defeasible Logics. In this paper we place ourselves in the setting of inconsistent knowledge bases expressed using existential rules and investigate how these approaches relate to each other. We run an experiment that checks how human intuitions align with those of either repair-based or defeasible methods and propose a new semantics combining both worlds.

1 Introduction

Conflicts in knowledge representation cause severe problems, notably due to the principle of explosion (from falsehood anything follows). These conflicts arise from two possible sources: either the facts are incorrect (known as *inconsistence*), or the rules themselves are contradictory (known as *incoherence*). In order to preserve the ability to reason in presence of conflicts, several approaches can be used, in particular Defeasible Logics [8,18] and Repair Semantics [16]. These two approaches stem from different needs and address conflicts in different ways. A key difference between defeasible logics and Repair Semantics is that the first was designed for incoherence while the latter was designed for inconsistence. However, since inconsistence is a special type of incoherence [11], defeasible logics can be applied to inconsistent but coherent knowledge, and thus be compared to the Repair Semantics. In this paper we want to investigate how the different intuitions of defeasible logics and Repair Semantics relate to each other. In order to attain the above mentioned objective, we make use of a combinatorial structure called Statement Graph [13]. Statement Graphs have been defined as way to reason defeasibly with existential rules using forward chaining. The reasoning is based on labeling functions shown to correspond to various flavors of Defeasible Logics. This paper proposes a new labeling for Repair Semantics and paves the way to combine both conflict-tolerant approaches in one unifying formalism.

© Springer Nature Switzerland AG 2020
M. Alam et al. (Eds.): ICCS 2020, LNAI 12277, pp. 3–17, 2020.
https://doi.org/10.1007/978-3-030-57855-8_1

2   Logical Language

We consider a first order language L with constants but no other function symbol composed of formulas built with the usual quantifiers ($\exists, \forall$) and the connectives ($\rightarrow, \wedge$), on a vocabulary constituted of infinite sets of predicates, constants and variables. A *fact* is a ground atom (an atom with only constants) or an existentially closed atom. An existential *rule* (a.k.a. a tuple generating dependency) r is a formula of the form $\forall \boldsymbol{X}, \boldsymbol{Y} \; \big(\mathcal{B}(\boldsymbol{X}, \boldsymbol{Y}) \rightarrow \exists \boldsymbol{Z} \; \mathcal{H}(\boldsymbol{X}, \boldsymbol{Z}) \big)$ where $\boldsymbol{X}, \boldsymbol{Y}$ are tuples of variables, $\boldsymbol{Z}$ is a tuple of *existential variables*, and $\mathcal{B}, \mathcal{H}$ are finite non-empty conjunctions of atoms respectively called *body* and *head* of r and denoted $Body(r)$ and $Head(r)$. In this paper we consider rules with atomic head (any rule can be transformed into a set of rules with atomic head [4]). A *negative constraint* is a rule of the form $\forall \boldsymbol{X} \, \mathcal{B}(\boldsymbol{X}) \rightarrow \bot$ where $\mathcal{B}$ is a conjunction of atoms and $\boldsymbol{X}$ is a set of variables with possibly constants. Negative constraints are used to express conflicts. In this paper, we take into account binary negative constraints, which contain only two atoms in their body.[1] A knowledge base is a tuple $\mathcal{KB} = (\mathcal{F}, \mathcal{R}, \mathcal{N})$ where $\mathcal{F}$ is a finite set of facts, $\mathcal{R}$ is a finite set of rules, and $\mathcal{N}$ is a finite set of negative constraints.

We denote the set of ***models*** of a knowledge base by $models(\mathcal{F}, \mathcal{R} \cup \mathcal{N})$.

A ***derivation*** is a (potentially infinite) sequence of tuples $D_i = (\mathcal{F}_i, r_i, \pi_i)$ composed of a set of facts $\mathcal{F}_i$, a rule r_i and a homomorphism π_i from $Body(r_i)$ to $\mathcal{F}_i$, where $D_0 = (\mathcal{F}, \emptyset, \emptyset)$ and such that $\mathcal{F}_i$ results from the application of rule r_i to F_{i-1} according to π_i, i.e. $\mathcal{F}_i = \alpha(\mathcal{F}_{i-1}, r_i, \pi_i)$. A derivation from a set of facts $\mathcal{F}$ to a fact f is a minimal sequence of rules applications starting from $D_0 = (\mathcal{F}_0 \subseteq \mathcal{F}, \emptyset, \emptyset)$ and ending with $D_n = (\mathcal{F}_n, r_n, \pi_n)$ such that $f \in \mathcal{F}_n$.

A ***chase*** (a.k.a. forward chaining) is the exhaustive application of a set of rules over a set of facts in a breadth-first manner (denoted $chase(\mathcal{F}, \mathcal{R})$) until no new facts are generated, the resulting "saturated" set of all initial and generated facts is denoted $\mathcal{F}^*$. While this is not always guaranteed to stop, certain recognizable classes of existential rules that are decidable for forward chaining have been defined [3]; we limit ourselves to the recognizable FES (Finite Expansion Set) class [5] and use Skolem chase [17]. We consider ground atomic queries. We denote that a query is entailed from a knowledge base $\mathcal{KB}$ by $\mathcal{KB} \models Q$ (equivalent to $chase(\mathcal{F}, \mathcal{R}) \models Q$ [9]).

Inconsistence vs. Incoherence. Conflicts appear in a knowledge base whenever a negative constraint becomes applicable: we say that two facts f_1 and f_2 are in ***conflict*** if the body of a negative constraint can be mapped to $\{f_1, f_2\}$. There are two possible sources of conflicts, either the facts are incorrect (known as *inconsistence*), or the rules themselves are contradictory (known as *incoherence*). A $\mathcal{KB} = (\mathcal{F}, \mathcal{R}, \mathcal{N})$ is *inconsistent* iff it has an empty set of models (i.e. $models(\mathcal{F}, \mathcal{R} \cup \mathcal{N}) = \emptyset$). A knowledge base is *incoherent* iff $\mathcal{R} \cup \mathcal{N}$ are unsatisfiable, meaning that there does not exist any set of facts S (even outside

---

[1] It should be noted that this restriction does not lead to a loss of expressive power, as [2] shows.

the facts of the knowledge base) where all rules in $\mathcal{R}$ are applicable such that $models(S, \mathcal{R} \cup \mathcal{N}) \neq \emptyset$ [11].

Example 1 (Inconsistence). *Consider the following* $\mathcal{KB} = (\mathcal{F}, \mathcal{R}, \mathcal{N})$ *that describes a simplified legal situation: If there is a scientific evidence incriminating a defendant then he is responsible for the crime, if there is a scientific evidence absolving a defendant then he is not responsible for the crime. A defendant is guilty if responsibility is proven. If a defendant is guilty then he will be given a sentence. If a defendant has an alibi then he is innocent. There is a scientific evidence "e1" incriminating a female defendant "alice", while another scientific evidence "e2" is absolving her of the crime. She also has an alibi. Is Alice innocent (i.e. $Q_1 = innocent(alice)$)? Is she guilty (i.e. $Q_2 = guilty(alice)$)?*

- $\mathcal{F} = \{incrim(e1, alice), absolv(e2, alice), alibi(alice), female(alice)\}$
- $\mathcal{R} = \{r_1 : \forall X, Y\ incrim(X, Y) \rightarrow resp(Y),$
  $r_2 : \forall X, Y\ absolv(X, Y) \rightarrow notResp(X),$
  $r_3 : \forall X\ resp(X) \rightarrow guilty(X),$
  $r_4 : \forall X\ alibi(X) \rightarrow innocent(X),$
  $r_5 : \forall X\ guilty(X) \rightarrow \exists Y\ sentence(X, Y)\}$
- $\mathcal{N} = \{\forall X\ resp(X) \wedge notResp(X) \rightarrow \bot,$
  $\forall X\ guilty(X) \wedge innocent(X) \rightarrow \bot\}$

The saturated set of facts resulting from the chase is

- $\mathcal{F}^* = \{incrim(e1, alice),\ absolv(e2, alice),\ alibi(alice),\ female(alice),\ resp(alice),\ notResp(alice),\ guilty(alice),\ innocent(alice),\ sentence(alice,\ null_1)\}$.

*This knowledge base is **inconsistent**, because a negative constraint is applicable, (thus $models(\mathcal{F}, \mathcal{R} \cup \mathcal{N}) = \emptyset$). This inconsistency is due to an erroneous set of facts (either one of the evidences, the alibi, or all of them are not valid). The classical answer to the Boolean queries Q_1 and Q_2 is "true" (i.e. Alice is guilty and innocent), because from falsehood, anything follows. However, the knowledge base is **coherent** because the set of rules are satisfiable i.e. there exists a set of facts (e.g. $\mathcal{F}' = \{incrim(e1, \mathbf{bob}), absolv(e3, \mathbf{alice}), alibi(\mathbf{alice})\}$) such that all rules are applicable and $models(\mathcal{F}', \mathcal{R} \cup \mathcal{N})) \neq \emptyset$.*

Inconsistency Handling. Defeasible Logics and Repair Semantics are two approaches to handle conflicts. Defeasible Logics are applied to potentially incoherent situations were two types of rules are considered: strict rules expressing undeniable implications (i.e. if $\mathcal{B}(r)$ then definitely $\mathcal{H}(r)$), and defeasible rules expressing weaker implications (i.e. if $\mathcal{B}(r)$ then generally $\mathcal{H}(r)$). In this context, contradictions stem from either relying on incorrect facts, or from having exceptions to the defeasible implications.

Repair Semantics are applied to situations where rules are assumed to hold in the true state of affair and hence inconsistencies can only stem from incorrect facts. A *repair* $\mathcal{D}$ is an inclusion-maximal subset of the facts $\mathcal{D} \subseteq \mathcal{F}$ that is consistent with the rules and negative constraints (i.e. $models(\mathcal{D}, \mathcal{R} \cup \mathcal{N}) \neq \emptyset$). We denote the set of repairs of a knowledge base by $repairs(\mathcal{KB})$. In presence of an incoherent set of rules, Repair Semantics yield an empty set of repairs [10].

3 Statement Graphs for Defeasible Reasoning

A Statement Graph (SG) [13] is a representation of the reasoning process happening inside a knowledge base, it can be seen as an updated Inheritance Net [15] with a custom labeling function. An SG is built using logical building blocks (called statements) that describe a situation (premises) and a rule that can be applied on that situation.

A statement s is a pair that is either a 'query statement' $(Q, \emptyset)$ where Q is a query, a 'fact statement' $(\top, f)$ where f is a fact, or a 'rule application statement' $(\varPhi, \psi)$ that represents a rule application $\alpha(\mathcal{F}, r, \pi)$ s.t. $\pi(\mathcal{B}(r)) = \varPhi$ and $\pi(\mathcal{H}(r)) = \psi$. We denote by $Prem(s)$ the first element of the statement and by $Conc(s)$ the second element. A statement can be written as $Prem(s) \rightarrow Conc(s)$.

A statement s_1 **supports** another statement s_2 iff $\exists f \in Prem(s_2)$ s.t. $Conc(s_1) = f$. A statement s_1 **attacks** s_2 $\exists f \in Prem(s_2)$ s.t. $Conc(s_1)$ and f are in conflict.

Statements are generated from a knowledge base, they can be structured in a graph according to the support and attack relations they have between each other.

Definition 1 (Statement Graph). *A Statement Graph of a* $\mathcal{KB} = (\mathcal{F}, \mathcal{R}, \mathcal{N})$ *is a directed graph* $\mathbb{SG}_{\mathcal{KB}} = (\mathcal{V}, \mathcal{E}_A, \mathcal{E}_S)$: $\mathcal{V}$ *is the set of* **statements** *generated from* $\mathcal{KB}$; $\mathcal{E}_A \subseteq \mathcal{V} \times \mathcal{V}$ *is the set of* **attack edges** *and* $\mathcal{E}_S \subseteq \mathcal{V} \times \mathcal{V}$ *is the set of* **support edges**.

For an edge $e = (s_1, s_2)$, we denote s_1 by $Source(e)$ and s_2 by $Target(e)$. For a statement s we denote its incoming attack edges by $\mathcal{E}_A^-(s)$ and its incoming support edges by $\mathcal{E}_S^-(s)$. We also denote its outgoing attack edges by $\mathcal{E}_A^+(s)$ and outgoing support edges by $\mathcal{E}_S^+(s)$.

A Statement Graph (SG) is constructed from the chase of a knowledge base. Starting facts are represented by fact statements and rule applications are represented using rule application statements. Figure 1 shows SG of Example 1.

An SG provides statements and edges with a label using a *labeling function*. Query answering can then be determined based on the label of the query statement. Continuing the previous example, in an **ambiguity propagating** setting (such as [12]), *innocent(alice)* is ambiguous because *guilty(alice)* can be derived, thus the ambiguity of *guilty(alice)* is propagated to *innocent(alice)* and consequently $\mathcal{KB} \nvDash_{prop} innocent(alice)$ and $\mathcal{KB} \nvDash_{prop} guilty(alice)$ ($\vDash_{prop}$ denotes entailment in ambiguity propagating). On the other hand, in an **ambiguity blocking** setting (such as [18]), the ambiguity of *resp(alice)* blocks any ambiguity derived from it, meaning that *guilty(alice)* cannot be used to attack *innocent(alice)*. Therefore *innocent(alice)* is not ambiguous, thus

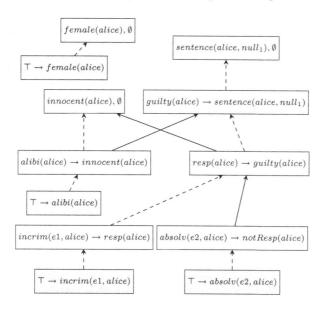

Fig. 1. Example 1's Statement Graph (fact statements are gray).

$\mathcal{KB} \models_{block} innocent(alice)$ and $\mathcal{KB} \not\models_{block} guilty(alice)$ ($\models_{block}$ denotes entailment in ambiguity blocking). The labeling function '**PDL**' (Propagating Defeasible Logic) was proposed for Statement Graphs in [13] that yields equivalent entailment results to Defeasible Logics with ambiguity propagating [1]. Similarily, the labeling function '**BDL**' (Blocking Defeasible Logic) was proposed by [13] to obtain entailment results equivalent to Defeasible Logics with ambiguity blocking [7].

4   Statement Graphs for Repair Semantics

In this paper we focus on two well-known semantics for inconsistent databases: IAR and ICAR repair Semantics. The Intersection of All Repairs semantic [16] is the most skeptical of the Repair Semantics. A query Q is IAR entailed ($\mathcal{KB} \models_{IAR} Q$) iff it is classically entailed by the intersection of all repairs constructed from the starting set of facts (i.e. $\bigcap repairs(\mathcal{KB}) \cup \mathcal{R} \models Q$). The Intersection of Closed ABox Repairs semantic [16] computes the repairs of the saturated set of facts. A query Q is ICAR entailed $\mathcal{KB} \models_{ICAR} Q$ iff it is classically entailed by the set of facts in the intersection of the repairs constructed after generating all facts.

Example 2. *Consider the $\mathcal{KB}$ in Example 1. The repairs constructed from the starting set of facts are:*

- $\mathcal{D}_1 = \{absolv(e2, alice),\ alibi(alice),\ female(alice)\}$
- $\mathcal{D}_2 = \{incrim(e1, alice),\ female(alice)\}$

$\mathcal{D}_1 \cap \mathcal{D}_2 = \{female(alice)\}$ *therefore only* $female(alice)$ *is entailed:* $\mathcal{KB} \vDash_{IAR}$ $female(alice)$. *The repairs constructed from the saturated set of facts are:*

- $\mathcal{D}'_1$ = $\{absolv(e2, alice),\ alibi(alice),\ female(alice),\ notResp(alice),\ sentence(alice, null_1)\}$
- $\mathcal{D}'_2$ = $\{incrim(e1, alice),\ female(alice),\ resp(alice),\ guilty(alice),\ sentence(alice, null_1)\}$

$\mathcal{D}'_1 \cap \mathcal{D}'_2$ = $\{female(alice), sentence(alice, null_1)\}$ *thus* $\mathcal{KB}$ $\vDash_{ICAR}$ $female(alice) \land sentence(alice, null_1)$.

4.1   New Labeling for IAR Semantics

The intuition behind IAR is to reject any fact that can be used to generate conflicting atoms, meaning that only the facts that produce no conflict will be accepted. From an SG point of view, any statement that is attacked, or that supports statements that lead by an attack or support edge to an attacked statement is discarded. This can be obtained by first detecting all conflicts, then discarding any statement that either leads to a conflict or is generated from conflicting atoms. In order to detect conflicts using Statement Graphs, we need to ensure that all conflicts are represented. Given that statements attack each other on the premise, it is necessary to handle in a particular way statements with no outgoing edges (i.e. statements that do not support or attack other statements) as they might still generate conflicting atoms. That is why any statement with no outgoing edges must be linked to a query statement. We first apply PDL to detect ambiguous statements, then backwardly broadcast this ambiguity to any statement that is linked (by a support or attack edge) to an ambiguous statement (cf. Fig. 2). Labelings for Defeasible Logics start from fact statements and propagate upward towards query statements, however, for Repair Semantics, the labelings have to conduct a second pass from query statements and propagate downward towards fact statements. We use the labeling function 'IAR' to obtain entailment results equivalent to IAR [16]. IAR is defined as follows: edges have the same (i.e. given an edge e, $IAR(e) = IAR(Source(e))$). Given a statement s:

(a) $\textbf{\textit{IAR}}(s) = \textbf{\textit{IN}}$ *iff* $IAR(s) \neq AMBIG$ *and* $PDL(s) = IN$.
(b) $\textbf{\textit{IAR}}(s) = \textbf{\textit{AMBIG}}$ *iff either* $PDL(s) = AMBIG$ *or* $\exists e \in \mathcal{E}_S^+(s) \cup \mathcal{E}_A^+(s)$ *such that* $IAR(Target(e)) = AMBIG$.
(c) $\textbf{\textit{IAR}}(s) = \textbf{\textit{OUT}}$ *iff* $PDL(s) = OUT$.

A statement is labeled AMBIG if it was labeled ambiguous by PDL or if it leads to an ambiguous statement. Otherwise, it is IN if it has an IN complete support and is not attacked (i.e. PDL labels it IN).

In the following proposition, we will denote by $\text{SG}_{\mathcal{KB}}^{\text{IAR}}$ an SG built on the KB $\mathcal{KB}$ that uses the ICAR labeling function and by $\text{SG}_{\mathcal{KB}}^{\text{IAR}}\langle s \rangle$ the label of a statement s.

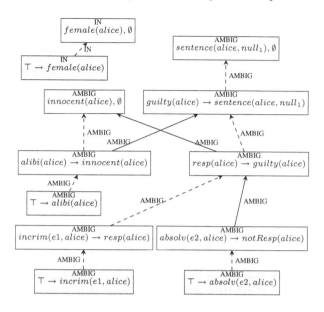

Fig. 2. IAR applied to Example 1's Statement Graph.

Proposition 1. *Let f be a fact in a $\mathcal{KB}$ that contains only defeasible facts and strict rules. $\mathcal{KB} \models_{IAR} f$ iff $\mathsf{SG}^{IAR}_{\mathcal{KB}}\langle(f, \emptyset)\rangle = IN$ and $\mathcal{KB} \not\models_{IAR} f$ iff $\mathsf{SG}^{IAR}_{\mathcal{KB}}\langle(f, \emptyset)\rangle \in \{AMBIG, OUT\}$.*

We split the proof of (1.) in two parts, first we prove by contradiction that if $\mathcal{KB} \models_{IAR} f$ then $\mathsf{SG}^{IAR}_{\mathcal{KB}}\langle(f, \emptyset)\rangle = $ IN: Suppose we have a fact f such that $\mathcal{KB} \models_{IAR} f$ and $\mathsf{SG}^{IAR}_{\mathcal{KB}}\langle(f, \emptyset)\rangle \neq$ IN:

1. $\mathcal{KB} \models_{IAR} f$ means that there is a derivation for f from an initial set of facts $T \subseteq \mathcal{F}$ and there is no consistent set of initial facts $S \subseteq \mathcal{F}$ such that $S \cup T$ is inconsistent (i.e. $models(S, \mathcal{R} \cup \mathcal{N}) \neq \emptyset$ and $models(S \cup T, \mathcal{R} \cup \mathcal{N}) = \emptyset$), which means that there is no derivation for an atom conflicting with an atom used in the derivation for f i.e. f is not generated from or used to generate ambiguous atoms, thus $PDL((f \rightarrow \emptyset)) = $ IN.
2. $\mathsf{SG}^{IAR}_{\mathcal{KB}}\langle(f, \emptyset)\rangle \neq$ IN means that either:
   (a) $\mathsf{SG}^{IAR}_{\mathcal{KB}}\langle(f, \emptyset)\rangle = $ OUT which is impossible given 1. (i.e. $PDL(f, \emptyset) = $ IN)
   (b) or $\mathsf{SG}^{IAR}_{\mathcal{KB}}\langle(f, \emptyset)\rangle = $ AMBIG which means either:
      i. $PDL(f, \emptyset) = $ AMBIG (impossible given 1.),
      ii. or $\exists e \in \mathcal{E}^{+}_{S}(\mathfrak{s}) \cup \mathcal{E}^{+}_{A}(\mathfrak{s})$ such that $IAR(Target(e)) = $ AMBIG which means that f is used to generate ambiguous atoms (impossible given 1.).

Now we prove by contradiction that if $\mathsf{SG}^{IAR}_{\mathcal{KB}}\langle(f, \emptyset)\rangle = $ IN then $\mathcal{KB} \models_{IAR} f$: Suppose we have a fact f such that $\mathsf{SG}^{IAR}_{\mathcal{KB}}\langle(f, \emptyset)\rangle = $ IN and $\mathcal{KB} \not\models_{IAR} f$:

1. $\mathsf{SG}^{IAR}_{\mathcal{KB}}\langle(f, \emptyset)\rangle = $ IN means that $IAR(f, \emptyset) \neq $ AMBIG and $PDL(f, \emptyset) = $ IN, which means that $(f, \emptyset)$ is not attacked (i.e. there is no derivation for an atom

conflicting with f) and is not used to generate conflicting atoms (no outgoing edge leads to an AMBIG statement).

2. $\mathcal{KB} \nvDash_{IAR} f$ means that either f is generated by conflicting atoms (impossible given 1.) or is used to generate conflicting atoms (impossible given 1.).

From (1.) the proposition (2.) directly holds ($\mathrm{SG}_{\mathcal{KB}}^{IAR}\langle(f \to \emptyset)\rangle \neq \mathrm{IN}$ means $\mathrm{SG}_{\mathcal{KB}}^{IAR}\langle(f \to \emptyset)\rangle \in \{\mathrm{AMBIG}, \mathrm{OUT}\}$ given that IAR is a function).

4.2   New Labeling for ICAR Semantics

The intuition behind ICAR is to reject any fact that is used to generate conflict, while accepting those that do not (even if they were generated after a conflict). From an SG point of view, any statement that is attacked or that supports statements that lead to an attack is considered "ambiguous". This is done by first applying PDL to detect ambiguous and accepted statements then the ICAR labeling starts from query statements and propagates downward towards fact statements (cf. Fig. 3). We use the labeling function '**ICAR**' to obtain entailment results equivalent to ICAR [16]. ICAR is defined as follows: given an edge e, $ICAR(e) = ICAR(Source(e))$. Given a statement s:

(a) **$ICAR(s) = IN$** iff $ICAR(s) \neq AMBIG$ and $PDL(s) \in \{IN, AMBIG\}$.
(b) **$ICAR(s) = AMBIG$** iff
   1. *either* $PDL(s) = AMBIG$ and $\exists e \in \mathcal{E}_A^-(s)$ s.t. $PDL(e) \in \{IN, AMBIG\}$,
   2. *or* $\exists e \in \mathcal{E}_S^+(s) \cup \mathcal{E}_A^+(s)$ such that $ICAR(Target(e)) = AMBIG$.
(c) **$ICAR(s) = OUT$** iff $PDL(s) = Out$.

A statement is labeled AMBIG if it was labeled ambiguous by PDL and it is attacked, or if it leads to an ambiguous statement. It is labeled IN if it was labeled IN or AMBIG by PDL and does not lead to an ambiguous statement.

In the following proposition, we will denote by $\mathrm{SG}_{\mathcal{KB}}^{ICAR}$ an SG built on the KB $\mathcal{KB}$ that uses the ICAR labeling function and by $\mathrm{SG}_{\mathcal{KB}}^{ICAR}\langle s \rangle$ the label of a statement s.

Proposition 2. *Let f be a fact in a $\mathcal{KB}$ that contains only defeasible facts and strict rules: $\mathcal{KB} \vDash_{ICAR} f$ iff $\mathrm{SG}_{\mathcal{KB}}^{ICAR}\langle(f, \emptyset)\rangle = IN$ and $\mathcal{KB} \nvDash_{ICAR} f$ iff $\mathrm{SG}_{\mathcal{KB}}^{ICAR}\langle(f, \emptyset)\rangle \in \{AMBIG, OUT\}$.*

We split the proof of (1.) in two parts, first we prove by contradiction that if $\mathcal{KB} \vDash_{ICAR} f$ then $\mathrm{SG}_{\mathcal{KB}}^{ICAR}\langle(f, \emptyset)\rangle = \mathrm{IN}$. Suppose we have a fact f such that $\mathcal{KB} \vDash_{ICAR} f$ and $\mathrm{SG}_{\mathcal{KB}}^{ICAR}\langle(f, \emptyset)\rangle \neq \mathrm{IN}$:

1. $\mathcal{KB} \vDash_{ICAR} f$ means that there is a derivation for f and there is no consistent set of facts $S \subseteq \mathcal{F}^*$ such that $S \cup \{f\}$ is inconsistent ($models(S, \mathcal{R} \cup \mathcal{N}) \neq \emptyset$ and $models(S \cup \{f\}, \mathcal{R} \cup \mathcal{N}) = \emptyset$) i.e. f is not used to generate ambiguous atoms.
2. $\mathrm{SG}_{\mathcal{KB}}^{ICAR}\langle(f, \emptyset)\rangle \neq \mathrm{IN}$ means that either:
   (a) $\mathrm{SG}_{\mathcal{KB}}^{ICAR}\langle(f, \emptyset)\rangle = \mathrm{OUT}$ which is impossible given 1. (there is a derivation for f i.e. $PDL(f, \emptyset) \in \{\mathrm{IN}, \mathrm{AMBIG}\}$).

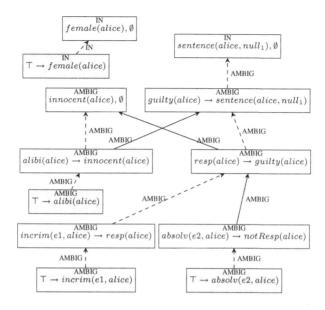

Fig. 3. ICAR applied to Example 1's Statement Graph.

(b) or $\mathrm{SG}_{\mathcal{KB}}^{\mathrm{ICAR}}\langle(f, \emptyset)\rangle = \mathrm{AMBIG}$ which means either:

   i. $\mathrm{PDL}(f, \emptyset) = \mathrm{AMBIG}$ and there is an edge attacking it (impossible given 1. i.e. there is no derivable conflicting atom with f).

   ii. or $\exists e \in \mathcal{E}_S^+(\mathbb{s}) \cup \mathcal{E}_A^+(\mathbb{s})$ such that $\mathrm{ICAR}(Target(e)) = \mathrm{AMBIG}$ which means that f is used to generate ambiguous atoms (impossible given 1.).

Now we prove by contradiction that if $\mathrm{SG}_{\mathcal{KB}}^{\mathrm{ICAR}}\langle(f, \emptyset)\rangle = \mathrm{IN}$ then $\mathcal{KB} \models_{ICAR} f$: Suppose we have a fact f such that $\mathrm{SG}_{\mathcal{KB}}^{\mathrm{ICAR}}\langle(f, \emptyset)\rangle = \mathrm{IN}$ and $\mathcal{KB} \nvDash_{ICAR} f$:

1. $\mathrm{SG}_{\mathcal{KB}}^{\mathrm{ICAR}}\langle(f, \emptyset)\rangle = \mathrm{IN}$ means that $\mathrm{ICAR}(f, \emptyset) \neq \mathrm{AMBIG}$ and $\mathrm{PDL}(f, \emptyset) \in \{\mathrm{IN}, \mathrm{AMBIG}\}$, which means that $(f, \emptyset)$ is not attacked (i.e. there is no derivation for an atom conflicting with f) and it is used to generate ambiguous atoms (no outgoing edge leads to an AMBIG statement).

2. $\mathcal{KB} \nvDash_{ICAR} f$ means that either f is not derivable (impossible given 1. since $\mathrm{PDL}(f, \emptyset) \in \{\mathrm{IN}, \mathrm{AMBIG}\}$), or there is a derivation for an atom conflicting with f, or f is used to generate ambiguous atoms (impossible given 1.).

From (1.) the proposition (2.) directly holds ($\mathrm{SG}_{\mathcal{KB}}^{\mathrm{ICAR}}\langle(f, \emptyset)\rangle \neq \mathrm{IN}$ means $\mathrm{SG}_{\mathcal{KB}}^{\mathrm{ICAR}}\langle(f, \emptyset)\rangle \in \{\mathrm{AMBIG}, \mathrm{OUT}\}$ given that ICAR is a function).

5 Human Intuitions for Conflict Management

The contribution of the paper is two fold. On one hand we have provided new labelings for Statement Graphs shown to capture repair semantics. In this section we go one step further and show (1) there is practical value into combining defeasible reasoning and repair semantics and (2) provide a Statement Graph labeling for this new semantics.

In order to get an idea of what intuitions humans follow in an abstract context, we ran an experiment with 41 participants in which they were told to place themselves in the shoes of an engineer trying to analyze a situation based on a set of sensors. These sensors (with unknown reliability) give information about the properties of an object called "o", e.g. "Object 'o' has the property P" (which could be interpreted for example as 'o' is red). Also, as an engineer, they have a knowledge that is always true about the relations between these properties, e.g. "All objects that have the property P, also have the property Q". Some of the properties cannot be true at the same time on the same object, e.g. "An object cannot have the properties P and T at the same time". Using abstract situations allowed us to avoid unwanted effects of *a priori* knowledge while at the same time representing formal concepts (facts, rules and negative constraints) in a textual simplified manner. A transcript of the original text that the experiment participants have received is shown in the following Example 3.

Example 3 (Situation 1). *Textual representation: Three sensors are respectively indicating that "o" has the properties S, Q, and T. We know that any object that has the property S also has the property V. Moreover, an object cannot have the properties S and Q at the same time, nor the properties V and T at the same time.* **Question:** *Can we say that the object "o" has the property T?*

Let us also provide here the logical representation of the above text. Please note that the participants have not also received the logical transcript.

- $\mathcal{F} = \{s(o), q(o), t(o)\}$

- $\mathcal{R} = \{\forall X \, s(X) \rightarrow v(X)\}$

- $\mathcal{N} = \{\forall X \, s(X) \wedge q(X) \rightarrow \bot, \\ \forall X \, v(X) \wedge t(X) \rightarrow \bot\}$
- *Query* $Q = t(o)$

Participants were shown in a random order 5 situations containing inconsistencies. For each situation, the participant was presented with a textual description of an inconsistent knowledge base and a query. Possible answers for a query is "Yes" (entailed) or "No" (not entailed). The 41 participants are second year university students in computer science, 12 female and 29 male aged between 17 and 46 years old.

Table 1 presents the situations and the semantics under which their queries are entailed ($\checkmark$) or not entailed ($-$). The "% of Yes" column indicates the percentage of participants that answered "Yes". The aim of each situation is to identify if a set of semantics coincides with the majority, for example the query in Situation 1 (Example 3) is only entailed under $\models_{block}$ [2]. Not all cases can be represented, for example $\models_{IAR} f$ and $\not\models_{prop} f$, due to *productivity* (c.f. Sect. 4.2).

---

[2] Situations and detailed results are available at https://www.dropbox.com/s/4wkblgdx7hzj7s8/situations.pdf.

Table 1. Situations entailment and results.

Situations	$\models_{block}$	$\models_{prop}$	$\models_{IAR}$	$\models_{ICAR}$	% of "Yes"	$\models_{IAR}^{block}$
#1	✓	−	−	−	73.17%	✓
#2	✓	✓	−	−	21.95%	−
#3	✓	✓	−	✓	21.95%	−
#4	−	−	−	✓	4.87%	−
#5	✓	✓	✓	✓	78.04%	✓

From the results in Table 1, we observe that blocking and IAR are the most intuitive (Situations 1 and 5), however blocking alone is not sufficient as shown by Situations 2 and 3, and IAR alone is not sufficient either (Situation 1). One possible explanation is that participants are using a semantics that is a mix of IAR and ambiguity blocking ($\models_{IAR}^{block}$). Such a semantics is absent from the literature as it is interestingly in between Repair Semantics and Defeasible Logics. Please note that we do not argue that this particular semantics is better than existing ones, our aim is to bridge Defeasible Logics and Repair Semantics by defining new inference relations based on intuitions coming from both of them, and then studying properties of these new inference relations.

5.1 New Semantics for Reasoning in Presence of Conflict

The intuition behind this new semantics is to apply IAR or ICAR on an SG which has been labeled using BDL rather than PDL. This would amount to replacing PDL by BDL in the definitions of IAR and ICAR. As it turns out, IAR with BDL fully coincides with the answers given by the majority of the participants in our experiment. To illustrate this semantics, consider Example 4.

Example 4. *Applying IAR with ambiguity blocking on Example 1's SG gives* $\mathcal{KB} \models_{IAR}^{block} female(alice) \wedge alibi(alice) \wedge innocent(alice)$. *Note that the difference with BDL is that* $\mathcal{KB} \not\models_{IAR}^{block} incrim(e1, alice)$ *and* $\mathcal{KB} \not\models_{IAR}^{block} absolv(e2, alice)$. *The difference with IAR is that* $\mathcal{KB} \not\models_{IAR} alibi(alice)$ *and* $\mathcal{KB} \not\models_{IAR} innocent(alice)$.

Let us now analyse the productivity and complexity of new semantics. We say that a semantics $\models_1$ is less productive than $\models_2$ (represented as $\models_1 \rightarrow \models_2$) if, for every $\mathcal{KB}$ and every f, it results in fewer conclusions being drawn (i.e. if $\mathcal{KB} \models_1 f$ then $\mathcal{KB} \models_2 f$). Productivity comparison of Repair Semantics has been discussed in [6] while the productivity between Defeasible Logics semantics can be extracted from the inclusion theorem in [8]. It can be seen that $\models_{IAR} \rightarrow \models_{prop}$ since $\models_{prop}$ only rejects facts that are challenged or generated from challenged facts, while $\models_{IAR}$ also rejects facts that would lead to a conflict. The results from the following Proposition 3 are summarized in Fig. 4.

Proposition 3. *Let* $\mathcal{KB}$ *be a knowledge base with only defeasible facts and strict rules. Given a fact f:*

1. *if* $\mathcal{KB} \models_{IAR} f$ *then* $\mathcal{KB} \models_{prop} f$
2. *if* $\mathcal{KB} \models_{IAR} f$ *then* $\mathcal{KB} \models_{IAR}^{block} f$
3. *if* $\mathcal{KB} \models_{IAR}^{block} f$ *then* $\mathcal{KB} \models_{block} f$
4. *if* $\mathcal{KB} \models_{IAR}^{block} f$ *then* $\mathcal{KB} \models_{ICAR}^{block} f$
5. *if* $\mathcal{KB} \models_{ICAR} f$ *then* $\mathcal{KB} \models_{ICAR}^{block} f$

We prove (1.) by contradiction. Suppose there is a fact f such that $\mathcal{KB} \models_{IAR} f$ and $\mathcal{KB} \not\models_{prop} f$. $\mathcal{KB} \models_{IAR} f$ means that there is a derivation for f from an initial set of facts $T \subseteq \mathcal{F}$ and there is no consistent set of initial facts $S \subseteq \mathcal{F}$ such that $S \cup T$ is inconsistent (i.e. $models(S, \mathcal{R} \cup \mathcal{N}) \neq \emptyset$ and $models(S \cup T, \mathcal{R} \cup \mathcal{N}) = \emptyset$) [16]. This means that f is derivable and does not rely conflicting facts, therefore the statement $(f \rightarrow \emptyset)$ has a complete IN support and no IN or AMBIG attack edges, i.e. $\mathsf{SG}_{\mathcal{KB}}^{PDL}\langle(f, \emptyset)\rangle = \mathrm{IN}$, thus $\mathcal{KB} \models_{prop} f$ which is a contradiction.

We prove (2.) by contradiction, suppose we have $\mathcal{KB} \models_{IAR} f$ and $\mathcal{KB} \not\models_{IAR}^{block} f$:

1. $\mathcal{KB} \models_{IAR} f$ means that there is a derivation for f from an initial set of facts $T \subseteq \mathcal{F}$ and there is no consistent set of initial facts $S \subseteq \mathcal{F}$ such that $S \cup T$ is inconsistent (i.e. $models(S, \mathcal{R} \cup \mathcal{N}) \neq \emptyset$ and $models(S \cup T, \mathcal{R} \cup \mathcal{N}) = \emptyset$), which means that f is not generated by conflicting atoms and is not used to generate conflicting atoms i.e. $\mathrm{PDL}(f, \emptyset) = \mathrm{IN}$ which implies that $\mathrm{BDL}(f, \emptyset) = \mathrm{IN}$ [8].
2. $\mathcal{KB} \not\models_{IAR}^{block} f$ means that either $\mathrm{BDL}(f, \emptyset) \neq \mathrm{IN}$ (impossible given 1.) or f is used to generate conflicting atoms (impossible given 1.)

We prove (3.) by contradiction, suppose we have $\mathcal{KB} \models_{IAR}^{block} f$ and $\mathcal{KB} \not\models_{block} f$:

1. $\mathcal{KB} \models_{IAR}^{block} f$ means that $\mathrm{BDL}(f, \emptyset) = \mathrm{IN}$ and f is not used to generate conflicting atoms.
2. $\mathcal{KB} \not\models_{block} f$ means that $\mathrm{BDL}(f, \emptyset) \neq \mathrm{IN}$ (impossible given 1.).

We prove (4.) by contradiction, suppose we have $\mathcal{KB} \models_{IAR}^{block} f$ and $\mathcal{KB} \not\models_{ICAR}^{block} f$:

1. $\mathcal{KB} \models_{IAR}^{block} f$ means that $\mathrm{BDL}(f, \emptyset) = \mathrm{IN}$ and f is not used to generate conflicting atoms.
2. $\mathcal{KB} \not\models_{ICAR}^{block} f$ means that either $\mathrm{BDL}(f, \emptyset) \neq \mathrm{IN}$ (impossible given 1.) or there is a derivable atom conflicting with f or f is used to generate conflicting atoms (impossible given 1.)

We prove (5.) by contradiction, suppose we have $\mathcal{KB} \models_{ICAR} f$ and $\mathcal{KB} \not\models_{ICAR}^{block} f$:

1. $\mathcal{KB} \models_{ICAR} f$ means that $\mathrm{PDL}((f \rightarrow \emptyset)) \in \{\mathrm{IN}, \mathrm{AMBIG}\}$, there is no derivable fact conflicting with f, and f is not used to derive conflicting atoms.
2. $\mathcal{KB} \not\models_{ICAR}^{block} f$ means that $\mathrm{BDL}((f \rightarrow \emptyset)) \neq \mathrm{IN}$ and $\mathrm{BDL}((f \rightarrow \emptyset)) = \mathrm{AMBIG}$ and either there is a derivable fact that is conflicting with f (impossible given 1.) or f is used to generate conflicting atoms (impossible given 1.).

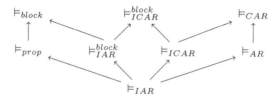

Fig. 4. Productivity and complexity of different semantics under Skolem-FES fragment of existential rules.

6   Discussion

In this paper we build upon Statement Graphs for existential rules and their labeling functions for ambiguity blocking, ambiguity propagating [13], and provide custom labeling functions for IAR, and ICAR. These labelings explicitly show how to transition from ambiguity propagating to IAR and ICAR, and how to obtain a combination of blocking with IAR and ICAR. Using an experiment, we have shown that bringing together Defeasible reasoning and Repair semantics allows for the definition of new and potentially interesting semantics with respect to human reasoning. Implementing these new labelings, for instance in the platform presented in [14], would allow to study further the links between labeling functions and human reasoning.

The modeling choices used in this paper (the use of forward chaining, specific Repair Semantics, particular intuitions of Defeasible Logics, and no account for preferences) stem from several rationale. More precisely:

- *Skolem chase*: the focus on the forward chaining mechanism is due to its ability to handle transitive rules [19] contrary to backward chaining [3]. Regarding the choice of chase, we focused on the Skolem chase given its relatively low cost and its ability to stay decidable for all known concrete classes of the FES fragment [5].
- *Language*: Repair Semantics make the assumption of a coherent set of rules because incoherence might yield to the trivial solution of an empty set of repairs [10]. Therefore allowing defeasible rules with the restriction of coherence defeats the purpose of having defeasible rules in the first place.
- *Considered Repair Semantics*: the appeal of IAR and ICAR is in their simplicity and low complexity. Considering other Repair Semantics such as ICR, AR, etc. would require using and defining a more complex version of SG and defeasible reasoning such as well founded semantics which is one favored future research avenue.
- *Defeasible reasoning intuitions*: ambiguity handling is, of course, not the only intuition in defeasible reasoning, however other intuitions such as team defeat, handling of strict rules, etc. are meaningless in this context given the absence of preferences and defeasible rules. However, floating conclusions are applicable in the considered language, nevertheless, neither Defeasible Logics nor IAR/ ICAR accept floating conclusion.

Acknowledgement. We would like to thanks the anonymous reviewers for their helpful and constructive comments.

References

1. Antoniou, G., Billington, D., Governatori, G., Maher, M.J., Rock, A.: A family of defeasible reasoning logics and its implementation. In: Proceedings of the 14th European Conference on Artificial Intelligence, pp. 459–463 (2000)
2. Bacchus, F., Chen, X., van Beek, P., Walsh, T.: Binary vs. non-binary constraints. Artif. Intell. **140**(1/2), 1–37 (2002). https://doi.org/10.1016/S0004-3702(02)00210-2
3. Baget, J.F., Garreau, F., Mugnier, M.L., Rocher, S.: Extending acyclicity notions for existential rules. In: ECAI, pp. 39–44 (2014)
4. Baget, J.F., Garreau, F., Mugnier, M.L., Rocher, S.: Revisiting chase termination for existential rules and their extension to nonmonotonic negation. arXiv preprint arXiv:1405.1071 (2014)
5. Baget, J.F., Leclère, M., Mugnier, M.L., Salvat, E.: On rules with existential variables: walking the decidability line. Artif. Intell. **175**(9–10), 1620–1654 (2011)
6. Benferhat, S., Bouraoui, Z., Croitoru, M., Papini, O., Tabia, K.: Non-objection inference for inconsistency-tolerant query answering. In: IJCAI, pp. 3684–3690 (2016)
7. Billington, D.: Defeasible logic is stable. J. Log. Comput. **3**(4), 379–400 (1993)
8. Billington, D., Antoniou, G., Governatori, G., Maher, M.: An inclusion theorem for defeasible logics. ACM Trans. Comput. Log. (TOCL) **12**(1), 6 (2010)
9. Calì, A., Gottlob, G., Lukasiewicz, T.: A general datalog-based framework for tractable query answering over ontologies. Web Semant. Sci. Serv. Agents World Wide Web **14**, 57–83 (2012)
10. Deagustini, C.A., Martinez, M.V., Falappa, M.A., Simari, G.R.: On the influence of incoherence in inconsistency-tolerant semantics for Datalog+-. In: JOWO@ IJCAI (2015)
11. Flouris, G., Huang, Z., Pan, J.Z., Plexousakis, D., Wache, H.: Inconsistencies, negations and changes in ontologies. In: Proceedings of the National Conference on Artificial Intelligence, vol. 21, p. 1295. AAAI Press; MIT Press, Menlo Park, Cambridge, London (1999, 2006)
12. Governatori, G., Maher, M.J., Antoniou, G., Billington, D.: Argumentation semantics for defeasible logic. J. Log. Comput. **14**(5), 675–702 (2004). https://doi.org/10.1093/logcom/14.5.675.1
13. Hecham, A., Bisquert, P., Croitoru, M.: On a flexible representation of defeasible reasoning variants. In: Proceedings of the 17th Conference on Autonomous Agents and MultiAgent Systems, pp. 1123–1131 (2018)
14. Hecham, A., Croitoru, M., Bisquert, P.: DAMN: defeasible reasoning tool for multi-agent reasoning. In: AAAI 2020–34th AAAI Conference on Artificial Intelligence. Association for the Advancement of Artificial Intelligence, New York, United States, February 2020. https://hal-lirmm.ccsd.cnrs.fr/lirmm-02393877
15. Horty, J.F., Thomason, R.H., Touretzky, D.S.: A skeptical theory of inheritance in nonmonotonic semantic networks. Artif. Intell. **42**(2–3), 311–348 (1990)
16. Lembo, D., Lenzerini, M., Rosati, R., Ruzzi, M., Savo, D.F.: Inconsistency-tolerant semantics for description logics. In: Hitzler, P., Lukasiewicz, T. (eds.) RR 2010. LNCS, vol. 6333, pp. 103–117. Springer, Heidelberg (2010). https://doi.org/10.1007/978-3-642-15918-3_9

17. Marnette, B.: Generalized schema-mappings: from termination to tractability. In: Proceedings of the Twenty-Eighth ACM SIGMOD-SIGACT-SIGART Symposium on Principles of Database Systems, pp. 13–22. ACM (2009)
18. Nute, D.: Defeasible reasoning: a philosophical analysis in prolog. In: Fetzer, J.H. (ed.) Aspects of Artificial Intelligence. Studies in Cognitive Systems, vol. 1, pp. 251–288. Springer, Dordrecht (1988). https://doi.org/10.1007/978-94-009-2699-8_9
19. Rocher, S.: Querying existential rule knowledge bases: decidability and complexity. Ph.D. thesis, Université de Montpellier (2016)

Using Grammar-Based Genetic Programming for Mining Disjointness Axioms Involving Complex Class Expressions

Thu Huong Nguyen$^{(\boxtimes)}$ and Andrea G. B. Tettamanzi

Université Côte d'Azur, CNRS, Inria, I3S, Nice, France
{thu-huong.nguyen,andrea.tettamanzi}@univ-cotedazur.fr

Abstract. In the context of the Semantic Web, learning implicit knowledge in terms of axioms from Linked Open Data has been the object of much current research. In this paper, we propose a method based on grammar-based genetic programming to automatically discover disjointness axioms between concepts from the Web of Data. A training-testing model is also implemented to overcome the lack of benchmarks and comparable research. The acquisition of axioms is performed on a small sample of DBpedia with the help of a Grammatical Evolution algorithm. The accuracy evaluation of mined axioms is carried out on the whole DBpedia. Experimental results show that the proposed method gives high accuracy in mining class disjointness axioms involving complex expressions.

Keywords: Ontology learning · OWL axiom · Disjointness axiom · Genetic programming · Grammatical Evolution

1 Motivation

The growth of the Semantic Web (SW) and of its most prominent implementation, the Linked Open Data (LOD), has made a huge number of interconnected RDF (Resource Definition Framework) triples freely available for sharing and reuse. LOD have thus become a giant real-world data resource that can be exploited for mining implicit knowledge, i.e., for *Knowledge Discovery from Data (KDD)*. Such wealth of data can be organized and made accessible by *ontologies* [1,2], formal representations of shared domains of knowledge, which play an essential role in data and knowledge integration. Through a shared schema, ontologies support automatic reasoning such as query answering or classification over different data sources. In the structure of ontologies, the definition about the incompatibility between pairs of concepts, in the form of class disjointness axioms, is important to ensure the quality of ontologies. Specifically, like other types of axioms, class disjointness axioms allow to check the correctness of a knowledge base or to derive new information, a task that is sometimes called *knowledge enrichment*. For instance, a reasoner will be able to deduce an error,

© Springer Nature Switzerland AG 2020
M. Alam et al. (Eds.): ICCS 2020, LNAI 12277, pp. 18–32, 2020.
https://doi.org/10.1007/978-3-030-57855-8_2

i.e., a logical inconsistency of facts in the ontology, whenever the class *Fish* is associated to a resource related to the class *Planet*, if there is a constraint of disjointness between the two concepts *Fish* and *Planet*.

However, the manual acquisition of axioms, a central task in ontology construction, is exceedingly expensive and time-consuming and mainly depends on the availability of expert resources, i.e., domain specialists and knowledge engineers. We focus on a subtask of *ontology learning*, which goes under the name of *axiom learning*, and specifically on the learning of class disjointness axioms. Axiom learning is essentially bottom up. While top-down approaches require schema-level information built by domain experts to suggest axioms, bottom-up approaches use learning algorithms and rely on instances from several existing knowledge and information resources to mine axioms. Axiom learning algorithms can help alleviate the overall cost of extracting axioms and of building ontologies in general.

In terms of input data sources for the learning process, supporting dynamic data sources, where the facts are updated or changed in time, is preferable, if one wants to achieve scalability and evolution, instead of only focusing on mostly small and uniform data collections. Such dynamic information can be extracted from various data resources of LOD, which constitute an open world of information. Indeed, the advantages of LOD with respect to learning, as argued in [3], is that it is publicly available, highly structured, relational, and large compared to other resources.

As a consequence of the general lack of class disjointness axioms in existing ontologies, learning implicit knowledge in terms of axioms from a LOD repository in the context of the Semantic Web has been the object of research using several different methods. Prominent research towards the automatic creation of class disjointness axioms from RDF facts include supervised classification, like in the *LeDA* system [4], statistical schema induction via associative rule mining, like in the *GoldMiner* system [5], and learning general class descriptions (including disjointness) from training data, like in the DL-Learner framework [6]. Furthermore, recent research has proposed using unsupervised statistical approaches like Formal Concept Analysis (FCA) [7] or Terminological Cluster Trees (TCT) [8], to discover disjointness axioms.

Along the lines of extensional (i.e., instance-based, bottom-up) methods and expanding on the Grammatical Evolution(GE) method proposed in [9,10], we propose a new approach to overcome its limitations as well as to enhance the diversity of discovered types of axioms. Specifically, a set of axioms with more diverse topics is generated from a small sample of an RDF dataset which is randomly extracted from a full RDF repository, more specifically, DBpedia. Also, the type of mined class disjointness axioms is extended to include the existential quantification ($\exists r.C$) and value restriction ($\forall r.C$) constructors, where r is a property and C a class, which cannot be mechanically derived from a given set of atomic axioms. Indeed, it is not because one knows that, for instance, the two classes Person and City are disjoint, that one can conclude that, say, Person and $\forall$birthPlace.City (i.e., who was born in a city) are disjoint too; indeed we all know they are not! Conversely, knowing that Person and Writer are *not* disjoint does not allow us to conclude that Person and ∀author.Writer are not disjoint either. We propose a specific axiom grammar that generates the axioms of the type we target. A set of candidate axioms is improved thanks to an evolutionary process through the use of the evolutionary operators of crossover and mutation. Finally, the final population of generated axioms is evaluated on the full RDF dataset, specifically the whole DBpedia, which can be considered as an objective benchmark, thus eliminating the need of domain experts to assess the quality of the generated axioms on a wide variety of topics. The evaluation of generated axioms in each generation of the evolutionary process is thus performed on a reasonably sized data sample, which alleviates the computational cost of query execution and enhances the performance of the method. Following [9], we apply a method based on possibility theory to score candidate axioms. It is important to mention that, to the best of our knowledge, no other method has been proposed so far in the literature to mine the Web of data for class disjointness axioms involving complex class expressions with existential quantifications and value restrictions in addition to conjunctions.

The rest of the paper is organized as follows: some basics in GE are provided in Sect. 2. The method to discover class disjointness axioms with a Grammar-based Genetic Programming approach is presented in Sect. 3. Section 4 describes the experimental settings. Results are presented and discussed in Sect. 5. A brief survey of current related work in the field of learning class disjointness axioms is provided in Sect. 6. Finally, conclusions and directions for future research are given in Sect. 7.

2 Basic Concepts of Grammar-Based Genetic Programming

Genetic Programming (GP) [11,12] is an evolutionary approach that extends genetic algorithms (GA) to allow the exploration of the space of computer programs. Inspired by biological evolution and its fundamental mechanisms, these programs are "bred" using iterative improvement of an initially random population of programs. That is an *evolutionary process*. At each iteration, known as a *generation*, improvements are made possible by stochastic variation, i.e., by a set of *genetic operators*, usually *crossover* and *mutation* and probabilistic selection according to pre-specified criteria for judging the quality of an individual (solution). According to the levels of fitness, the process of selecting individuals, called *fitness-based selection*, is performed to create a list of better qualified individuals as input for generating a new set of candidate solutions in the next generation. The new solutions of each generation are bred by applying genetic operators on the selected old individuals. Then, *replacement* is the last step and decides which individuals stay in a population and which are replaced on a par, with selection influencing convergence.

A grammar-based form of GP, namely *Grammatical Evolution* (GE) [13], differs from traditional GP in that it distinguishes the search space from the solution space, through the use of a grammar-mediated representation.

Programs, viewed as *phenotypic solutions* or *phenotypes*, are decoded from variable-length binary strings, i.e., *genotypic individuals* or *genotypes*, through a transformation called *mapping process*. According to it, the variable-length binary string genomes, or *chromosomes*, are split into consecutive groups of bits, called *codons*, representing an integer value, used to select, at each step, one of a set of production rules from a formal grammar, typically in *Backus-Naur form (BNF)*, which specifies the syntax of the desired programs. A *BNF grammar* is a context-free grammar consisting of terminals and non-terminals and being represented in the form of a four-tuple $\{N, T, P, S\}$, where N is the sets of non-terminals, which can be extended into one or more terminals; T is the set of terminals which are items in the language; P is the set of the production rules that map N to T; S is the start symbol and a member of N. When there are a number of productions that can be used to rewrite one specific non-terminal, they are separated by the '|' symbol.

In the mapping process, codons are used consecutively to choose production rules from P in the BNF grammar according to the function:

$$production = codon \textbf{ modulo } \begin{bmatrix} \text{Number of productions} \\ \text{for the current non-} \\ \text{terminal} \end{bmatrix} \quad (1)$$

3   A Grammar-Based GP for Disjointness Axioms Discovery

We consider axiom discovery as an evolutionary process and reuse the GE method of [9,10] to mine class disjointness axioms with a few modifications. As said, we focus on axioms involving class expressions with existential quantification and value restriction. Also, a "training-testing" model is applied. Specifically, the learning process is performed with the input data source derived from a training RDF dataset, a random sample of DBpedia, whereas the evaluation of discovered axioms is based on a testing one, namely the full DBpedia. In terms of GE, axioms are "programs" or "phenotypes", obeying a given BNF grammar. A population of candidate genotypic axioms, encoded as variable-length integer strings, i.e., numerical chromosomes, is randomly generated. Then, a mapping process based on the BNF grammar is performed to translate these chromosomes to phenotypic axioms. The set of axioms is maintained and iteratively refined to discover axioms that satisfy two key quality measures: generality and credibility. The quality of generated axioms can be enhanced gradually during the evolutionary process by applying variation operators, i.e., crossover and mutation, on phenotypic axioms. In this section, we first introduce the BNF grammar construction and a specific example illustrating the decoding phase to form well-formed class disjointness axioms. A possibilistic framework for the evaluation of the discovered axioms is then presented in detail.

3.1   BNF Grammar Construction

The functional-style grammar[1] used by the W3C is applied to design the grammar for generating well-formed OWL class disjointness axioms. Like in [9,10] and without loss of generality, we only focus on the case of binary axioms of the form DisjointClasses(C_1, C_2), where C_1 and C_2 may be atomic or complex classes involving relational operators and possibly including more than one single class identifier, like DisjointClasses(VideoGame, ObjectAllValuesFrom(hasStadium, Sport)). The structure of the BNF grammar here aims at mining well-formed axioms expressing the facts, i.e., instances, contained in a given RDF triple store. Hence, only resources that actually occur in the RDF dataset should be generated. We follow the approach proposed by [9,10] to organize the structure of a BNF grammar which ensures that changes in the contents of RDF repositories will not require the grammar to be rewritten. The grammar is split into a static and a dynamic part. The static part defines the syntax of the types of axioms to be extracted. The content of this part is loaded from a hand-crafted text file. Unlike [9,10], we specify it to mine only disjointness axioms involving at least one complex axiom, containing a relational operator of existential quantification $\exists$ or value restriction $\forall$, i.e., of the form $\exists r.C$ or $\forall r.C$, where r is a property and C is an atomic class. The remaining class expression can be an atomic class or a complex class expression involving an operator out of $\sqcap$, $\exists$ or $\forall$. The static part of the grammar is thus structured as follows.

```
(r1) Axiom := ClassAxiom
(r2) ClassAxiom := DisjointClasses
(r3) DisjointClasses := 'DisjointClasses' '(' ClassExpression1 ' 'ClassExpression2 ')'
(r4) ClassExpression1 :=    Class                (0)
                          | ObjectSomeValuesFrom  (1)
                          | ObjectAllValuesFrom   (2)
                          | ObjectIntersection    (3)
(r5) ClassExpression2 :=    ObjectSomeValuesFrom  (0)
                          | ObjectAllValuesFrom   (1)
(r6) ObjectIntersectionOf := 'ObjectIntersectionOf' '(' Class ' ' Class ')'
(r7) ObjectSomeValuesFrom := 'ObjectSomeValuesFrom' '(' ObjectPropertyOf ' ' Class ')'
(r8) ObjectAllValuesFrom  := 'ObjectAllValuesFrom' '(' ObjectPropertyOf ' ' Class ')'
```

The dynamic part contains production rules for the low-level non-terminals, called *primitives* in [9,10]. These production rules are automatically filled at run-time by querying the SPARQL endpoint of the RDF data source at hand. The data source here is a training RDF dataset and the primitives are Class and ObjectPropertyOf. The production rules for these two primitives are filled by the following SPARQL queries to extract atomic classes and properties (represented by their IRI) from the RDF dataset.

```
SELECT ?class WHERE { ?instance rdf:type ?class.}
SELECT ?property WHERE { ?subject ?property ?object.
                         FILTER (isIRI(?object))}
```

Let us consider an example representing a small sample of an RDF dataset:

---

[1] https://www.w3.org/TR/owl2-syntax/#Disjoint_Classes.

```
PREFIX dbr: http://dbpedia.org/resource/
PREFIX dbo: http://dbpedia.org/ontology/
PREFIX dbprop: http://dbpedia.org/property/
PREFIX rdf: http://www.w3.org/1999/02/22\-rdf-syntax-ns\#
```

```
dbr:Amblycera        rdf:type          dbo:Animal.
dbr:Salweenia        rdf:type          dbo:Plant.
Dbr:Himalayas        rdf:type          dbo:NaturalPlace.
dbr:Amadeus          rdf:type          dbo:Work.
dbr:Cat_Napping      dbprop:director   dbr:William_Hanna.
dbr:With_Abandon     dbprop:artist     dbr:Chasing_Furies.
dbr:Idris_Muhammad   dbprop:occupation dbr:Drummer.
dbr:Genes_Reunited   dbo:industry      dbr:Genealogy.
```

The productions for Class and ObjectPropertyOf would thus be:

```
(r9) Class :=  dbo:Animal        (0)     (r10) ObjectPropertyOf :=  dbprop:director    (0)
            |  dbo:Plant         (1)                            |  dbprop:artist      (1)
            |  dbo:NaturalPlace  (2)                            |  dbprop:occuptation (2)
            |  dbo:Work          (3)                            |  dbo:industry       (3)
```

3.2 Translation to Class Disjointness Axioms

We illustrate the decoding of an integer chromosome into an OWL class disjointness axiom in functional-style syntax through a specific example. Let the chromosome be 352, 265, 529, 927, 419. There is only one production for the non-terminals Axiom, ClassAxiom, DisjointClasses, ObjectIntersectionOf, ObjectSome- ValuesFrom and ObjectAllValuesFrom as it can be seen from Rules 1–3, and 6–8. In these cases, we skip using any codons for mapping and concentrate on reading codons for non-terminals having more than one production, like in Rules 4, 5, 9 and 10. We begin by decoding the first codon, i.e. 352, by Eq. 1. The result, i.e 352 modulo 4 = 0, is used to determine which production is chosen to replace the leftmost non-terminal (ClassExpression1) from its relevant rule (Rule 4). In this case, the leftmost ClassExpression1 will be replaced by the value of Class. Next, the next codon will determine the production rule for the leftmost Class and dbo:Plant is selected by the value from 265 mod 4 = 1. The mapping goes on like this until eventually there is no non-terminal left in the expression. Not all codons were required and extra codons have been simply ignored in this case.

3.3 Evaluation Framework

We follow the evaluation framework based on possibility theory, presented in [10] (see [14] for the theoretical background) to determine the fitness value of generated axioms in each generation, i.e., the credibility and generality of axioms. To make the paper self-contained, we recall the most important aspects of the approach, but we refer the interested reader to [10,14] for an in-depth treatment.

Possibility theory [15] is a mathematical theory of epistemic uncertainty. Given a finite universe of discourse Ω, whose elements $\omega \in \Omega$ may be regarded as events, values of a variable, possible worlds, or states of affairs, a possibility distribution is a mapping $\pi : \Omega \rightarrow [0,1]$, which assigns to each ω a degree of possibility ranging from 0 (impossible, excluded) to 1 (completely possible, normal). A possibility distribution π for which there exists a completely possible state of affairs ($\exists \omega \in \Omega : \pi(\omega) = 1$) is said to be *normalized*.

A possibility distribution π induces a *possibility measure* and its dual *necessity measure*, denoted by Π and N respectively. Both measures apply to a set $A \subseteq \Omega$ (or to a formula ϕ, by way of the set of its models, $A = \{\omega : \omega \models \phi\}$), and are usually defined as follows:

$$\Pi(A) = \max_{\omega \in A} \pi(\omega); \tag{2}$$

$$N(A) = 1 - \Pi(\bar{A}) = \min_{\omega \in \bar{A}}\{1 - \pi(\omega)\}. \tag{3}$$

In other words, the possibility measure of A corresponds to the greatest of the possibilities associated to its elements; conversely, the necessity measure of A is equivalent to the impossibility of its complement $\bar{A}$. A generalization of the above definition can be obtained by replacing the min and the max operators with any dual pair of triangular norm and co-norm.

Given incomplete knowledge like RDF datasets, where there exist some missing and erroneous facts (instances) as a result of the heterogeneous and collaborative character of the LOD, adopting an axiom scoring heuristic based on possibility theory is a well-suited approach. Accordingly, a candidate axiom ϕ is viewed as a hypothesis that has to be tested against the evidence contained in an RDF dataset. Its *content* is defined as a finite set of logical consequences

$$\text{content}(\phi) = \{\psi : \phi \models \psi\}, \tag{4}$$

obtained through the instantiation of ϕ to the vocabulary of the RDF repository; every $\psi \in \text{content}(\phi)$ may be readily tested by means of a SPARQL ASK query. The *support* of axiom ϕ, u_ϕ, is defined as the cardinality of content(ϕ). The support, together with the number of confirmations u_ϕ^+ (i.e., the number of ψ for which the test is successful) and the number of counterexamples u_ϕ^- (i.e., the number of ψ for which the test is unsuccessful), are used to compute a degree of *possibility* $\Pi(\phi)$ for axiom ϕ, defined, for $u(\phi) > 0$, as

$$\Pi(\phi) = 1 - \sqrt{1 - \left(\frac{u_\phi - u_\phi^-}{u_\phi}\right)^2}.$$

Alongside $\Pi(\phi)$, the dual degree of *necessity* $N(\phi)$ could normally be defined. However, for reasons explained in [10], the necessity degree of a formula would not give any useful information for scoring class disjointness axioms against real-world RDF datasets. Possibility alone is a reliable measure of the *credibility* of a class disjointness axiom, all the more so because (and this is a very important point), in view of the open world assumption, for two classes that do not share any instance, disjointness *can only be hypothetical* (i.e., fully possible, if not contradicted by facts, but *never* necessary).

In terms of the generality scoring, an axiom is the more general, the more facts are in the extension of its components. In [9], the generality of an axiom is defined as the cardinality of the sets of the facts in the RDF repository reflecting the support of each axiom, i.e., u_ϕ. However, in case one of the components of an axiom is not supported by any fact, its generality should be zero. Hence, the generality of an axiom should be measured by *the minimum* of the cardinalities of the extensions of the two class expressions involved, i.e., $g_\phi = \min\{\|[C]\|, \|[D]\|\}$ where C, D are class expressions. For the above reasons, instead of the fitness function in [9],

$$f(\phi) = u_\phi \cdot \frac{\Pi(\phi) + N(\phi)}{2}, \tag{5}$$

we resorted to the following improved definition, proposed in [10]:

$$f(\phi) = g_\phi \cdot \Pi(\phi). \tag{6}$$

The fitness value of a class disjointness axiom DisjointClasses(C, D) (or Dis(C, D) in Description Logic notation) is measured by defining the numbers of counterexamples and the support. These values are counted by executing the corresponding SPARQL queries based on *graph patterns*, via an accessible SPARQL endpoint. Each SPARQL graph pattern here is a mapping $Q(E, \texttt{?x}, \texttt{?y})$ translated from the corresponding OWL expression in axiom where E is an OWL expression, $\texttt{x}$ and $\texttt{y}$ are variables such that the query SELECT DISTINCT ?x ?y WHERE $\{Q(E, \texttt{?x}, \texttt{?y})\ \}$ returns all individuals that are instances of E.

The definition of $Q(E, \texttt{?x}, \texttt{?y})$ is based on different kinds of OWL expressions.

– E is an atomic expression.

• For an atomic class A,

$$Q(A, \texttt{?x}, \texttt{?y}) = \texttt{?x} \quad \text{rdf}: \text{type} \quad A. \tag{7}$$

where A is a valid IRI.

• For a simple relation R,

$$Q(R, \texttt{?x}, \texttt{?y}) = \texttt{?x} \quad R \quad \texttt{?y}. \tag{8}$$

where R is a valid IRI.

– E is a complex expression. We only focus on the case of complex class expressions involving relational operators, i.e., intersection, existential quantification and value restriction and skip complex relation expressions, i.e., we only allow simple relations in the expressions. In this case, Q can be inductively extended to complex expressions:

• if $E = C_1 \sqcap \ldots \sqcap C_n$ is an intersection of classes,

$$Q(E, \texttt{?x}, \texttt{?y}) = Q(C_1, \texttt{?x}, \texttt{?y}) \ldots Q(C_n, \texttt{?x}, \texttt{?y}). \tag{9}$$

• if E is an existential quantification of a class expression C,

$$Q(\exists R.C, \texttt{?x}, \texttt{?y}) = Q(R, \texttt{?x}, \texttt{?z1}) \quad Q(C, \texttt{?z1}, \texttt{?z2}) \tag{10}$$

where R is a simple relation.

- if E is a value restriction of a class expression C,

$$Q(\forall R.C, ?\mathrm{x}, ?\mathrm{y}) = \{ \ Q(R, ?\mathrm{x}, ?\mathrm{z0}) \tag{11}$$

```
FILTER NOT EXISTS {
    Q(R, ?x, ?z1)
    FILTER NOT EXISTS {
        Q(C, ?z1, ?z2)
} } } .
```

where R is a simple relation.

The support $u_{\mathsf{Dis}(C,D)}$ can thus be computed with the following SPARQL query:

$$\begin{aligned} &\texttt{SELECT (count (DISTINCT ?x AS ?u)WHERE } \{Q(C, ?\mathrm{x}, ?\mathrm{y}) \\ &\quad\texttt{UNION} \quad Q(D, ?\mathrm{x}, ?\mathrm{y})\} \end{aligned} \tag{12}$$

To compute the generality $g_{\mathsf{Dis}(C,D)} = \min(u_C, u_D)$, u_C and u_D are required, which are returned by the following SPARQL queries:

$$\texttt{SELECT (count (DISTINCT ?x) AS ?u\_C)WHERE } \{Q(C, ?\mathrm{x}, ?\mathrm{y})\} \tag{13}$$

$$\texttt{SELECT (count (DISTINCT ?x) AS ?u\_D)WHERE } \{Q(D, ?\mathrm{x}, ?\mathrm{y})\} \tag{14}$$

Finally, we must figure out the number of counterexamples $u^-_{\mathsf{Dis}(C,D)}$. Counterexamples are individuals i such that $i \in [Q(\texttt{C}, ?\mathrm{x}, ?\mathrm{y})]$ and $i \in [Q(\texttt{D}, ?\mathrm{x}, ?\mathrm{y})]$; this may be translated into a SPARQL query to compute $u^-_{\mathsf{Dis}(C,D)}$:

$$\begin{aligned} &\texttt{SELECT (count (DISTINCT ?x) AS ?counters)} \\ &\texttt{WHERE } \{Q(\texttt{C}, ?\mathrm{x}, ?\mathrm{y}) \quad Q(\texttt{D}, ?\mathrm{x}, ?\mathrm{y})\} \end{aligned} \tag{15}$$

4   Experimental Setup

The experiments are divided into two phases: (1) mining class disjointness axioms with the GE framework introduced in Sect. 3 from a training RDF dataset, i.e., a random sample of DBpedia 2015-04, and (2) testing the resulting axioms against the test dataset, i.e., the entire DBpedia 2015-04, which can be considered as an objective benchmark to evaluate the effectiveness of the method.

4.1   Training Dataset Preparation

We randomly collect 1% of the RDF triples from DBpedia 2015-04 (English version), which contains 665,532,306 RDF triples, to create the *Training Dataset (TD)*.[2] Specifically, a small linked dataset is generated where RDF triples are interlinked with each other and the number of RDF triples accounts for 1% of the triples of DBpedia corresponding to each type of resource, i.e., subjects and objects. An illustration of this mechanism to extract the sample training dataset

---

[2] Available for download at http://bit.ly/2OtFqHp.

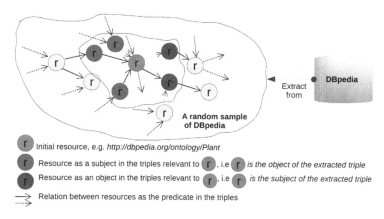

Initial resource, e.g. *http://dbpedia.org/ontology/Plant*

Resource as a subject in the triples relevant to (r) , i.e (r) *is the object of the extracted triple*

Resource as an object in the triples relevant to (r) , i.e (r) *is the subject of the extracted triple*

Relation between resources as the predicate in the triples

Fig. 1. An illustration of the Training Dataset sampling procedure

is provided in Fig. 1. Let r be an initial resource for the extraction process, e.g., http://dbpedia.org/ontology/Plant; 1% of the RDF triples having r as their subject, of the form $\langle r\ p\ r'\rangle$, and 1% of the triples having r as their object, of the form $\langle r''\ p'\ r\rangle$, will be randomly extracted from DBpedia. Then, the same will be done for every resource r' and r'' mentioned in the extracted triples, until the size of the training dataset reaches 1% of the size of DBpedia. If the number of triples to be extracted for a resource is less than 1 (according to the 1% proportion), we round it to 1 triple.

We applied the proposed mechanism to extract a training dataset containing 6,739,240 connected RDF triples with a variety of topics from DBpedia.

4.2 Parameters

We use the BNF grammar introduced in Sect. 3.1. Given how the grammar was constructed, the mapping of any chromosome of length ≥ 6 will always be successful. Hence, we can set $maxWrap = 0$. We ran our algorithm in 20 different runs on different parameter settings. In addition, to make fair comparisons possible, a set of milestones of total effort k (defined as the total number of fitness evaluations) corresponding to each population size are also recorded for each run, namely 100,000; 200,000; 300,000 and 400,000, respectively. The maximum numbers of generations $maxGenerations$ (used as the stopping criterion of the algorithm) are automatically determined based on the values of the total effort k so that $popSize \cdot maxGenerations = k$. The parameters are summarized in Table 1.

4.3 Performance Evaluation

We measure the performance of the method using the entire DBpedia 2015-04 as a test set, measuring possibility and generality for every distinct axiom discovered by our algorithm. To avoid overloading DBpedia's SPARQL endpoint, we set up a local mirror using the Virtuoso Universal Server.[3]

---

[3] https://virtuoso.openlinksw.com/.

5   Results and Discussions

We ran the GE method 20 times with the parameters shown in Table 1 on the BNF grammar defined in Sect. 3.1. Full results are available online.[4]

Table 1. Parameter values for GE.

Parameter	Value
Total effort k	100,000; 200,000; 300,000; 400,000
$initLenChrom$	6
$pCross$	80%
$pMut$	1%
$popSize$	1000; 2000; 5000; 10000

Table 2. Number of valid distinct axioms discovered over 20 runs.

k	popSize			
	1000	2000	5000	10000
100000	8806	11389	4684	4788
200000	6204	13670	10632	9335
300000	5436	10541	53021	14590
400000	5085	9080	35102	21670

The number of valid distinct axioms, i.e., axioms ϕ such that $\Pi(\phi) > 0$ and $g_\phi > 0$, discovered is listed in Table 2. For measuring the accuracy of our results, given that the discovered axioms come with an estimated degree of possibility, which is essentially a fuzzy degree of membership, we propose to use a fuzzy extension of the usual definition of *precision*, based on the most widely used definition of fuzzy set cardinality, introduced in [16] as follows: given a fuzzy set F defined on a countable universe set Δ,

$$\|F\| = \sum_{x \in \Delta} F(x), \tag{16}$$

In our case, we may view $\Pi(\phi)$ as the degree of membership of axiom ϕ in the (fuzzy) set of the "positive" axioms. The value of precision can thus be computed against the test dataset, i.e., DBpedia 2015-04, according to the formula

$$\text{precision} = \frac{\|\text{true positives}\|}{\|\text{discovered axioms}\|} = \frac{\sum_\phi \Pi_{\text{DBpedia}}(\phi)}{\sum_\phi \Pi_{\text{TD}}(\phi)}, \tag{17}$$

where Π_{TD} and Π_{DBpedia} are the possibility measures computed on the training dataset and DBpedia, respectively.

The results in Table 3 confirm the high accuracy of our axiom discovery method with a precision ranging from 0.969 to 0.998 for all the different considered sizes of population and different numbers of generations (reflected through the values of total effort). According the results, we have statistically compared the performance of using different settings of *popSize* and k. The best setting $\{popSize = 5,000; k = 300,000\}$ allows the method to discover 53,021 distinct valid axioms with very high accuracy, i.e., $precision = 0.993 \pm 0.007$. Indeed, the plot in Fig. 2 illustrating the distribution of axioms in terms of possibility and generality shows that most discovered axioms with this setting are highly possible ($\Pi(\phi) > \frac{2}{3}$).

---

[4] http://bit.ly/32YEQH1.

In order to obtain a more objective evaluation, we analyze in detail the axioms discovered by the algorithm with this best setting. First, we observe that together with the mandatory class expression containing the ∀ or ∃ operator, most extracted disjointness axioms contain an atomic class expression. This may be due to the fact that the support of atomic classes is usually larger than the support of a complex class expression. We also analyse axioms containing complex expressions in both their members. These axioms are less general, even though they are completely possible. An example is the case with DisjointClasses(ObjectAllValuesFrom(dbprop:author dbo:Place) ObjectAllValuesFrom(dbprop:placeofBurial dbo:Place)) ($\Pi(\phi) = 1.0$; $g_\phi = 4$), which states that "what can only be buried in a place cannot be what can only have a place as its author".

Table 3. Average precision per run ($\pm std$)

k	popSize			
	1,000	2,000	5,000	10,000
100,000	0.981 ± 0.019	0.999 ± 0.002	0.998 ± 0.002	0.998 ± 0.003
200,000	0.973 ± 0.024	0.979 ± 0.011	0.998 ± 0.001	0.998 ± 0.002
300,000	0.972 ± 0.024	0.973 ± 0.014	0.993 ± 0.007	0.998 ± 0.001
400,000	0.972 ± 0.024	0.969 ± 0.018	0.980 ± 0.008	0.998 ± 0.001

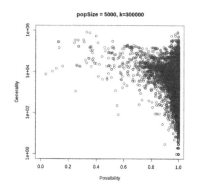

popSize = 5000, k=300000

Fig. 2. Possibility and generality distribution of the discovered axioms

We also observe that some discovered axioms have a particularly high generality, as it is the case with DisjointClasses(dbo:Writer ObjectAllValuesFrom(dbo:writer dbo:Agent)) ($\Pi(\phi) = 0.982$; $g_\phi = 79,464$). This can be explained by the existence of classes supported by a huge number of instances (like dbo:Agent or dbo:Writer). From it, we might say that it is quite possible that "writers are never written by agents". Another similar case is axiom DisjointClasses(dbo:Journalist ObjectAllValuesFrom(dbo:distributor dbo:Agent)) ($\Pi(\phi) = 0.992$; $g_\phi = 32,533$) whereby in general "journalists are not distributed by agents", although it would appear that some journalists are, since $\Pi(\phi) < 1$!

Finally, we analyze an example of a completely possible and highly general axiom, DisjointClasses(dbo:Stadium ObjectAllValuesFrom(dbo:birthPlace dbo:Place)) ($\Pi(\phi) = 1.0$; $g_\phi = 10,245$), which we can paraphrase as "stadiums cannot have a place as their birthplace". Knowing that Stadium and Place are not disjoint, this axiom states that Stadium and ∀birthPlace.Place are in fact disjoint; in addition, ∀.birthPlace.Place, i.e., "(people) whose birthplace is a place" is a class with many instances, hence the high generality of the axiom.

6   Related Work

Some prominent works are introduced in Sect. 1 and are also analysed in [9,10]. In this paper, we only focus on recent contributions relevant to class disjointness discovery. For instance, Reynaud *et al.* [7] use *Redescription Mining (RM)* to learn class equivalence and disjointness axioms with the *ReReMi* algorithm. *RM* is about extracting a category definition in terms of a description shared by all the instances of a given class, i.e., equivalence axioms, and finding incompatible categories which do not share any instance, i.e., class disjointness axioms. Their method, based on *Formal Concept Analysis (FCA)*, a mathematical framework mainly used for classification and knowledge discovery, aims at searching for data subsets with multiple descriptions, like different views of the same objects. While category redescriptions, i.e., equivalence axioms, refer to complex types, defined with the help of relational operators like $A \equiv \exists r.C$ or $A \equiv B \sqcap \exists r.C$, in the case of incompatible categories, the redescriptions are only based on the set of attributes with the predicates of dct:subject, i.e., axioms involving atomic classes only. Another procedure for extracting disjointness axioms [8] requires a *Terminological Cluster Tree (TCT)* to search for a set of pairwise disjoint clusters. A decision tree is built and each node in it corresponds to a concept with a logical formula. The tree is traversed to create concept descriptions collecting the concepts installed in the leaf-nodes. Then, by exploring the paths from the root to the leaves, intensional definitions of disjoint concepts are derived. Two concept descriptions are disjoint if they lie on different leaf nodes. An important limitation of the method is the time-consuming and computationally expensive process of growing a *TCT*. A small change in the data can lead to a large change in the structure of the tree. Also, like other intensional methods, that work relies on the services of a reasoning component, but suffers from scalability problems for the application to large datasets, like the ones found on the LOD, caused by the excessive growth of the decision tree.

In [9,10], a heuristic method by using *Grammatical Evolution (GE)* is applied to generate class disjointness axioms from an RDF repository. Extracted axioms include both atomic and complex axioms, i.e., defined with the help of relational operators of intersection and union; in other words, axioms like $\mathsf{Dis}(C_1, C_2)$, where C_1 and C_2 are complex class expressions including $\sqcap$ and $\sqcup$ operators. The use of a grammar allows great flexibility: only the grammar needs to be changed to mine different data repositories for different types of axioms. However, the dependence on SPARQL endpoints (i.e., query engines) for testing mined axioms against facts, i.e., instances, in large RDF repositories limits the performance of the method. In addition, evaluating the effectiveness of the method requires the participation of experts in specific domains, i.e., the use of a *Gold Standard*, which is proportional to the number of concepts. Hence, the extracted axioms are limited to the classes relevant to a small scope of topics, namely the *Work* topic of DBpedia.[5] Also, complex axioms are defined with the help of relational operators of intersection and union, which can also be mechanically derived from the known atomic axioms.

---

[5] https://wiki.dbpedia.org/.

7   Conclusion

We have proposed an extension of a grammar-based GP method for mining disjointness axioms involving complex class expressions. These expressions consist of the relational operators of existential quantification and value restriction. The use of a training-testing model allows to objectively validate the method, while also alleviating the computational bottleneck of SPARQL endpoints. We analyzed some examples of discovered axioms. The experimental results confirm that the proposed method is capable of discovering highly accurate and general axioms.

In the future, we will focus on mining disjointness axioms involving further types of complex classes, by bringing into the picture other relational operators such as `owl:hasValue` and `owl:OneOf`. We might also forbid the occurrence of atomic classes at the root of class expressions. We also plan on refining the evaluation of candidate axioms with the inclusion of some measurement of their complexity in the fitness function.

Acknowledgments. This work has been supported by the French government, through the 3IA Côte d'Azur "Investments in the Future" project managed by the National Research Agency (ANR) with the reference number ANR-19-P3IA-0002.

References

1. Guarino, N., Oberle, D., Staab, S.: What is an ontology? In: Staab, S., Studer, R. (eds.) Handbook on Ontologies. IHIS, pp. 1–17. Springer, Heidelberg (2009). https://doi.org/10.1007/978-3-540-92673-3_0
2. Gruber, T.R.: Toward principles for the design of ontologies used for knowledge sharing? Int. J. Hum. Comput. Stud. **43**(5–6), 907–928 (1995)
3. Zhu, M.: DC proposal: ontology learning from noisy linked data. In: Aroyo, L., et al. (eds.) ISWC 2011. LNCS, vol. 7032, pp. 373–380. Springer, Heidelberg (2011). https://doi.org/10.1007/978-3-642-25093-4_31
4. Völker, J., Vrandečić, D., Sure, Y., Hotho, A.: Learning disjointness. In: Franconi, E., Kifer, M., May, W. (eds.) ESWC 2007. LNCS, vol. 4519, pp. 175–189. Springer, Heidelberg (2007). https://doi.org/10.1007/978-3-540-72667-8_14
5. Völker, J., Fleischhacker, D., Stuckenschmidt, H.: Automatic acquisition of class disjointness. J. Web Semant. **35**, 124–139 (2015)
6. Lehmann, J.: Dl-learner: learning concepts in description logics. J. Mach. Learn. Res. **10**, 2639–2642 (2009)
7. Reynaud, J., Toussaint, Y., Napoli, A.: Redescription mining for learning definitions and disjointness axioms in linked open data. In: Endres, D., Alam, M., Şotropa, D. (eds.) ICCS 2019. LNCS (LNAI), vol. 11530, pp. 175–189. Springer, Cham (2019). https://doi.org/10.1007/978-3-030-23182-8_13
8. Rizzo, G., d'Amato, C., Fanizzi, N., Esposito, F.: Terminological cluster trees for disjointness axiom discovery. In: Blomqvist, E., Maynard, D., Gangemi, A., Hoekstra, R., Hitzler, P., Hartig, O. (eds.) ESWC 2017. LNCS, vol. 10249, pp. 184–201. Springer, Cham (2017). https://doi.org/10.1007/978-3-319-58068-5_12

9. Nguyen, T.H., Tettamanzi, A.G.B.: Learning class disjointness axioms using grammatical evolution. In: Sekanina, L., Hu, T., Lourenço, N., Richter, H., García-Sánchez, P. (eds.) EuroGP 2019. LNCS, vol. 11451, pp. 278–294. Springer, Cham (2019). https://doi.org/10.1007/978-3-030-16670-0_18

10. Nguyen, T.H., Tettamanzi, A.G.B.: An evolutionary approach to class disjointness axiom discovery. In: WI, pp. 68–75. ACM (2019)

11. Koza, J.R.: Genetic Programming: On the Programming of Computers by Means of Natural Selection. MIT Press, Cambridge (1992)

12. Vanneschi, L., Poli, R.: Genetic programming – introduction, applications, theory and open issues. In: Rozenberg, G., Bäck, T., Kok, J.N. (eds.) Handbook of Natural Computing, pp. 709–739. Springer, Heidelberg (2012). https://doi.org/10.1007/978-3-540-92910-9_24

13. O'Neill, M., Ryan, C.: Grammatical evolution. Trans. Evol. Comput. 5(4), 349–358 (2001). https://doi.org/10.1109/4235.942529

14. Tettamanzi, A.G.B., Faron-Zucker, C., Gandon, F.: Possibilistic testing of OWL axioms against RDF data. Int. J. Approx. Reason. **91**, 114–130 (2017)

15. Zadeh, L.A.: Fuzzy sets as a basis for a theory of possibility. Fuzzy Sets Syst. **1**, 3–28 (1978)

16. De Luca, A., Termini, S.: A definition of a nonprobabilistic entropy in the setting of fuzzy sets theory. Inf. Control **20**, 301–312 (1972)

An Incremental Algorithm for Computing All Repairs in Inconsistent Knowledge Bases

Bruno Yun[1(✉)] and Madalina Croitoru[2]

[1] University of Aberdeen, Aberdeen, UK
`bruno.yun@abdn.ac.uk`
[2] University of Montpellier, Montpellier, France

Abstract. Repair techniques are used for reasoning in presence of inconsistencies. Such techniques rely on optimisations to avoid the computation of all repairs while certain applications need the generation of all repairs. In this paper, we show that the problem of all repair computation is not trivial in practice. To account for a scalable solution, we provide an incremental approach for the computation of all repairs when the conflicts have a cardinality of at most three. We empirically study its performance on generated knowledge bases (where the knowledge base generator could be seen as a secondary contribution in itself).

Keywords: Repairs · Knowledge base · Existential rule

1 Introduction

We place ourselves in the context of reasoning with knowledge bases (KBs) expressed using Datalog± [11] and investigate *inconsistent KBs*, i.e. KBs with the inconsistency solely stemming from the factual level and a coherent ontology. For instance, a prominent practical application in this setting is Ontology Based Data Access (OBDA) [22] that considers the querying of multiple heterogeneous data sources via an unifying ontology. With few exceptions [7], approaches performing query answering under inconsistency in the aforementioned setting rely on repairs [3]. Repairs, originally defined for database approaches [1] are maximal subsets of facts consistent with the ontology. Inconsistency tolerant semantics [21] avoid the computational overhead of computing all repairs by various algorithmic strategies [10]. Unfortunately, certain tasks need the repair enumeration problem, such as inconsistency-based repair ranking frameworks [26] or argumentation-based decision-making [12,25].

We focus on the problem of *computing possibly some or all repairs from* Datalog± *inconsistent KBs*. Our proposal relies on the notion of conflict (i.e. set of facts that trigger an inconsistency). Although approaches exist for computing conflicts in SAT instances or propositional logic [16,17], there are few works addressing conflict computation for Datalog± that come with additional

© Springer Nature Switzerland AG 2020
M. Alam et al. (Eds.): ICCS 2020, LNAI 12277, pp. 33–47, 2020.
https://doi.org/10.1007/978-3-030-57855-8_3

challenges given the expressivity of the language [23]. In this paper we extend the state of the art with a *computationally efficient manner* to generate the set of all repairs using an incremental algorithm adapted from stable set computation in hypergraphs [9]. To this end, we make the hypothesis that the KB allows for bounded sized conflicts (limited here at three). Our proposed algorithm, in a first step, finds the conflicts of the KBs using specific sequences of directed hyperedges (derivations) of the Graph of Atom Dependency (GAD) [19] leading to *falsum*. In the second step, we use an efficient incremental algorithm for finding all repairs of a set of facts from the set of conflicts of a given KB. This efficient algorithm was inspired by the problem of extending a given list of maximal independent sets in hypergraphs when hyperedges have a bounded dimension [9]. The aforementioned graph theoretical problem was proven to be in the NC complexity class if the size of the hyperedges were bounded by three [9,13] which means that the task can be efficiently solved on a parallel computer where processors are permitted to flip coins. Please note that although conflicts of size more than three can easily occur even when the arity of the negative constraints is limited to two, we do not find that this condition is limiting as, in reality, it is not unlikely to find KBs with only conflicts of size two.

Therefore, the proposed algorithm is more efficient than the approach of [23] for two reasons: (1) We do not compute all the "causes" and "consequences" of all the atoms and restrict ourselves to the derivations that lead to an inconsistency. (2) We use an efficient algorithm for incrementally computing repairs from conflicts.

When implementing our technique we noticed two key aspects of our approach: (1) getting some repairs from a KB can be relatively easy as the average number of repairs found during the allotted time did not change when the KB grew and (2) finding the last repairs was comparatively harder than the first repairs. Please note that although the computational problem of getting all repairs is in EXPTIME as the number of repairs can be exponential w.r.t. the number of facts [8], the proposed algorithm has a two fold significance: (1) it improves upon the state of the art for the task of all repair computation and (2) it is a viable alternative for applications that require the *repair enumeration*.

2   Background Notions

We introduce some notions of the Datalog$\pm$ language. A *fact* is a ground atom of the form $p(t_1, \ldots, t_k)$ where p is a predicate of arity k and for every $i \in \{1, \ldots, k\}, t_i$ is a constant. An existential *rule* is of the form $r = \forall \overrightarrow{X}, \overrightarrow{Y}$ $B[\overrightarrow{X}, \overrightarrow{Y}] \rightarrow \exists \overrightarrow{Z} H[\overrightarrow{Z}, \overrightarrow{X}]$ where B (called the body) and H (called the head) are existentially closed atoms or conjunctions of existentially closed atoms and $\overrightarrow{X}, \overrightarrow{Y}, \overrightarrow{Z}$ their respective vectors of variables. A *rule is applicable* on a set of facts $\mathcal{F}$ iff there exists a homomorphism from the body of the rule to $\mathcal{F}$. Applying a rule to a set of facts (also called *chase*) consists of adding the set of atoms of the conclusion of the rule to the facts according to the application homomorphism. Different *chase* mechanisms use different simplifications that prevent infinite redundancies [5]. We use recognisable classes of existential rules where the chase is guaranteed to stop [5]. A *negative constraint* is a rule of the form $\forall \overrightarrow{X}, \overrightarrow{Y}\ B[\overrightarrow{X}, \overrightarrow{Y}] \rightarrow \bot$ where B is an existentially closed atom or conjunctions of existentially closed atoms, $\overrightarrow{X}, \overrightarrow{Y}$, their respective vectors of variables and $\bot$ is *falsum*.

Definition 1. *A KB is a tuple $\mathcal{K} = (\mathcal{F}, \mathcal{R}, \mathcal{N})$ where $\mathcal{F}$ is a finite set of facts, $\mathcal{R}$ a set of rules and $\mathcal{N}$ a set of negative constraints.*

Example 1. Let $\mathcal{K} = (\mathcal{F}, \mathcal{R}, \mathcal{N})$ with $\mathcal{F} = \{a(m), b(m), c(m), d(m), e(m), f(m),$ $g(m), h(m), i(m), j(m)\}$, $\mathcal{R} = \{\forall x(f(x) \wedge h(x) \rightarrow k(x)), \forall x(i(x) \wedge j(x) \rightarrow l(x))\}$ and $\mathcal{N} = \{\forall x(a(x) \wedge b(x) \wedge c(x) \rightarrow \bot), \forall x(c(x) \wedge d(x) \rightarrow \bot), \forall x(e(x) \wedge f(x) \wedge d(x) \rightarrow \bot), \forall x(e(x) \wedge f(x) \rightarrow \bot), \forall x(i(x) \wedge k(x) \rightarrow \bot), \forall x(l(x) \wedge h(x) \rightarrow \bot)\}$.

In a KB $\mathcal{K} = (\mathcal{F}, \mathcal{R}, \mathcal{N})$, the saturation $Sat_\mathcal{R}(X)$ of a set of facts X is the set of atoms obtained after successively applying the set of rules $\mathcal{R}$ on X until a fixed point. A set $X \subseteq \mathcal{F}$ is $\mathcal{R}$-inconsistent iff *falsum* can be entailed from the saturation of X by $\mathcal{R} \cup \mathcal{N}$, i.e. $Sat_{\mathcal{R} \cup \mathcal{N}}(X) \models \bot$. A conflict of a KB is a minimal $\mathcal{R}$-inconsistent subset of facts.

Definition 2. *Let us consider $\mathcal{K} = (\mathcal{F}, \mathcal{R}, \mathcal{N})$. $X \subseteq \mathcal{F}$ is a conflict of $\mathcal{K}$ iff $Sat_{\mathcal{R} \cup \mathcal{N}}(X) \models \bot$ and for every $X' \subset X$, $Sat_{\mathcal{R} \cup \mathcal{N}}(X') \not\models \bot$.*

The set of all conflicts of $\mathcal{K}$ is denoted $Conflict(\mathcal{K})$.

Example 2 [(Cont'd Example 1]. We have $Conflict(\mathcal{K}) = \{\{a(m), b(m), c(m)\}, \{c(m), d(m)\}, \{e(m), f(m)\}, \{f(m), h(m), i(m)\}, \{h(m), i(m), j(m)\}\}$. The set $\{d(m), e(m), f(m)\}$ is not a conflict since $Sat_{\mathcal{R} \cup \mathcal{N}}(\{e(m), f(m)\}) \models \bot$.

To practically compute the conflicts, we use a special directed hypergraph [14] called the Graph of Atom Dependency (GAD) and defined by [19].

Definition 3. *Given a KB $\mathcal{K} = (\mathcal{F}, \mathcal{R}, \mathcal{N})$, the GAD of $\mathcal{K}$, denoted by $GAD_\mathcal{K}$, is a pair (V, D) such that V is the set of atoms in $Sat_{\mathcal{R} \cup \mathcal{N}}(\mathcal{F})$ and $D = \{(U, W) \in 2^V \times 2^V$ s.t. there exists $r \in \mathcal{R} \cup \mathcal{N}$ and a homomorphism π such that W is obtained by applying r on U using $\pi\}$.*

Example 3 [Cont'd Example 1]. Here, we have that $V = \{\bot, a(m), b(m), c(m), \ldots, l(m)\}$ and $D = \{D_1, D_2, \ldots, D_8\}$ where $D_1 = (\{f(m), h(m)\}, \{k(m)\}), D_2 = (\{i(m)\}, j(m)\}, \{l(m)\}), D_3 = (\{a(m), c(m), b(m)\}, \{\bot\}), D_4 = (\{c(m), d(m)\}, \{\bot\}), D_5 = (\{k(m), i(m)\}, \{\bot\}), D_6 = (\{h(m), l(m)\}, \{\bot\}), D_7 = (\{e(m), f(m)\}, \{\bot\})$ and $D_8 = (\{d(m), e(m), f(m)\}, \{\bot\})$.

A derivation is a sequence of rule applications such that each rule can be applied successively. A derivation for a specific atom a is a finite minimal sequence of rule applications starting from a set of facts and ending with a rule application that generates a. We now define the notion of fix and repair w.r.t. a set $Y \subseteq 2^\mathcal{F}$ of a KB $\mathcal{K} = (\mathcal{F}, \mathcal{R}, \mathcal{N})$, that will be used in the proposed algorithms.

Definition 4. *Let $\mathcal{F}$ be a set of facts, $F \subseteq \mathcal{F}$ is a fix of $\mathcal{F}$ w.r.t. $Y \subseteq 2^{\mathcal{F}}$ iff for every $X \in Y, X \cap F \neq \emptyset$. A fix F of $\mathcal{F}$ w.r.t. Y is called a minimal fix of $\mathcal{F}$ w.r.t. Y iff for all $F' \subset F$, it holds that F' is not a fix of $\mathcal{F}$ w.r.t. Y. The set of all minimal fixes of $\mathcal{F}$ w.r.t. Y is denoted by $MFix(\mathcal{F}, Y)$.*

The notion of KB reparation is linked to that of conflict via the minimal fixes. We define a repair of a set of facts $\mathcal{F}$ w.r.t. a set $Y \subseteq 2^{\mathcal{F}}$.

Definition 5. *Let $\mathcal{F}$ be a set of facts, $X \subseteq \mathcal{F}$ is a repair of $\mathcal{F}$ w.r.t. $Y \subseteq 2^{\mathcal{F}}$ iff there exists $F \in MFix(\mathcal{F}, Y)$ such that $X = \mathcal{F} \setminus F$.*

Please note that there is a bijection between the set of repairs and the set of minimal fixes of a set $\mathcal{F}$ w.r.t. a set $Y \subseteq 2^{\mathcal{F}}$. We denote the set of all repairs of $\mathcal{F}$ w.r.t. Y by $Repair(\mathcal{F}, Y)$. Moreover, the repairs of $\mathcal{F}$ w.r.t. $Conflict(\mathcal{K})$ are the maximal, for set inclusion, consistent subsets of $\mathcal{F}$.

3   Repairs Generation

In this section, we detail a framework for computing all maximal consistent sets of a KB. The approach is given in Algorithm 1 and composed of two steps:

1. **(Conflicts Generation).** First, the GAD is constructed. Then, all conflicts are computed by extracting the facts used in the minimal derivations for $\bot$.
2. **(From Conflicts to Repairs).** Second, repairs of $\mathcal{F}$ w.r.t. $Conflict(\mathcal{K})$ are constructed using the *FindAllRepairs* call. The provided algorithm is efficient for computing repairs in the case where the conflicts are at most of size 3.

Algorithm 1: Finding all maximal consistent sets of $\mathcal{K}$

---

   input : A KB $\mathcal{K} = (\mathcal{F}, \mathcal{R}, \mathcal{N})$
   output: A set I of repairs of $\mathcal{F}$ w.r.t. $Conflict(\mathcal{K})$
1 $GAD_{\mathcal{K}} \leftarrow$ GADConstructor($\mathcal{K}$);
2 $C \leftarrow$ FindAllConflicts($\mathcal{K}, GAD_{\mathcal{K}}$);
3 $Result \leftarrow$ FindAllRepairs($\mathcal{K}, C$);
4 **return** $Result$;

Conflicts are subsets of $\mathcal{F}$ but there is not always a negative constraint directly triggered by the conflict (since the actual "clash" can be between the atoms generated using rules). These two kinds of conflicts are referred to as "conflicts" and "naive conflicts" in Rocher [23]. The use of the GAD allows to keep track of all the rule applications and to propagate those "clashes" into $\mathcal{F}^1$.

---

[1] The algorithms avoid the problem of derivation loss [19] which is important for the completeness of our approach. Note that in Hecham et al. [19] the authors discuss how finding all derivations for an atom is practically feasible despite the problem being exponential for combined complexity but polynomial for data complexity.

FindAllConflicts takes as input a KB $\mathcal{K}$ and $GAD_{\mathcal{K}}$ and outputs the set of all conflicts of this KB. It is based on three steps: (1) It builds the GAD. This step has been proven to be efficient as the GAD can be constructed alongside the chase [18]. (2) The GAD is used for finding the set of all possible minimal derivations for $\bot$. (3) For each derivation for $\bot$, the facts in $\mathcal{F}$ that enabled the generation of this derivation are extracted. They correspond to conflicts of $\mathcal{K}$.

Example 4 (Cont'd Example 2). The set of all minimal derivations for $\bot$ is $\{(D_2, D_6),\ (D_1, D_5),\ (D_7),\ (D_4),\ (D_3)\}$. The set of conflicts is $\{\{h(m),$ $i(m), j(m)\},\ \{f(m), h(m), i(m)\}, \{e(m),\ f(m)\},\ \{c(m),\ d(m)\}, \{a(m), b(m),$ $c(m)\}\}$.

3.1 From Conflicts to Repairs

Our approach for computing the set of maximal consistent sets of a KB from the set of conflicts is composed of four algorithms: *FindAllRepairs, NewMinimalFix, FindRepairs* and *SubRepair*. In order to compute the repairs of $\mathcal{F}$ w.r.t. the set of conflicts of $\mathcal{K}$, we need to first compute the set of all minimal fixes of $\mathcal{F}$ w.r.t. $Conflict(\mathcal{K})$. *FindAllRepairs* computes the repairs of $\mathcal{F}$ w.r.t. $Conflict(\mathcal{K})$ by iteratively computing the set of all minimal fixes of $\mathcal{F}$ w.r.t. $Conflict(\mathcal{K})$ before converting them into repairs of $\mathcal{F}$ w.r.t. $Conflict(\mathcal{K})$. More precisely, *FindAllRepairs* repeatedly calls *NewMinimalFix* which returns a new minimal fix of $\mathcal{F}$ w.r.t. $Conflict(\mathcal{K})$ not previously found. The idea behind *NewMinimalFix* is that it produces new sets (U and A) depending on the minimal fixes of $\mathcal{F}$ w.r.t. $Conflict(\mathcal{K})$ that were previously found. A repair for U w.r.t. A can be modified in order to return a new fix of $\mathcal{F}$ w.r.t. $Conflict(\mathcal{K})$. Lastly, *FindRepair* computes a repair for U w.r.t. a set $A \subseteq 2^U$ by relying on *SubRepair* for iteratively constructing the repair. In the rest of this section, we detail the general outline of *FindAllRepairs* and *NewMinimalFix*.

FindAllRepairs (see Algorithm 2) takes as input a KB $\mathcal{K}$ and its set of conflicts $Conflict(\mathcal{K})$ and returns the set of all repairs of $\mathcal{F}$ w.r.t. $Conflict(\mathcal{K})$. The sets B and I contain the set of minimal fixes and repairs of $\mathcal{F}$ w.r.t. $Conflict(\mathcal{K})$ respectively and are initially empty. $NewMinimalFix(\mathcal{K}, Conflict(\mathcal{K}), B)$ is called for finding a new minimal fix of $\mathcal{F}$ w.r.t. $Conflict(\mathcal{K})$ that is not contained in B. If $NewMinimalFix(\mathcal{K}, Conflict(\mathcal{K}), B)$ returns the empty set then B already contains all possible minimal fixes of $\mathcal{F}$ w.r.t. $Conflict(\mathcal{K})$. Otherwise, the new minimal fix of $\mathcal{F}$ w.r.t. $Conflict(\mathcal{K})$ is stored in B and converted into a repair of $\mathcal{F}$ w.r.t. $Conflict(\mathcal{K})$ that is stored in I.

NewMinimalFix (see Algorithm 3) takes as input a KB $\mathcal{K}$, the corresponding set of conflicts $Conflict(\mathcal{K})$ and a set of minimal fixes B of $\mathcal{F}$ w.r.t. $Conflict(\mathcal{K})$ and returns the empty set if B contains all the minimal fixes of $\mathcal{F}$ w.r.t. $Conflict(\mathcal{K})$, otherwise it returns a new minimal fix of $\mathcal{F}$ w.r.t. $Conflict(\mathcal{K})$ that is not contained in B. First, the facts in $\mathcal{F}$ that are not in any conflict of $\mathcal{K}$ are removed. By definition, these facts cannot be in a minimal fix of $\mathcal{F}$ w.r.t. $Conflict(\mathcal{K})$. Then, we check whether or not each fact is at least in one element of B. If this is not the case, we can build a minimal fix of $\mathcal{F}$ w.r.t.

Algorithm 2: FindAllRepairs

---

    input : A KB $\mathcal{K} = (\mathcal{F}, \mathcal{R}, \mathcal{N})$ and a set of conflicts $Conflict(\mathcal{K})$
    output: A set I of repairs of $\mathcal{F}$ w.r.t. $Conflict(\mathcal{K})$
1 $B \leftarrow \emptyset, I \leftarrow \emptyset, stops \leftarrow false$;
2 **while** $stops = false$ **do**
3     $MF \leftarrow \texttt{NewMinimalFix}(\mathcal{K}, Conflict(\mathcal{K}), B)$;
4   **if** $MF = \emptyset$ **then**
5        $stops = true$;
6   **else**
7        $B \leftarrow B \cup \{MF\}$;
8        $I \leftarrow I \cup (\mathcal{F} \setminus MF)$;

9 **return** I;

$Conflict(\mathcal{K})$ that is not in B (line 6 to 10). To do so, we first pick an arbitrary fact u that is not in any set of B. Then, we pick an arbitrary conflict A_u containing u and find a repair Rep of U w.r.t. $\mathcal{A}'$ where $\mathcal{A}'$ is the set of restricted conflicts by U^2 where $U = \mathcal{F} \setminus A_u$. The resulting $U \setminus Rep$ is a minimal fix of U w.r.t. $\mathcal{A}'$. It is extended to a minimal fix of $\mathcal{F}$ w.r.t. $Conflict(\mathcal{K})$ by adding the fact u. It can thus be added to B as the first minimal fix containing u.

Example 5 (Cont'd Example 4). At step 1 in Table 1, $g(m)$ is removed because it is in no conflicts. Then, since $\bigcup B = \emptyset$ is included in $\mathcal{F}$, an arbitrary fact $u = a(m)$ in $\mathcal{F}$ is picked. Then, an arbitrary conflict $A_u = \{a(m), b(m), c(m)\}$ that contains u is selected. $U = \mathcal{F} \setminus A_u$ is $\{d(m), e(m), f(m), h(m), i(m), j(m)\}$ and the restricted set of conflict by U is $\{\{d(m)\}, \{e(m), f(m)\}, \{f(m), h(m), i(m)\}, \{h(m), i(m), j(m)\}\}$. The repair of U w.r.t. $\mathcal{A}'$ returned is $\{j(m), i(m), f(m)\}$ which means that $\{d(m), e(m), h(m)\}$ is a minimal fix of U w.r.t. $\mathcal{A}'$. We conclude that the set $\{a(m), d(m), e(m), h(m)\}$ is a minimal fix of $\mathcal{F}$ w.r.t. $Conflict(\mathcal{K})$. This process is repeated by iteratively selecting the facts $b(m), c(m), f(m), i(m)$ and $j(m)$. As the reader can note, after step 6, we have that $\bigcup B = \mathcal{F}$.

If each fact is at least in one element of B then each conflict a' of $\mathcal{K}$ is a fix of $\mathcal{F}$ w.r.t. B. However, if a' is not a minimal fix of $\mathcal{F}$ w.r.t. B then we can find u such that $a' \setminus \{u\}$ is still a fix of $\mathcal{F}$ w.r.t. B (line 13 to 17). We use the previous method and find a repair Rep of U w.r.t. $\mathcal{A}'$ where $\mathcal{A}'$ is the restricted set of conflicts by U with $U = \mathcal{F} \setminus (a' \setminus \{u\})$. $U \setminus Rep$ is thus a minimal fix of U w.r.t. $\mathcal{A}'$ but also a minimal fix of $\mathcal{F}$ w.r.t. $Conflict(\mathcal{K})$. In the example, we skipped this as each a' in $Conflict(\mathcal{K})$ is a minimal fix of $\mathcal{F}$ w.r.t. B.

In the case where each fact is at least in one minimal fix of $\mathcal{F}$ w.r.t. B and each conflict is a minimal fix of $\mathcal{F}$ w.r.t. B, we can still find new minimal fix $\mathcal{F}$ w.r.t. $Conflict(\mathcal{K})$ that is not in B (line 18 to 28). We first find subsets S of $\mathcal{F}$

---

[2] The set of restricted conflicts by a set U is the set containing each intersection of a conflict with U. Namely, it is equal to $\{X \cap U \mid X \in Conflict(\mathcal{K})\}$.

Algorithm 3: NewMinimalFix

---

input : A KB $\mathcal{K} = (\mathcal{F}, \mathcal{R}, \mathcal{N})$, the corresponding set of conflicts $Conflict(\mathcal{K})$
 and a set B of minimal fixes of $\mathcal{F}$ w.r.t. $Conflict(\mathcal{K})$

output: Either a new minimal fix of $\mathcal{F}$ w.r.t. $Conflict(\mathcal{K})$ that is not in B or $\emptyset$
 if B contains all of them

1 $V \leftarrow \mathcal{F}$;
2 **for** $v \in V$ **do**
3 $\quad$ **if** *there is no* $a \in Conflict(\mathcal{K})$ *such that* $v \in a$ **then**
4 $\quad\quad$ $V \leftarrow V \setminus \{v\}$;

5 **if** $\bigcup B \subset V$ **then**
6 $\quad$ $u \leftarrow$ random fact in $V \setminus \bigcup B$;
7 $\quad$ $A_u \leftarrow$ random conflict in $Conflict(\mathcal{K})$ that contains u;
8 $\quad$ $U \leftarrow V \setminus A_u$;
9 $\quad$ $A' \leftarrow \{a \cap U \mid a \in Conflict(\mathcal{K}), u \notin a\}$;
10 $\quad$ **return** $\{u\} \cup (U \setminus \texttt{FindRepair}(A', U))$;
11 **else**
12 $\quad$ **for** $a' \in Conflict(\mathcal{K})$ **do**
13 $\quad\quad$ **if** a' *is not a minimal fix of* $\mathcal{F}$ *w.r.t.* B **then**
14 $\quad\quad\quad$ $u \leftarrow$ fact in a' s.t. a' is still a fix of $\mathcal{F}$ w.r.t. B after its removal;
15 $\quad\quad\quad$ $U \leftarrow V \setminus (a' \setminus \{u\})$;
16 $\quad\quad\quad$ $A' \leftarrow \{a \cap U \mid a \in Conflict(\mathcal{K})\}$;
17 $\quad\quad\quad$ **return** $U \setminus \texttt{FindRepair}(A', U)$;

18 $\quad$ **for** $S \subseteq V, |S| \leq 3, S \not\subseteq a$ *and* $a \not\subseteq S$, *for every* $a \in Conflict(\mathcal{K})$ **do**
19 $\quad\quad$ **for** $v \in S$ **do**
20 $\quad\quad\quad$ $BS_v \leftarrow \{X \in B \text{ such that } B \cap S = \{v\}\}$;
21 $\quad\quad$ $BS_0 \leftarrow \{X \in B \text{ such that } B \cap S = \emptyset\}$;
22 $\quad\quad$ **for** $\{B_v \mid v \in S\} \subseteq \prod_{v \in S} BS_v$ **do**
23 $\quad\quad\quad$ **if** $B_v \neq \emptyset$ *for every* $v \in S$ **then**
24 $\quad\quad\quad\quad$ **if** *for every* $X \in BS_0, X \not\subseteq \bigcup_{v \in S} B_v$ **then**
25 $\quad\quad\quad\quad\quad$ $Z \leftarrow S \cup \left(V \setminus \bigcup_{v \in S} B_v \right)$;
26 $\quad\quad\quad\quad\quad$ $U \leftarrow V \setminus Z$;
27 $\quad\quad\quad\quad\quad$ $A' \leftarrow \{a \cap U \mid a \in Conflict(\mathcal{K})\}$;
28 $\quad\quad\quad\quad\quad$ **return** $U \setminus \texttt{FindRepair}(A', U)$;

29 $\quad$ **return** $\emptyset$;

---

that have a size equal or less than 3^3, that are not be included in any conflict of $\mathcal{K}$ and such that any conflict of $\mathcal{K}$ are not be included in S. If there is a set S that satisfies every aforementioned conditions then it can be extended into a

---

[3] The computational problem of finding a single repair of $\mathcal{F}$ w.r.t. a set $Y \subseteq 2^{\mathcal{F}}$ is only in the NC complexity class when every $y \in Y$ is such that $|y| \leq 3$, otherwise it has been proven to be in the RNC complexity class [6,20].

Table 1. List of minimal fixes and repairs for $\mathcal{F}$ w.r.t. $Conflict(\mathcal{K})$ found at each step.

Step	New elements of B	New elements of I
1	$\{d, e, h, a\}$	$\{b, c, f, g, i, j\}$
2	$\{d, e, h, b\}$	$\{a, c, f, g, i, j\}$
3	$\{e, h, c\}$	$\{a, b, d, f, g, i, j\}$
4	$\{c, h, f\}$	$\{a, b, d, e, g, i, j\}$
5	$\{c, e, i\}$	$\{a, b, d, f, g, h, j\}$
6	$\{c, f, j\}$	$\{a, b, d, e, g, h, i\}$
7	$\{a, d, f, h\}$	$\{b, c, e, g, i, j\}$
8	$\{b, d, f, h\}$	$\{a, c, e, g, i, j\}$
$\vdots$	$\vdots$	$\vdots$

minimal fix of B. If that is the case, the set Z does not contain any conflict of $\mathcal{K}$ [9]. Then, we use the previous method and find a repair Rep of U w.r.t. $\mathcal{A}'$ where $\mathcal{A}'$ is the set of restricted conflicts by U with $U = \mathcal{F} \setminus (V \setminus Z)$. $U \setminus Rep$ is a minimal fix of U w.r.t. $\mathcal{A}'$ but also a minimal fix of $\mathcal{F}$ w.r.t. $Conflict(\mathcal{K})$ (line 28) because Z does not contain any conflict of $\mathcal{K}$. Note that this algorithm relies on Algorithm 4 for finding a repair w.r.t. some restricted conflicts.

Example 6 (Cont'd Example 5). Let us consider $S = \{c(m), e(m)\}$ at step 7 in Table 1. We have $|S| \leq 3$, $S \not\subseteq a$ and $a \not\subseteq S$ for every $a \in Conflict(\mathcal{K})$. We have $BS_{c(m)} = \{\{c(m), h(m), f(m)\}, \{c(m), f(m), j(m)\}\}$ and $BS_{e(m)} = \{\{d(m), e(m), h(m), a(m)\}, \{d(m), e(m), h(m), b(m)\}\}$. Since $BS_0 = \emptyset$, for every $X \in BS_0$, $X \not\subseteq \bigcup E$ where $E = \{\{d(m), e(m), h(m), a(m)\}, \{c(m), h(m), f(m)\}\} \in BS_{c(m)} \times BS_{e(m)}$. Thus, we have $Z = \{c(m), e(m), b(m), i(m), j(m)\}$, $U = \{a(m), d(m), f(m), h(m)\}$ and $\mathcal{A}' = \{\{a(m)\}, \{d(m)\}, \{f(m)\}, \{f(m), h(m)\}, \{h(m)\}\}$. The only repair of U w.r.t. $\mathcal{A}'$ is $\emptyset$. We conclude that the set U is a minimal fix of $\mathcal{F}$ w.r.t. $Conflict(\mathcal{K})$.

3.2 Generating a Repair Efficiently

We show how to efficiently find a single repair of U w.r.t. $\mathcal{A} \subseteq 2^U$ when $|a| \leq 3$ for every $a \in \mathcal{A}$. The problem of finding a single repair is in the NC complexity class (but as soon as $|a| > 3$, it falls into the RNC complexity class [6,20]). *FindRepair* gradually build a repair by successively finding subrepairs C of large size with *SubRepair* and by restricting U and $\mathcal{A}$[4]. We now detail the general outline of the two algorithms *FindRepair* and *SubRepair*.

$\quad$ **FindRepair** (see Algorithm 4) takes as input a set of facts U and a set $\mathcal{A} \subseteq 2^U$ and returns a repair of U w.r.t. $\mathcal{A}$. We first initialise the algorithm with $\mathcal{A}' = \mathcal{A}$, $V' = U$ and $I = \emptyset$ (I will eventually be the repair of U w.r.t. $\mathcal{A}$).

---

[4] A subrepair of U w.r.t. $\mathcal{A}$ is a subset of a repair of U w.r.t. $\mathcal{A}$.

As long as the set $\mathcal{A}'$ is not empty, we update $\mathcal{A}'$ and V' by removing the facts found in a large subset of a repair of V' w.r.t. $\mathcal{A}'$. The two for-loop at line 10 and 13 remove supersets and sets of size one that may arise in $\mathcal{A}'$. The reason behind the removal of supersets is that they do not change the sets of repairs obtained. Furthermore, at line 14, we remove facts that are in a set of size one in $\mathcal{A}'$ because they cannot be in any repairs. Finally, when $\mathcal{A}' = \emptyset$, I is returned with the remaining facts in V'.

Algorithm 4: FindRepair

---

input : A set of facts U and a set $\mathcal{A} \subseteq 2^U$ such that $|a| \leq 3$ for every $a \in \mathcal{A}$
output: A repair of U w.r.t. $\mathcal{A}$

1   $\mathcal{A}' \leftarrow \mathcal{A}, V' \leftarrow U, I \leftarrow \emptyset$;
2   **while** $\mathcal{A}' \neq \emptyset$ **do**
3      $C \leftarrow \texttt{SubRepair}(V', \mathcal{A}')$;
4      $I \leftarrow I \cup C$;
5      $V' \leftarrow V' \setminus C$;
6   **for** $a' \in \mathcal{A}'$ **do**
7        $a' \leftarrow a' \cap V'$;
8   **for** $a' \in \mathcal{A}'$ **do**
9   **if** *there exists* $a'' \in \mathcal{A}'$ *such that* $a'' \subset a'$ **then**
10          $\mathcal{A}' \leftarrow \mathcal{A}' \setminus \{a'\}$;
11   **for** $a' \in \mathcal{A}'$ **do**
12   **if** $|a'| = 1$ **then**
13          $V' \leftarrow V' \setminus a'$;
14          $\mathcal{A}' \leftarrow \mathcal{A}' \setminus \{a'\}$;
15   **return** $I \cup V'$;

SubRepair (see Algorithm 5) is used for finding a large subrepair of U w.r.t. $\mathcal{A} \subseteq 2^U$. This algorithm uses two constants d_0 and d_1. When these constants are initialised with $d_0 = 0.01$ and $d_1 = 0.25$, [13] showed that SubRepair returns either a subrepair j such that $|j \cup N(j, \mathcal{A}, U)| \geq d_0 \times \frac{p}{\log(p)}$ or a subrepair that is at least of size $d_0 \times \frac{p}{\log(p)}$ where p is the size of V'. SubRepair maintains a collection of sets J initialised with sets of the form $\{v\}$ for all facts $v \in U$ such that $\{v\}$ is not a set in $\mathcal{A}$. The sets in J are subrepairs and will remain mutually disjoint throughout the algorithm. The algorithm iteratively checks if there is a set in J that is large enough to be returned and if not, it will select which sets of J should be merged and merge them (lines 12 to 21). However, merging subrepairs does not always produce a subrepair, that is why it removes some facts after the merging. Although the procedure for finding a matching M of Q at line 18 is not described, the reader can find it in [15]. Note that the functions N and D are defined as $N(C, \mathcal{A}, U) = \{u \in U \setminus C \mid \exists a \in \mathcal{A}, a \setminus C = \{u\}\}$ and $D(C, C', \mathcal{A}, U) = (N(C, \mathcal{A}, U) \cap C') \cup (N(C', \mathcal{A}, U) \cap C)$. It has been proven that SubRepair runs in

$O(log^2 n)$ time on $n + m$ processors and since FindRepair makes at most $O(log^2 n)$ calls to SubRepair (because the subrepairs have a minimal size), FindRepair runs in time $O(log^4 n)$ on $n + m$ EREW processors.

Algorithm 5: SubRepair

---

input : A set of facts U and a set $\mathcal{A} \subseteq 2^U$ such that $|a| \leq 3$ for every $a \in \mathcal{A}$
output: A subrepair of U w.r.t. $\mathcal{A}$

1   $Q \leftarrow \emptyset, p \leftarrow |U|, J \leftarrow \emptyset$;
2   **for** $u \in U$ **do**
3   **if** $\{u\} \notin \mathcal{A}$ **then**
4       $J \leftarrow J \cup \{\{u\}\}$;

5   $stops \leftarrow false$;
6   **while** $stops = false$ **do**
7   **for** $j \in J$ **do**
8   **if** $|j \cup N(j, \mathcal{A}, U)| \geq d_0 \times \frac{p}{log(p)}$ **then**
9         $stops \leftarrow true$;
10        $result \leftarrow j$;

11   **if** $stops = false$ **then**
12   **for** $j \in J$ **do**
13   **for** $j' \in J$ **do**
14   **if** $|D(j, j', \mathcal{A}, U)| \leq \frac{d_1 \times p}{|J| \times log(p)}$ **then**
15           $Q \leftarrow Q \cup \{\{j, j'\}\}$;

16      $M \leftarrow$ matching of Q of size $\lceil \left(\frac{1}{4} - 2\frac{d_0}{d_1} \right) \times |J| \rceil$;
17   **for** $\{j, j'\} \in M$ **do**
18        $J \leftarrow J \setminus j$;
19        $J \leftarrow J \setminus j'$;
20        $J \leftarrow J \cup \{(j \cup j') \setminus D(j, j', \mathcal{A}, U)\}$;

21 **return** $result$;

Example 7 (Cont'd Example 6). Suppose that $U = \{d(m), e(m), f(m), h(m),$ $i(m), j(m)\}$ and $\mathcal{A} = \{\{d(m)\}, \{e(m), f(m)\}, \{f(m), h(m), i(m)\}, \{h(m), i(m),$ $j(m)\}\}$, SubRepair returns the set $\{j(m)\}$. We remove $j(m)$ from V' and $\mathcal{A}'$. Thus, $V' = \{d(m), e(m), f(m), h(m), i(m)\}$ and $\mathcal{A}' = \{\{d(m)\}, \{e(m), f(m)\},$ $\{f(m), i(m), h(m)\}, \{h(m), i(m)\}\}$. $\{f(m), i(m), h(m)\}$ and $\{d(m)\}$ are removed from $\mathcal{A}'$ because they are respectively a superset and a set of size one. The same process is repeated and *FindRepair* returns $\{i(m), j(m), f(m)\}$. Here, the condition $|j \cup N(j, \mathcal{A}, U)| \geq \frac{c_0 \times p}{log(p)}$ is always satisfied with $d_0 = 0.01$.

The approach is correct since (1) *FindAllConflicts* returns the set of all conflicts, (2) *FindAllRepairs* returns the set of all repairs of $\mathcal{F}$ w.r.t. $Conflict(\mathcal{K})$ [9] and (3) *FindRepair* returns a repair of U w.r.t. $\mathcal{A} \subseteq 2^U$ [13].

4   Evaluation

Since the benchmarks of [10] was too large to be handled by the algorithm with a reasonable duration, we created a generator for Datalog$\pm$ KBs as follows:

1. **(Facts Generation)** We generates N_1 facts with a fixed probability p_0 of generating a new predicate. The arity of the predicates are randomly picked between two fixed constants c_0 and c_1. We used the idea that some constants only appear at a specific position in a predicate. Thus, we linked multiple positions of atoms into groups that share a distinct pool of constants with a probability p_1. The size of each pool of constants is increased such that for every predicate $pred_i$, the product of the size of all the pools of constants of positions in predicate $pred_i$ is superior to the number of atoms with predicate $pred_i$. Last, we created the necessary constants and "filled" the positions of atoms with constants from the corresponding pool of constants such that N_1 distinct facts are generated.

2. **(Rules Generation)** We generate N_2 rules and the number of atoms in the head and body of each rule is picked between four fixed constants c_2, c_3, c_4 and c_5 respectively. In order to avoid infinite rule applications, we only use new predicates in the head of the rules. We used the idea that rules should be split in levels such that a rule in level i can be applied to the N_1 original facts but also to the atoms generated by the all the rules in the level $j < i$. Thus, we split the rules randomly in each level such that $|L_i| \geq 1$ for $i \in \{1, \ldots, c_6\}$ and $|\bigcup_{1 \leq i \leq c_6} L_i| = N_2$ where c_6 is a constant corresponding to the maximum level of a rule. In order to build the rules in level one, we randomly "filled" the body of the rules with the N_1 ground atom that were previously generated. The heads of the rules are filled with atoms with new predicates but, within the same rule, there is a probability p_0 that the same predicate is reused. The positions of the new predicates in the head of a rule r_1 are also linked to the position of the predicates in the body of r_1 with a probability p_2. At this point, the atoms in the heads of the rules are also filled with constants from the corresponding pool of constants and each rule contains only ground atoms. Variables are added into the bodies of the rules by replacing constants with a probability p_3. There is a probability p_4 that a variable is reused when replacing a constant at a position belonging to the same group. Each constant in the heads of the rules is replaced by a variable that is used in the body at a position that belongs to the same group with a probability p_5. The process is repeated for the rules in level superior to one by filling the bodies of the rules with the N_1 original facts and the atoms in the head of the rules in inferior levels instead of only the original facts.

3. **(Negative constraints Generation)** We generate N_3 negative constraints and the number of atoms in the body of each negative constraint is randomly fixed between two fixed constants c_7 and c_8. In order to generate the negative constraints, one has to be careful not to make the set of rules incoherent, i.e. the union of the set of rules with the set of negative constraints has to

be satisfiable. $GAD_{\mathcal{K}} = (V, D)$ is constructed on the KB with the facts and rules generated according to the aforementioned steps. For each ground atom $v \in V$, we compute the set $W_v = \bigcup\limits_{S \in S_v} \bigcup\limits_{D_i \in S} U(D_i)$ where S_v is the set of all possible derivations for v and D_i is a rule application in S. Thus, in order to create a negative constraint neg_1 of size K, we first pick an atom v_1 in V and add it in the body of neg_1. We then remove W_{v_1} from V and pick an atom v_2 in $V \setminus W_{v_1}$ such that every atom in the body of neg_1 does not belong to W_{v_2}, we add v_2 to the body of neg_1 and remove W_{v_2} from $V \setminus W_{v_1}$. The process is repeated until the body of neg_1 reaches the size K.

In order to generate a set of different KBs, we decided to vary some parameters and fix others. Namely: N_1 varies between $10, 100, 1000$ and 10000, p_1 varies between 0 and 0.05, N_2 varies between $10, 100$ and 200, c_6 varies between 1 and 3 and N_3 varies between $20, 40$ and 60. The other parameters were fixed such that $p_0 = 0.5$, $p_2 = 0.05$, $c_1 = 3$, $c_0 = c_2 = c_4 = 1$, $c_3 = c_5 = 2$, $p_3 = 0.7$ and $p_4 = p_5 = 0.8$. This resulted in the generation of 144 different combinations of the parameters and a total of 720 different KBs since we generated 5 different KBs for each combination. The generated KBs are in DLGP format [4], the tool for generating the KBs and the tool for computing all the repairs are all available online at: https://gite.lirmm.fr/yun/Generated-KB.

4.1 Evaluation Results

The algorithm for finding the repairs was launched on each KB with a timeout after 10 min. We recorded both the time for finding each repair and the time for the conflict computation. We made the following observations: (1) On KBs with 10 facts, the tool successfully terminated with a total median time of 418 ms and an average of 11.7 repairs. Although all instances with 100, 1000 and 10000 facts did not finish before the timeout, the program returned an average number of 86.5 repairs by KB and this number seems to be independent of the number of facts. (2) The last repairs are harder to find: Across all KBs, the first repair takes an average of 763 ms to be computed whereas the last found repair took an average of 64461 ms. Lastly, finding all the conflicts takes a small part of the total computational time as it amounts to only an average of 12.8% of the total time. (3) On the one hand, the parameter c_6 does not impact the average number of repairs (66.8 with $c_6 = 1$ and 68.7 with $c_6 = 3$) but the median time for finding the conflicts does slightly increase (479 ms with $c_6 = 1$ and 800 ms with $c_6 = 3$). On the other hand, we noticed a sharp increase in the average time for finding the conflicts when the parameter N_3 is increased (888.1 ms for $N_3 = 20$, 1477.5 ms for $N_3 = 40$ and 3737.7 ms for $N_3 = 60$).

4.2 Conclusion

We showed an efficient incremental algorithm that allows for some or all repairs computation and empirically evaluated the proposed algorithm with a benchmark on inconsistent KBs expressed using Datalog±. We empirically showed that our approach is able to find the first repairs after a reasonable amount of time. We argue that our approach is useful for applications where an enumeration, even partial, of the repairs is necessary. For example, in life science applications such as biodegradable packaging selection [24] or wheat transformation [2] the repairs are used by the experts in order to enrich the KB with further information. In this setting, enumerating the set of repairs could be of practical value.

Last but not least, let us also highlight that the paper also provides a knowledge base generator, a contribution in itself for the OBDA community.

Acknowledgement. The second author acknowledges the support of the Docamex project, funded by the French Ministry of Agriculture.

References

1. Arenas, M., Bertossi, L.E., Chomicki, J.: Consistent query answers in inconsistent databases. In: Proceedings of the Eighteenth ACM SIGACT-SIGMOD-SIGART Symposium on Principles of Database Systems, Philadelphia, Pennsylvania, USA, 31 May–2 June 1999, pp. 68–79 (1999). https://doi.org/10.1145/303976.303983
2. Arioua, A., Croitoru, M., Buche, P.: DALEK: a tool for dialectical explanations in inconsistent knowledge bases. In: Computational Models of Argument - Proceedings of COMMA 2016, Potsdam, Germany, 12–16 September 2016, pp. 461–462 (2016). https://doi.org/10.3233/978-1-61499-686-6-461
3. Baget, J.F., et al.: A general modifier-based framework for inconsistency-tolerant query answering. In: Principles of Knowledge Representation and Reasoning: Proceedings of the Fifteenth International Conference, KR 2016, Cape Town, South Africa, 25–29 April 2016, pp. 513–516 (2016)
4. Baget, J.F., Gutierrez, A., Leclère, M., Mugnier, M.L., Rocher, S., Sipieter, C.: DLGP: An extended Datalog Syntax for Existential Rules and Datalog± Version 2.0, June 2015
5. Baget, J.F., Leclère, M., Mugnier, M.L., Salvat, E.: On rules with existential variables: walking the decidability line. Artif. Intell. **175**(9–10), 1620–1654 (2011)
6. Beame, P., Luby, M.: Parallel search for maximal independence given minimal dependence. In: Proceedings of the First Annual ACM-SIAM Symposium on Discrete Algorithms, San Francisco, California, USA, 22–24 January 1990, pp. 212–218 (1990)
7. Benferhat, S., Bouraoui, Z., Croitoru, M., Papini, O., Tabia, K.: Non-objection inference for inconsistency-tolerant query answering. In: Proceedings of the Twenty-Fifth International Joint Conference on Artificial Intelligence, IJCAI 2016, New York, NY, USA, 9–15 July 2016, pp. 3684–3690 (2016)
8. Bienvenu, M.: On the complexity of consistent query answering in the presence of simple ontologies. In: Proceedings of the Twenty-Sixth AAAI Conference on Artificial Intelligence, Toronto, Ontario, Canada, 22–26 July 2012 (2012). http://www.aaai.org/ocs/index.php/AAAI/AAAI12/paper/view/4928
9. Boros, E., Elbassioni, K.M., Gurvich, V., Khachiyan, L.: An efficient incremental algorithm for generating all maximal independent sets in hypergraphs of bounded dimension. Parallel Process. Lett. **10**(4), 253–266 (2000)

10. Bourgaux, C.: Inconsistency Handling in Ontology-Mediated Query Answering. Ph.D. thesis, Université Paris-Saclay, Paris, September 2016. https://tel.archives-ouvertes.fr/tel-01378723
11. Calì, A., Gottlob, G., Lukasiewicz, T., Marnette, B., Pieris, A.: Datalog±: a family of logical knowledge representation and query languages for new applications. In: Proceedings of the 25th Annual IEEE Symposium on Logic in Computer Science, LICS 2010, Edinburgh, United Kingdom, 11–14 July 2010, pp. 228–242 (2010). https://doi.org/10.1109/LICS.2010.27
12. Croitoru, M., Vesic, S.: What can argumentation do for inconsistent ontology query answering? In: Liu, W., Subrahmanian, V.S., Wijsen, J. (eds.) SUM 2013. LNCS (LNAI), vol. 8078, pp. 15–29. Springer, Heidelberg (2013). https://doi.org/10.1007/978-3-642-40381-1_2
13. Dahlhaus, E., Karpinski, M., Kelsen, P.: An efficient parallel algorithm for computing a maximal independent set in a hypergraph of dimension 3. Inf. Process. Lett. **42**(6), 309–313 (1992). https://doi.org/10.1016/0020-0190(92)90228-N
14. Gallo, G., Longo, G., Pallottino, S.: Directed hypergraphs and applications. Discrete Appl. Math. **42**(2), 177–201 (1993). https://doi.org/10.1016/0166-218X(93)90045-P
15. Goldberg, M.K., Spencer, T.H.: A new parallel algorithm for the maximal independent set problem. SIAM J. Comput. **18**(2), 419–427 (1989). https://doi.org/10.1137/0218029
16. Grégoire, É., Mazure, B., Piette, C.: Boosting a complete technique to find MSS and MUS thanks to a local search oracle. In: IJCAI 2007, Proceedings of the 20th International Joint Conference on Artificial Intelligence, Hyderabad, India, 6–12 January 2007, pp. 2300–2305 (2007). http://ijcai.org/Proceedings/07/Papers/370.pdf
17. Grégoire, É., Mazure, B., Piette, C.: Using local search to find MSSes and MUSes. Eur. J. Oper. Res. **199**(3), 640–646 (2009). https://doi.org/10.1016/j.ejor.2007.06.066
18. Hecham, A.: Defeasible reasoning for existential rules. (Raisonnement defaisable dans les règles existentielles). Ph.D. thesis (2018). https://tel.archives-ouvertes.fr/tel-01904558
19. Hecham, A., Bisquert, P., Croitoru, M.: On the chase for all provenance paths with existential rules. In: Proceedings of the Rules and Reasoning - International Joint Conference, RuleML+RR 2017, London, UK, 12–15 July 2017, pp. 135–150 (2017)
20. Kelsen, P.: On the parallel complexity of computing a maximal independent set in a hypergraph. In: Proceedings of the 24th Annual ACM Symposium on Theory of Computing, Victoria, British Columbia, Canada, 4–6 May 1992, pp. 339–350 (1992). https://doi.org/10.1145/129712.129745
21. Lembo, D., Lenzerini, M., Rosati, R., Ruzzi, M., Savo, D.F.: Inconsistency-tolerant semantics for description logics. In: Hitzler, P., Lukasiewicz, T. (eds.) RR 2010. LNCS, vol. 6333, pp. 103–117. Springer, Heidelberg (2010). https://doi.org/10.1007/978-3-642-15918-3_9
22. Poggi, A., Lembo, D., Calvanese, D., Giacomo, G.D., Lenzerini, M., Rosati, R.: Linking data to ontologies. J. Data Semant. **10**, 133–173 (2008)
23. Rocher, S.: Interrogation tolérante aux incohérences, Technical report. Université de Montpellier (2013)
24. Tamani, N., et al.: Eco-efficient packaging material selection for fresh produce: industrial session. In: Hernandez, N., Jäschke, R., Croitoru, M. (eds.) ICCS 2014. LNCS (LNAI), vol. 8577, pp. 305–310. Springer, Cham (2014). https://doi.org/10.1007/978-3-319-08389-6_27

25. Yun, B., Bisquert, P., Buche, P., Croitoru, M.: Arguing about end-of-life of packagings: preferences to the rescue. In: Garoufallou, E., Subirats Coll, I., Stellato, A., Greenberg, J. (eds.) MTSR 2016. CCIS, vol. 672, pp. 119–131. Springer, Cham (2016). https://doi.org/10.1007/978-3-319-49157-8_10
26. Yun, B., Vesic, S., Croitoru, M., Bisquert, P.: Inconsistency measures for repair semantics in OBDA. In: Proceedings of the Twenty-Seventh International Joint Conference on Artificial Intelligence, IJCAI 2018, Stockholm, Sweden, 13–19 July 2018, pp. 1977–1983 (2018). https://doi.org/10.24963/ijcai.2018/273

Knowledge-Based Matching of n-ary Tuples

Pierre Monnin$^{(\boxtimes)}$ ⓘ, Miguel Couceiro ⓘ, Amedeo Napoli, and Adrien Coulet ⓘ

Université de Lorraine, CNRS, Inria, LORIA, 54000 Nancy, France
{pierre.monnin,miguel.couceiro,amedeo.napoli,adrien.coulet}@loria.fr

Abstract. An increasing number of data and knowledge sources are accessible by human and software agents in the expanding Semantic Web. Sources may differ in granularity or completeness, and thus be complementary. Consequently, they should be reconciled in order to unlock the full potential of their conjoint knowledge. In particular, units should be matched within and across sources, and their level of relatedness should be classified into equivalent, more specific, or similar. This task is challenging since knowledge units can be heterogeneously represented in sources (*e.g.*, in terms of vocabularies). In this paper, we focus on matching n-ary tuples in a knowledge base with a rule-based methodology. To alleviate heterogeneity issues, we rely on domain knowledge expressed by ontologies. We tested our method on the biomedical domain of pharmacogenomics by searching alignments among 50,435 n-ary tuples from four different real-world sources. Results highlight noteworthy agreements and particularities within and across sources.

Keywords: Alignment · Matching · n-ary tuple · Order · Ontology

1 Introduction

In the Semantic Web [4], data or knowledge sources often describe similar units but may differ in quality, completeness, granularity, and vocabularies. Unlocking the full potential of the knowledge that these sources conjointly express requires matching equivalent, more specific, or similar knowledge units within and across sources. This matching process results in alignments that enable the reconciliation of these sources, *i.e.*, the harmonization of their content [7]. Such a reconciliation then provides a consolidated view of a domain that is useful in many applications, *e.g.*, in knowledge fusion and fact-checking.

Here, we illustrate the interest of such a matching process to reconcile knowledge within the biomedical domain of pharmacogenomics (PGx), which studies the influence of genetic factors on drug response phenotypes. PGx knowledge originates from distinct sources: reference databases such as PharmGKB,

Supported by the *PractiKPharma* project, founded by the French National Research Agency (ANR) under Grant ANR15-CE23-0028, by the IDEX "Lorraine Université d'Excellence" (15-IDEX-0004), and by the *Snowball* Inria Associate Team.

biomedical literature, or the mining of Electronic Health Records of hospitals. Knowledge represented in these sources may differ in levels of validation, completeness, and granularity. Consequently, reconciling these sources would provide a consolidated view on the knowledge of this domain, certainly beneficial in precision medicine, which aims at tailoring drug treatments to patients to reduce adverse effects and maximize drug efficacy [5,6]. PGx knowledge consists of n-ary relationships, here represented as tuples relating sets of drugs, sets of genomic variations, and sets of phenotypes. Such an n-ary tuple states that a patient being treated with the specified sets of drugs, while having the specified genomic variations will be more likely to experience the given phenotypes, $e.g.$, adverse effects. For example, Fig. 1 depicts the tuple pgt_1, which states that patients treated with warfarin may experience cardiovascular diseases because of variations in the CYP2C9 gene. If a source contained the same tuple but with the genetic factor unknown, then it should be identified as less specific than pgt_1. Conversely, if a source contained the same tuple but with myocardial infarction as phenotype, then it should be identified as more specific than pgt_1.

Fig. 1. Representation of a PGx relationship between gene CYP2C9, drug warfarin and phenotype cardiovascular_diseases. It can be seen as an n-ary tuple pgt_1 = ({warfarin}, {CYP2C9}, {cardiovascular_diseases}). This tuple is reified through the individual pgt_1, connecting its components through the causes predicate.

Motivated by this application, we propose a general and mathematically wellfounded methodology to match n-ary tuples. Precisely, given two n-ary tuples, we aim at deciding on their relatedness among five levels such as being equivalent or more specific. We suppose that such tuples are represented within a knowledge base that is expressed using Semantic Web standards. In such standards, only binary predicates exist, which requires the reification of n-ary tuples to represent them: tuples are individualized and linked to their components by predicates (see Fig. 1) [12]. In these knowledge bases, entities can also be associated with ontologies, $i.e.$, formal representations of a domain [9]. Ontologies consist of classes and predicates, partially ordered by the subsumption relation, denoted by $\sqsubseteq$. This relation states that a class (respectively a predicate) is more specific than another.

The process of matching n-ary tuples appears naturally in the scope of ontology matching [7], $i.e.$, finding equivalences or subsumptions between classes, predicates, or instances of two ontologies. Here, we match individuals representing reified n-ary tuples, which is somewhat related to instance matching and the extraction of *linkkeys* [2]. However, we allow ourselves to state that a tuple is more specific than another, which is unusual in instance matching but common when matching classes or predicates with systems such as PARIS [14] and

AMIE [8]. Besides, to the best of our knowledge, works available in the literature do not deal with the complex task of matching n-ary tuples with potentially unknown arguments formed by sets of individuals. See Appendix A for further details.

In our approach, we assume that the tuples to match have the same arity, the same indices for their arguments, and that they are reified with the same predicates and classes. Arguments are formed by sets of individuals (no literal values) and may be unknown. This matching task thus reduces to comparing each argument of the tuples and aggregating these comparisons to establish their level of relatedness. We achieve this process by defining five general rules, designed to satisfy some desired properties such as transitivity and symmetry. To tackle the heterogeneity in the representation of tuples, we enrich this structure-based comparison with domain knowledge, *e.g.*, the hierarchy of ontology classes and links between individuals.

This paper is organized as follows. In Sect. 2, we formalize the problem of matching n-ary tuples. To tackle it, we propose two preorders in Sect. 3 to compare sets of individuals by considering domain knowledge: links between individuals, instantiations, and subsumptions. These preorders are used in Sect. 4 to define matching rules that establish the level of relatedness between two n-ary tuples. These rules are applied to PGx knowledge in Sect. 5. We discuss our results in Sect. 6 and present some directions of future work in Sect. 7. Appendices are available online (https://arxiv.org/abs/2002.08103).

2   Problem Setting

We aim at matching n-ary tuples represented within a knowledge base $\mathcal{K}$, *i.e.*, we aim at determining the relatedness level of two tuples t_1 and t_2 (*e.g.*, whether they are equivalent, more specific, or similar). $\mathcal{K}$ is represented in the formalism of Description Logics (DL) [3] and thus consists of a TBox and an ABox.

Precisely, we consider a set $\mathcal{T}$ of n-ary tuples to match. This set is formed by tuples whose matching makes sense in a given application. For example, in our use-case, $\mathcal{T}$ consists of all PGx tuples from the considered sources. All tuples in $\mathcal{T}$ have the same arity n, and their arguments are sets of individuals of $\mathcal{K}$. Such a tuple t can be formally represented as $t = (\pi_1(t), \ldots, \pi_n(t))$, where $\pi_i : \mathcal{T} \to 2^\Delta$ is a mapping that associates each tuple t to its i-th argument $\pi_i(t)$, which is a set of individuals included in the domain of interpretation Δ. The index set is the same for all tuples in $\mathcal{T}$. Tuples come from potentially noisy sources and some arguments may be missing. As $\mathcal{K}$ verifies the Open World Assumption, such arguments that are not explicitly specified as empty, can only be considered unknown and they are set to Δ to express the fact that all individuals may apply. To illustrate, `pgt_1` in Fig. 1 could be seen as a ternary tuple `pgt_1` = ({`warfarin`}, {`CYP2C9`}, {`cardiovascular_diseases`}), where arguments respectively represent the sets of involved drugs, genetic factors, and phenotypes.

In view of our formalism, matching two n-ary tuples t_1 and t_2 comes down to comparing their arguments $\pi_i(t_1)$ and $\pi_i(t_2)$ for each $i \in \{1, \ldots, n\}$. For instance, if $\pi_i(t_1) = \pi_i(t_2)$ for all i, then t_1 and t_2 are representing the same knowledge unit, highlighting an agreement between their sources. In the next section, we propose other tests between arguments that are based on domain knowledge.

3 Ontology-Based Preorders

As previously illustrated, the matching of two n-ary tuples t_1 and t_2 relies on the comparison of each of their arguments $\pi_i(t_1)$ and $\pi_i(t_2)$, which are sets of individuals. Such a comparison can be achieved by testing their inclusion or equality. Thus, if $\pi_i(t_1) \subseteq \pi_i(t_2)$, then $\pi_i(t_1)$ can be considered as more specific than $\pi_i(t_2)$. It is noteworthy that testing inclusion or equality implicitly considers `owl:sameAs` links that indicate identical individuals. For example, the comparison of $\{e_1\}$ with $\{e_2\}$ while knowing that `owl:sameAs`(e_1, e_2) results in an equality. However, additional domain knowledge can be considered to help tackle the heterogeneous representation of tuples. For instance, some individuals can be *part of* others. Individuals may also instantiate different ontological classes, which are themselves comparable through subsumption. To consider this domain knowledge in the matching process, we propose two preorders, *i.e.*, reflexive and transitive binary relations.

3.1 Preorder $\preccurlyeq^P$ Based on Links Between Individuals

Several links may associate individuals in $\pi_i(t_j)$ with other individuals in $\mathcal{K}$. Some links involve a transitive and reflexive predicate (*i.e.*, a preorder). Then, for each such predicate p, we define a preorder $\preccurlyeq^P$ parameterized by p as follows[1]:

$$\pi_i(t_1) \preccurlyeq^P \pi_i(t_2) \Leftrightarrow \forall e_1 \in \pi_i(t_1),\ \exists e_2 \in \pi_i(t_2),\ \mathcal{K} \models p(e_1, e_2) \qquad (1)$$

Note that, from the reflexivity of p and the use of quantifiers $\forall$ and $\exists$, $\pi_i(t_1) \subseteq \pi_i(t_2)$ implies $\pi_i(t_1) \preccurlyeq^P \pi_i(t_2)$. The equivalence relation $\sim^P$ associated with $\preccurlyeq^P$ is defined as usual by:

$$\pi_i(t_1) \sim^P \pi_i(t_2) \Leftrightarrow \pi_i(t_1) \preccurlyeq^P \pi_i(t_2) \text{ and } \pi_i(t_2) \preccurlyeq^P \pi_i(t_1) \qquad (2)$$

3.2 Preorder $\preccurlyeq^O$ Based on Instantiation and Subsumption

The second preorder we propose takes into account classes of an ontology $\mathcal{O}$ ordered by subsumption and instantiated by individuals in $\pi_i(t_j)$. We denote by classes$(\mathcal{O})$ the set of all classes of $\mathcal{O}$. As it is standard in DL, $\top$ denotes the largest class in $\mathcal{O}$. Given an individual e, we denote by ci$(\mathcal{O}, e)$ the set of classes of $\mathcal{O}$ instantiated by e and distinct from $\top$, *i.e.*,

$$\text{ci}(\mathcal{O}, e) = \{C \in \text{classes}(\mathcal{O}) \setminus \{\top\} \mid \mathcal{K} \models C(e)\}.$$

---

[1] See Appendix B and Appendix C for the proof and examples.

Note that $\mathrm{ci}(\mathcal{O}, e)$ may be empty. We explicitly exclude $\top$ from $\mathrm{ci}(\mathcal{O}, e)$ since $\mathcal{K}$ may be incomplete. Indeed, individuals may lack instantiations of specific classes but instantiate $\top$ by default. Thus, $\top$ is excluded to prevent $\preccurlyeq^{\mathcal{O}}$ from inadequately considering these individuals more general than individuals instantiating classes other than $\top$[2].

Given $\mathcal{C} = \{C_1, C_2, \ldots, C_k\} \subseteq \mathrm{classes}(\mathcal{O})$, we denote by $\mathrm{msc}(\mathcal{C})$ the set of the most specific classes of $\mathcal{C}$, i.e., $\mathrm{msc}(\mathcal{C}) = \{C \in \mathcal{C} \mid \nexists D \in \mathcal{C}, \ D \sqsubset C\}$[3]. Similarly, we denote by $\mathrm{msci}(\mathcal{O}, e)$ the set of the most specific classes of $\mathcal{O}$, except $\top$, instantiated by an individual e, i.e., $\mathrm{msci}(\mathcal{O}, e) = \mathrm{msc}(\mathrm{ci}(\mathcal{O}, e))$.

Given an ontology $\mathcal{O}$, we define the preorder $\preccurlyeq^{\mathcal{O}}$ based on set inclusion and subsumption as follows[4]:

$$\pi_i(t_1) \preccurlyeq^{\mathcal{O}} \pi_i(t_2) \Leftrightarrow \forall e_1 \in \pi_i(t_1), \ \underbrace{\left[e_1 \in \pi_i(t_2) \right]}_{(3a)} \bigvee \left[\mathrm{msci}(\mathcal{O}, e_1) \neq \emptyset \ \wedge \right.$$

$$\left. \underbrace{\forall C_1 \in \mathrm{msci}(\mathcal{O}, e_1), \ \exists e_2 \in \pi_i(t_2), \ \exists C_2 \in \mathrm{msci}(\mathcal{O}, e_2), \ C_1 \sqsubseteq C_2}_{(3b)} \right] \quad (3)$$

Clearly, if $\pi_i(t_1)$ is more specific than $\pi_i(t_2)$ and $e_1 \in \pi_i(t_1)$, then (3a) $e_1 \in \pi_i(t_2)$, or (3b) all the most specific classes instantiated by e_1 are subsumed by at least one of the most specific classes instantiated by individuals in $\pi_i(t_2)$. Thus individuals in $\pi_i(t_2)$ can be seen as "more general" than those in $\pi_i(t_1)$. As before, $\preccurlyeq^{\mathcal{O}}$ induces the equivalence relation $\sim^{\mathcal{O}}$ defined by:

$$\pi_i(t_1) \sim^{\mathcal{O}} \pi_i(t_2) \Leftrightarrow \pi_i(t_1) \preccurlyeq^{\mathcal{O}} \pi_i(t_2) \text{ and } \pi_i(t_2) \preccurlyeq^{\mathcal{O}} \pi_i(t_1) \quad (4)$$

The preorder $\preccurlyeq^{\mathcal{O}}$ can be seen as parameterized by the ontology $\mathcal{O}$, allowing to consider different parts of the TBox of $\mathcal{K}$ for each argument $\pi_i(t_j)$, if needed.

4   Using Preorders to Define Matching Rules

Let $t_1, t_2 \in \mathcal{T}$ be two n-ary tuples to match. We assume that each argument $i \in \{1, \ldots, n\}$ is endowed with a preorder $\preccurlyeq_i \in \{\subseteq, \preccurlyeq^{\mathrm{P}}, \preccurlyeq^{\mathcal{O}}\}$ that enables the comparison of $\pi_i(t_1)$ and $\pi_i(t_2)$. We can define rules that aggregate such comparisons for all $i \in \{1, \ldots, n\}$ and establish the relatedness level of t_1 and t_2. Hence, our matching approach comes down to applying these rules to every ordered pair (t_1, t_2) of n-ary tuples from $\mathcal{T}$.

Here, we propose the following five relatedness levels: $=$, $\sim$, $\preccurlyeq$, $\lesssim$, and $\propto$, from the strongest to the weakest. Accordingly, we propose five matching rules of the form $B \Rightarrow H$, where B expresses the conditions of the rule, testing equalities, equivalences, or inequalities between arguments of t_1 and t_2. Classically, these conditions can be combined using conjunctions or disjunctions, respectively

---

[2] See Appendix D for a detailed example.
[3] $D \sqsubset C$ means that $D \sqsubseteq C$ and $D \not\equiv C$.
[4] See Appendix E and Appendix F for the proof and examples.

denoted by $\wedge$ and $\vee$. If B holds, H expresses the relatedness between t_1 and t_2 to add to $\mathcal{K}$. Rules are applied from Rule 1 to Rule 5. Once conditions in B hold for a rule, H is added to $\mathcal{K}$ and the following rules are discarded, meaning that at most one relatedness level is added to $\mathcal{K}$ for each pair of tuples. When no rule can be applied, t_1 and t_2 are considered incomparable and nothing is added to $\mathcal{K}$. The first four rules are the following:

Rule 1. $\forall i \in \{1, \ldots, n\}$, $\pi_i(t_1) = \pi_i(t_2) \Rightarrow t_1 = t_2$

Rule 2. $\forall i \in \{1, \ldots, n\}$, $\pi_i(t_1) \sim_i \pi_i(t_2) \Rightarrow t_1 \sim t_2$

Rule 3. $\forall i \in \{1, \ldots, n\}$, $\pi_i(t_1) \preccurlyeq_i \pi_i(t_2) \Rightarrow t_1 \preccurlyeq t_2$

Rule 4. $\forall i \in \{1, \ldots, n\}$, $[\,(\pi_i(t_1) = \pi_i(t_2)) \vee (\pi_i(t_2) \neq \Delta \wedge \pi_i(t_1) \preccurlyeq_i \pi_i(t_2)) \vee (\pi_i(t_1) \neq \Delta \wedge \pi_i(t_2) \preccurlyeq_i \pi_i(t_1))\,] \Rightarrow t_1 \lesssim t_2$

Rule 1 states that t_1 and t_2 are identical ($=$) whenever t_1 and t_2 coincide on each argument. Rule 2 states that t_1 and t_2 are equivalent ($\sim$) whenever each argument $i \in \{1, \ldots, n\}$ of t_1 is equivalent to the same argument of t_2. Rule 3 states that t_1 is more specific than t_2 ($\preccurlyeq$) whenever each argument $i \in \{1, \ldots, n\}$ of t_1 is more specific than the same argument of t_2 w.r.t. $\preccurlyeq_i$. Rule 4 states that t_1 and t_2 have comparable arguments ($\lesssim$) whenever they have the same specified arguments (*i.e.*, different from Δ), and these arguments are comparable w.r.t. $\preccurlyeq_i$. Rules 1 to 3 satisfy the transitivity property. Additionally, Rules 1, 2, and 4 satisfy the symmetry property.

In Rules 1 to 4, comparisons are made argument-wise. However, other relatedness cases may require to aggregate over arguments. For example, we may want to compare all individuals involved in two tuples, regardless of their arguments. Alternatively, we may want to consider two tuples as weakly related if their arguments have a specified proportion of comparable individuals. To this aim, we propose Rule 5. Let $\mathbb{I} = \{I_1, \ldots, I_m\}$ be a partition of $\{1, \ldots, n\}$, defined by the user at the beginning of the matching process. We define the aggregated argument I_k of t_j as the union of all specified $\pi_i(t_j)$ (*i.e.*, different from Δ) for $i \in I_k$. Formally,

$$\pi_{I_k}(t_j) = \bigcup_{\substack{i \in I_k \\ \pi_i(t_j) \neq \Delta}} \pi_i(t_j).$$

We assume that each aggregated argument $I_k \in \mathbb{I}$ is endowed with a preorder $\preccurlyeq_{I_k} \in \{\subseteq, \preccurlyeq^{\mathrm{P}}, \preccurlyeq^{\mathcal{O}}\}$. We denote by $\mathrm{SSD}(\pi_{I_k}(t_1), \pi_{I_k}(t_2))$ the semantic set difference between $\pi_{I_k}(t_1)$ and $\pi_{I_k}(t_2)$, *i.e.*,

$$\mathrm{SSD}(\pi_{I_k}(t_1), \pi_{I_k}(t_2)) = \{e_1 \mid e_1 \in \pi_{I_k}(t_1) \text{ and } \{e_1\} \not\preccurlyeq_{I_k} \pi_{I_k}(t_2)\}.$$

Intuitively, it is the set of elements in $\pi_{I_k}(t_1)$ preventing it from being more specific than $\pi_{I_k}(t_2)$ w.r.t. $\preccurlyeq_{I_k}$. We define the operator $\propto_{I_k}$ as follows:

$$\pi_{I_k}(t_1) \propto_{I_k} \pi_{I_k}(t_2) = \begin{cases} 1 \text{ if } \pi_{I_k}(t_1) \preccurlyeq_{I_k} \pi_{I_k}(t_2) \text{ or } \pi_{I_k}(t_2) \preccurlyeq_{I_k} \pi_{I_k}(t_1) \\ 1 - \dfrac{|\mathrm{SSD}(\pi_{I_k}(t_1), \pi_{I_k}(t_2)) \cup \mathrm{SSD}(\pi_{I_k}(t_2), \pi_{I_k}(t_1))|}{|\pi_{I_k}(t_1) \cup \pi_{I_k}(t_2)|} \text{ otherwise} \end{cases}$$

This operator returns a number measuring the similarity between $\pi_{I_k}(t_1)$ and $\pi_{I_k}(t_2)$. This number is equal to 1 if the two aggregated arguments are comparable. Otherwise, it is equal to 1 minus the proportion of incomparable elements. We denote by $\mathbb{I}_{\neq\Delta}(t_1, t_2) = \{I_k \mid I_k \in \mathbb{I} \text{ and } \pi_{I_k}(t_1) \neq \Delta \text{ and } \pi_{I_k}(t_2) \neq \Delta\}$ the set of aggregated arguments that are specified for both t_1 and t_2 (*i.e.*, different from Δ). Then, Rule 5 is defined as follows:

Rule 5. Let $\mathbb{I} = \{I_1, \ldots, I_m\}$ be a partition of $\{1, \ldots, n\}$, and let $\gamma_{\neq\Delta}$, γ_S, and γ_C be three parameters, all fixed at the beginning of the matching process.

$$\left(|\mathbb{I}_{\neq\Delta}(t_1, t_2)| \geq \gamma_{\neq\Delta} \right) \bigwedge \left(\left[\forall I_k \in \mathbb{I}_{\neq\Delta}(t_1, t_2), \ \pi_{I_k}(t_1) \propto_{I_k} \pi_{I_k}(t_2) \geq \gamma_S \right] \vee \right.$$
$$\left. \left[\left(\sum_{I_k \in \mathbb{I}_{\neq\Delta}(t_1, t_2)} \mathbb{1} \left(\pi_{I_k}(t_1) \propto_{I_k} \pi_{I_k}(t_2) = 1 \right) \right) \geq \gamma_C \right] \right) \Rightarrow t_1 \propto t_2$$

Rule 5 is applicable if at least $\gamma_{\neq\Delta}$ aggregated arguments are specified for both t_1 and t_2. Then, t_1 and t_2 are weakly related ($\propto$) whenever all these specified aggregated arguments have a similarity of at least γ_S or when at least γ_C of them are comparable. Notice that $\propto$ is symmetric.

5   Application to Pharmacogenomic Knowledge

Our methodology was motivated by the problem of matching pharmacogenomic (PGx) tuples. Accordingly, we tested this methodology on PGxLOD[5] [10], a knowledge base represented in the $\mathcal{ALHI}$ Description Logic [3]. In PGxLOD, 50,435 PGx tuples were integrated from four different sources: (i) 3,650 tuples from structured data of PharmGKB, (ii) 10,240 tuples from textual portions of PharmGKB called clinical annotations, (iii) 36,535 tuples from biomedical literature, and (iv) 10 tuples from results found in EHR studies. We obtained the matching results summarized in Table 1 and discussed in Sect. 6. Details about formalization, code and parameters are given in Appendix G.

6   Discussion

In Table 1, we observe only a few inter-source links, which may be caused by missing mappings between the vocabularies used in sources. Indeed, our matching process requires these mappings to compare individuals represented with different vocabularies. This result underlines the relevance of enriching the knowledge base with ontology-to-ontology mappings. We also notice that Rule 5 generates more links than the other rules, which emphasizes the importance of weaker relatedness levels to align sources and overcome their heterogeneity. Some results were expected and therefore seem to validate our approach. For example, some tuples from the literature appear more general than those of PharmGKB (with 15 and 42 `skos:broadMatch` links). These links are a foreseen consequence of

---

[5] https://pgxlod.loria.fr.

Table 1. Number of links resulting from each rule. Links are generated between tuples of distinct sources or within the same source. PGKB stands for "PharmGKB", sd for "structured data", and ca for "clinical annotations". As Rules 1, 2, 4, and 5 satisfy symmetry, links from t_1 to t_2 as well as from t_2 to t_1 are counted. Similarly, as Rules 1 to 3 satisfy transitivity, transitivity-induced links are counted. Regarding `skos:broadMatch` links, rows represent origins and columns represent destinations.

		PGKB (sd)	PGKB (ca)	Literature	EHRs
Links from Rule 1	PGKB (sd)	166	0	0	0
Encoded by `owl:sameAs`	PGKB (ca)	0	10,134	0	0
	Literature	0	0	122,646	0
	EHRs	0	0	0	0
Links from Rule 2	PGKB (sd)	0	5	0	0
Encoded by `skos:closeMatch`	PGKB (ca)	5	1,366	0	0
	Literature	0	0	16,692	0
	EHRs	0	0	0	0
Links from Rule 3	PGKB (sd)	87	3	15	0
Encoded by `skos:broadMatch`	PGKB (ca)	9,325	605	42	0
	Literature	0	0	75,138	0
	EHRs	0	0	0	0
Links from Rule 4	PGKB (sd)	20	0	0	0
Encoded by `skos:relatedMatch`	PGKB (ca)	0	110	0	0
	Literature	0	0	18,050	0
	EHRs	0	0	0	0
Links from Rule 5	PGKB (sd)	100,596	287,670	414	2
Encoded by `skos:related`	PGKB (ca)	287,670	706,270	1,103	19
	Literature	414	1,103	1,082,074	15
	EHRs	2	19	15	0

the completion process of PharmGKB. Indeed, curators achieve this completion after a literature review, inevitably leading to tuples more specific or equivalent to the ones in reviewed articles. Interestingly, our methodology could ease such a review by pointing out articles describing similar tuples. Clinical annotations of PharmGKB are in several cases more specific than structured data (9,325 `skos:broadMatch` links). This is also expected as structured data are a broad-level summary of more complex phenotypes detailed in clinical annotations.

Regarding our method, using rules is somehow off the current machine learning trend [1,11,13]. However, writing simple and well-founded rules constitutes a valid first step before applying machine learning approaches. Indeed, such explicit rules enable generating a "silver" standard for matching, which may be useful to either train or evaluate supervised approaches. Rules are readable and may thus be analyzed and confirmed by domain experts, and provide a basis of explanation for the matching results. Additionally, our rules are simple enough to be generally true and useful in other domains. By relying on instantiated classes and links between individuals, we illustrate how domain knowledge and reasoning mechanisms can serve a structure-based matching. In future works, conditions under which preorders $\preceq^P$ and $\preceq^O$ could be merged into one unique preorder deserve a deeper study. See Appendix H for further discussion.

7   Conclusion

In this paper, we proposed a rule-based approach to establish the relatedness level of n-ary tuples among five proposed levels. It relies on rules and preorders that leverage domain knowledge and reasoning capabilities. We applied our methodology to the real-world use case of matching pharmacogenomic relationships, and obtained insightful results. In the future, we intend to compare and integrate our purely symbolic approach with ML methodologies.

References

1. Alam, M., et al.: Reconciling event-based knowledge through RDF2VEC. In: Proceedings of HybridSemStats@ISWC 2017. CEUR Workshop Proceedings (2017)
2. Atencia, M., David, J., Euzenat, J.: Data interlinking through robust linkkey extraction. In: Proceedings of ECAI 2014. Frontiers in Artificial Intelligence and Applications, vol. 263, pp. 15–20 (2014)
3. Baader, F., et al. (eds.): The Description Logic Handbook: Theory, Implementation, and Applications. Cambridge University Press, Cambridge (2003)
4. Berners-Lee, T., Hendler, J., Lassila, O., et al.: The semantic web. Sci. Am. **284**(5), 28–37 (2001)
5. Caudle, K.E., et al.: Incorporation of pharmacogenomics into routine clinical practice: the clinical pharmacogenetics implementation consortium (CPIC) guideline development process. Curr. Drug Metab. **15**(2), 209–217 (2014)
6. Coulet, A., Smaïl-Tabbone, M.: Mining electronic health records to validate knowledge in pharmacogenomics. ERCIM News **2016**(104)(2016)
7. Euzenat, J., Shvaiko, P.: Ontology Matching, 2nd edn. Springer, Heidelberg (2013). https://doi.org/10.1007/978-3-642-38721-0
8. Galárraga, L.A., Preda, N., Suchanek, F.M.: Mining rules to align knowledge bases. In: Proceedings of AKBC@CIKM 2013, pp. 43–48. ACM (2013)
9. Gruber, T.R.: A translation approach to portable ontology specifications. Knowl. Acquis. **5**(2), 199–220 (1993)
10. Monnin, P., et al.: PGxO and PGxLOD: a reconciliation of pharmacogenomic knowledge of various provenances, enabling further comparison. BMC Bioinform. **20**(Suppl. 4), 139 (2019)
11. Nickel, M., Murphy, K., Tresp, V., Gabrilovich, E.: A review of relational machine learning for knowledge graphs: from multi-relational link prediction to automated knowledge graph construction. Proc. IEEE **104**(1), 11–33 (2016)
12. Noy, N., Rector, A., Hayes, P., Welty, C.: Defining N-ary relations on the semantic web. W3C Work. Group Note **12**(4) (2006)
13. Ristoski, P., Paulheim, H.: RDF2Vec: RDF graph embeddings for data mining. In: Groth, P., Simperl, E., Gray, A., Sabou, M., Krötzsch, M., Lecue, F., Flöck, F., Gil, Y. (eds.) ISWC 2016. LNCS, vol. 9981, pp. 498–514. Springer, Cham (2016). https://doi.org/10.1007/978-3-319-46523-4_30
14. Suchanek, F.M., Abiteboul, S., Senellart, P.: PARIS: probabilistic alignment of relations, instances, and schema. PVLDB **5**(3), 157–168 (2011)

Conceptual Structures

Some Programming Optimizations for Computing Formal Concepts

Simon Andrews[✉]

Conceptual Structures Research Group, Department of Computing,
College of Business, Technology and Engineering, The Industry and Innovation
Research Institute, Sheffield Hallam University, Sheffield, UK
s.andrews@shu.ac.uk

Abstract. This paper describes in detail some optimization approaches taken to improve the efficiency of computing formal concepts. In particular, it describes the use and manipulation of bit-arrays to represent FCA structures and carry out the typical operations undertaken in computing formal concepts, thus providing data structures that are both memory-efficient and time saving. The paper also examines the issues and compromises involved in computing and storing formal concepts, describing a number of data structures that illustrate the classical trade-off between memory footprint and code efficiency. Given that there has been limited publication of these programmatical aspects, these optimizations will be useful to programmers in this area and also to any programmers interested in optimizing software that implements Boolean data structures. The optimizations are shown to significantly increase performance by comparing an unoptimized implementation with the optimized one.

1 Introduction

Although there have been a number of advances and variations of the Close-By-One algorithm [14] for computing formal concepts, including [4,5,12,13], optimization approaches used when implementing such algorithms have not been described in detail. Mathematical and algorithmic aspects of FCA have been well covered, for example in [7,9,15], but less attention has been paid to programming. Using a bit-array to represent a formal context has previously been reported [5,11], but without the implementation details presented here. Providing detailed code for these optimizations will be useful to programmers in this area and also to any programmers interested in optimizing software that implements and manipulates Boolean data structures. Thus, this paper sets out to describe and explain these optimizations, with example code, and to explore the classical efficiency trade-offs between memory and speed in a CbO context. As an example CbO-type algorithm, this paper makes use of In-Close2 as presented in [6]. However, the optimization approaches detailed here should be generalizable for most, if not all, algorithms that compute formal concepts.

The programming language chosen is C++; it is often the language of choice for efficient coding as it facilitates low level programming and its compilers are extremely adept at producing efficient assembler.

© Springer Nature Switzerland AG 2020
M. Alam et al. (Eds.): ICCS 2020, LNAI 12277, pp. 59–73, 2020.
https://doi.org/10.1007/978-3-030-57855-8_5

2 Formal Concepts

A description of formal concepts [9] begins with a set of objects X and a set of attributes Y. A binary relation $I \subseteq X \times Y$ is called the *formal context*. If $x \in X$ and $y \in Y$ then xIy says that object x has attribute y. For a set of objects $A \subseteq X$, a derivation operator $\uparrow$ is defined to obtain the set of attributes common to the objects in A as follows:

$$A^\uparrow := \{\, y \in Y \mid \forall x \in A : xIy \,\}. \tag{1}$$

Similarly, for a set of attributes $B \subseteq Y$, the $\downarrow$ operator is defined to obtain the set of objects common to the attributes in B as follows:

$$B^\downarrow := \{\, x \in X \mid \forall y \in B : xIy \,\}. \tag{2}$$

(A, B) is a formal concept *iff* $A^\uparrow = B$ and $B^\downarrow = A$. The relations $A \times B$ are then a closed set of pairs in I. In other words, a formal concept is a set of attributes and a set of objects such that all of the objects have all of the attributes and there are no other objects that have all of the attributes. Similarly, there are no other attributes that all the objects have. A is called the *extent* of the formal concept and B is called the *intent* of the formal concept.

A formal context is typically represented as a cross table, with crosses indicating binary relations between objects (rows) and attributes (columns). The following is a simple example of a formal context:

	0	1	2	3	4
a	×			×	×
b		×	×	×	×
c	×		×		
d		×	×		×

Formal concepts in a cross table can be visualized as closed rectangles of crosses, where the rows and columns in the rectangle are not necessarily contiguous. The formal concepts in the example context are:

$$
\begin{aligned}
C_1 &= (\{a,b,c,d\}, \emptyset) & C_6 &= (\{b\}, \{1,2,3,4\}) \\
C_2 &= (\{a,c\}, \{0\}) & C_7 &= (\{b,d\}, \{1,2,4\}) \\
C_3 &= (\emptyset, \{0,1,2,3,4\}) & C_8 &= (\{b,c,d\}, \{2\}) \\
C_4 &= (\{c\}, \{0,2\}) & C_9 &= (\{a,b\}, \{3,4\}) \\
C_5 &= (\{a\}, \{0,3,4\}) & C_{10} &= (\{a,b,d\}, \{4\})
\end{aligned}
$$

For readers not familiar with Formal Concept Analysis, further background can be found in [17–19].

3 A Re-Cap of the In-Close2 Algorithm

In-Close2 [6] is a CbO variant that was 'bred' from In-Close [2] and FCbO [13,16] to combine the efficiencies of the partial closure canonicity test of In-Close with the full inheritance of the parent intent achieved by FCbO.

The In-Close2 algorithm is given below, with a line by line explanation, and is invoked with an initial $(A, B) = (X, \emptyset)$ and initial attribute $y = 0$, where A is the extent of a concept, B is the intent and X is a set of objects such that $A \subseteq X$.

In-Close2

ComputeConceptsFrom$((A, B), y)$

---

1 **for** $j \leftarrow y$ **upto** $n - 1$ **do**
2   **if** $j \notin B$ **then**
3        $C \leftarrow A \cap \{j\}^{\downarrow}$
4   **if** $A = C$ **then**
5           $B \leftarrow B \cup \{j\}$
6   **else**
7   **if** $B \cap Y_j = C^{\uparrow_j}$ **then**
8   PutInQueue(C, j)

9 ProcessConcept$((A, B))$
10 **while** GetFromQueue(C, j) **do**
11    $D \leftarrow B \cup \{j\}$
12   ComputeConceptsFrom$((C, D), j + 1)$

Line 1 - Iterate across the context, from starting attribute y up to attribute $n - 1$, where n is the number of attributes.

Line 2 - Skip inherited attributes.

Line 3 - Form an extent, C, by intersecting the current extent, A, with the next column of objects in the context.

Line 4 - If $C = A$, then...

Line 5 - ...add the current attribute j to the current intent being closed, B.

Line 7 - Otherwise, apply the partial-closure canonicity test to C (is this a new extent?). Note that $Y_j = \{y \in Y | y < j\}$. Similarly, $C^{\uparrow_j}$ is C closed up to (but not including) j: $C^{\uparrow_j} = \{ y \in Y_j \mid \forall x \in C : xIy \}$

Line 8 - If the test is passed, place the new (child) extent, C, and the location where it was found, j, in a queue for later processing.

Line 9 - Pass concept (A, B) to notional procedure **ProcessConcept** to process it in some way (for example, storing it in a set of concepts).

Lines 10 - The queue is processed by obtaining each child extent and associated location from the queue.

Line 11 - Each new partial intent, D, inherits all the attributes from its completed parent intent, B, along with the attribute, j, where its extent was found.

Line 12 - Call **ComputeConceptsFrom** to compute child concepts from $j + 1$ and to complete the closure of D.

4   Implementation of the Formal Context as a Bit Array

Common to most efficient implementations of CbO-type algorithms is the implementation of the formal context as a bit array, with each bit representing a
Boolean 'true/false' cell in the cross-table. Such an approach leads to efficient
computation in two ways: it allows for bit-wise operations to be performed over
multiple cells in the context at the same time and reducing the size of cells to
bits allows a much larger portion of the context to be held in cache memory. So,
for example, in a 64 bit architecture the formal context can be declared in the
heap using C++ thus:

```
1    unsigned __int64 **context;
```

Once the number of objects, m, and number of attributes, n, are known, the
required memory can be allocated thus:

```
1  /* create empty context */
2  //calculate size for attributes - 1 bit per attribute
3  nArray = (n−1)/64 + 1;
4  //create one dimension of the context
5  context = new unsigned __int64 *[m];
6  for (i = 0;i<m;i++){    //for each object
7      context[i] = new unsigned __int64[nArray];//create a row of
8      for(j=0;j<nArray;j++) context[i][j]=0;    //attributes
9  }
```

Clearly this is a memory efficient way of storing the context: not only are bits
being used to represent the individual cells, but dynamic memory allocation is
being used to declare only the number of bits required for a particular context.
Although dynamic memory allocation is a relatively time-consuming process,
here this does not matter as the context is being allocated once only, before the
invocation of the main algorithm.

It is important to declare the context so that attributes are contiguous in
memory, rather than objects. This structure allows the efficient use of cache
memory when the processing is operating on contiguous attributes, such as the
iteration across attributes in In-Close. A cache-line will be filled with row of the
table, rather than a column, so that contiguous attributes are readily available.
Arranging the context column-wise in memory would mean that the subsequent
processing would be operating 'against the grain' of memory, causing continuous
cache-misses when trying to access contiguous attributes, as the next attribute
would be a whole column-worth of memory away from the current one.

Obviously the use of bits to represent the Boolean cells of the cross-table
requires careful programming to identify specific cells in the cross-table. Each 64
bit unsigned integer represents 64 cells in a row of the cross-table, thus the arith-
metic required is the use of modulo-64 to identify a required cell. For example,
attribute 137 would be bit 9 of integer 3: $137 \ mod \ 64 = 9$ and $137 \ div \ 64 = 2$.

If the formal context is being input as a cxt file, for example, the program
will need to populate the bit array by reading and parsing rows of character

strings where '.' represents an empty cell and 'X' represents a cross. For example, a single row in the formal context in a `cxt` file will look something like this:

```
...X.....XX.........X........X...X.X...XX...........X....X.....X
```

The procedure to input the formal context will then look something like this:

```
 1    /* input instances (rows) and translate into temporary context */
 2      //for each row (object)
 3      for(i = 0; i < m; i++){
 4        //get instance
 5        cxtFile.getline(instance, instanceSize);
 6        //for each attribute
 7        for(j = 0;j < n; j++){
 8          //if object has the attribute
 9          if(instance[j] == 'X'){
10            //set context bit to true at byte: i div 8, bit: i mod 8
11            contextTemp[j][(i>>6)] |= (1i64<<(i%64));
12            //increment column support (density of Xs) for attribute j
13            colSup[j]++;
14          }
15        }
16      }
```

Because binary arithmetic is being used, the C++ bit shift operators `<<` and `>>` provide an efficient means of implementing modulo-64. Thus, `j>>6` shifts the bits in j rightwards by 6 bits, which is equivalent to integer division by 64 ($2^6 = 64$). This identifies the required 64 bit integer in the row of the bit array. The *mod* operator in C++ is `%` and the 64 bit literal integer representation of 1 is defined as `1i64` so, similarly, bit shifting `1i64` leftwards by `j%64` places 1 at the required bit position in a 64 bit integer, with all other bits being zero. The C++ bit-wise logical 'or' operator, `|`, can then be used to set the required bit to 1 in the context.

Bit shift operators and bit-wise logical operators are extremely efficient (typically taking only a single CPU clock-cycle to execute) and thus are fundamental to the fast manipulation of structures such as bit arrays. This becomes even more important in the main cycle of CbO-type algorithms and in efficient canonicity testing, as can be seen later in this paper. However, before considering the implementation of the algorithm itself, some consideration needs to be given to the data structures required for the storage and processing of formal concepts.

Note that a temporary bit array, `contextTemp`, is used to initially store the context in column-wise form, because we next wish to physically sort the columns (see Sect. 4: Physical Sorting of Context Columns, below). After sorting, the context will be translated into row-wise form in the permanent bit-array, `context`, for the main computation.

5   Physical Sorting of Context Columns

It is well-known that sorting context columns in ascending order of support (density of Xs) significantly improves the efficiency of computing formal concepts in CbO-type implementations. The typical approach is to sort pointers to the columns, rather than the columns themselves, as this takes less time. However, in actuality, physically sorting the columns in large formal contexts provides better results, because physical sorting makes more efficient use of cache memory. If data is contiguous in RAM, cache lines will be filled with data that are more likely to be used when carrying out column intersections and when finding an already closed extent in the canonicity test. This can significantly reduce level one data cache misses, particularly when large contexts are being processed [3]. The overhead of physically sorting the context is outweighed by the saving in memory loads.

Thus the column-wise bit array, `contextTemp`, is physically sorted by making use of an array of previously logically sorted column indexes, `colOriginal`:

```
1   /* rewrite sorted context (physical sort) */
2   int tempColNums[MAX_COLS];
3   int rank[MAX_COLS];
4     for(j = 0; j < n; j++){
5           //use the sorted original col nos to index the physical↩
                sort
6         tempColNums[j]=colOriginal[j];
7         rank[colOriginal[j]]=j; //record the ranking of the column
8     }
9     for(j = 0; j < n - 1; j++){
10      for(i = 0; i < mArray; i++){
11          unsigned __int64 temp = contextTemp[j][i];
12          contextTemp[j][i] = contextTemp[tempColNums[j]][i];
13          contextTemp[tempColNums[j]][i] = temp;
14      }
15      //make note of where swapped-out col has moved to using its ↩
                rank
16      tempColNums[rank[j]]=tempColNums[j];
17      rank[tempColNums[j]]=rank[j];
18    }
```

If, for example, `tempColNums = [4,7,0,2,1,6,5,3]`, it means that column 4 is the least dense column and column 3 the most dense. The array `rank` is used to record and maintain the relative ranking of the columns in terms of density. Thus, in this example, `rank = [2,4,3,7,0,6,5,1]`, which means that that column 0 has ranking 2, column 1 has ranking 4, column 2 has ranking 3, and so on.

Once the columns have been physically sorted, the column-wise context, `contextTemp`, is written, a bit at a time, into the row-wise context, `context`, ready for the main computation:

```
1   for(int i=0;i<m;i++){
2     for(int j=0;j<n;j++){
3       if(contextTemp[j][(i>>6)]&(1i64<<(i%64)))
4           context[i][(j>>6)] = context[i][(j>>6)]|(1i64<<(j%64));
5     }
6   }
```

6   Storing and Processing Formal Concepts

For the purposes of efficiency, it would be desirable to store each formal concept literally and completely, say as a two-dimensional array of objects (for the extents) and a corresponding two-dimensional array of attributes (for the intents). Adding a new formal concept as it is computed would require very little in the way of data management and processing the computed concepts would be via simple iteration of the arrays. However, if we wish to deal with large numbers of objects and attributes, and large numbers of formal concepts, it soon becomes impossible to store them in available memory and in any case would be a very inefficient means of storing them with very little of the allocated memory actually being used (if there are 10,000 objects, for example, each extent would need to be declared as size 10,000 even though most extents will contain far fewer objects). An alternative approach, in an attempt to avoid memory considerations altogether, would be to process each concept as it is computed and not to store them at all. However, it is often the case that the 'processing' is not specified. It may be more useful to compute all formal concepts as a service for later batch-type processing. Or, if the processing is simply to output the concepts to a file, outputting each concept as it is computed is a terribly inefficient process and would make any attempt to optimize the implementation of the algorithm redundant. The approach adopted here, for In-Close2, is a compromise: it is decided to store the formal concepts for later processing, but to store them in such a way as to reduce the memory required, whilst maintaining an efficient means of data management. For speed, the most efficient data structure to use to store intents and extents would be standard two-dimensional arrays, indexing each item in its entirety. However, given that the storage space for each extent would need to be of size m, and size n for each intent, it is quickly apparent that the memory required for a typical computation would be enormous and impractical. Compromises need to be made, and here extents are stored in full but in a list, with the memory required for an extent being the size of the extent. This still often requires a significant amount of memory, typically in the order of several MBs, which, although large, is generally practicable on today's standard PCs. Whilst managing a list requires additional indexing overheads (storing starting points and sizes for each extent) the number of additional computational operations required is not large, enabling extents to be stored for later processing but without drastically impacting speed. This illustrates, in the context of FCA, some typical trade-offs between memory and speed that are so common in dealing with optimization problems.

Another approach would be to employ dynamic memory allocation, allocating memory on the fly (e.g. using `malloc`) with the exact size required for storage. Whilst this intuitively seems like a sensible idea, the process of dynamic memory allocation is rather slow and employing it to store extents and intents increases run-time enormously.

Further computational details (and trade-offs) in the handling of intents and extents are given below.

6.1   Intents

In the In-Close2 algorithm, each child intent inherits fully its parent's attributes. Each child is then specialized by adding one or more new attributes which are then, along with its parental attributes, inherited by the next generation, and so on. Thus, it seems sensible to store the intents in that natural 'tree' structure, thus avoiding repetition of inherited attributes. To further save memory, a single dimensional, linear memory, structure can be used with the addition of meta-data to store the start of each intent in memory, the number of 'own' attributes in each intent (i.e. those attributes in an intent not inherited from its parent) and a pointer to a child intent's parent intent so as to be able to obtain the inherited attributes later when the concepts are 'processed'. The data structure can be declared in C++ as follows:

```
1  int *B;    //store for intents - memory will be allocated
2             //for B at start of main program
3  int sizeBnode[MAX_CONS]; //number of 'own' attributes in each ↩
      intent
4  int *startB[MAX_CONS];    //pointers to start of intents
5  int nodeParent[MAX_CONS]; //pointers to parent intents
6  int *bptr; //will point to next available location in B
```

At the start of the main program, the memory allocation for storing intents and pointer initialization is carried out:

```
1  B = new int[MAX_FOR_B];
2  bptr = B;
```

Note that there are some predefined literals here, namely MAX_CONS (the maximum number of concepts that can be computed) and MAX_FOR_B (the amount of memory to be allocated for storing intents). Although it would be possible to dynamically allocate memory on the fly, in the process of computing the concepts, the overheads in time required for this would reduce the efficiency of the implementation. Again, a compromise has been made, in this case to increase efficiency but at the expense of setting arbitrary limits on quantities and sizes.

6.2   Extents

In the In-Close2 algorithm, a new extent is formed as a sub-set of objects from its parent extent. With the breadth then depth approach of the algorithm, it would be possible to avoid repetition of objects (and thus save memory) by removing the child objects from the parent once all the children have been found and then adding meta-data to link the children to the parent. However, this amount of data management would incur significant time overheads, so again a compromise is chosen, in this case to store each extent in full, back-to-back, in memory, adding meta-data to record the starting address of each extent and its size. Thus, although individual objects may be repeated in a number of extents, there is no 'empty', wasted memory that would occur if a two-dimensional array was being used. The data structure can be declared in C++ as follows:

```
1  int* A;    //store for extents - memory will be allocated
2             //at start of main program
3  int* startA[MAX_CONS];    //pointers to start of extents
4  int sizeA[MAX_CONS];      //extent sizes
```

At the start of the program, the memory allocation for storing extents is made, making use of another arbitrary literal for the amount of memory to use:

```
1   A = new int[MAX_FOR_A];
```

Now that the underlying data structures are in place, it is possible to present the optimized implementation of the algorithm itself.

7   Implementation of the Algorithm

The optimized implementation of the InClose2 algorithm is presented below. A key optimization to note is the use of one-dimensional bit arrays (**Bparent** and **Bcurrent**) to represent intents in Boolean form. It was described above how intents are stored in a tree structure to save memory, as opposed to storing each intent separately and in full. Even if they were stored in bit form, the memory required for a large number of intents, each with a maximum size of n would be prohibitive. However, in the algorithm, to skip inherited attributes (line 2) it is necessary to search for j in B. To search the B tree data structure would require some significant time overhead. Searching the intent in Boolean form, however, is simply a logical 'and' bit-wise test (& in C++), locating the required bit in the same way as previously described above:

```
24   if (!(Bcurrent[j>>6] & (1i64 << (j % 64))))
```

The memory required for a single Boolean form intent is insignificant. The parent intent is passed down to the child intent at the next level of recursion, and thus the total number of Boolean-form intents being stored (on the stack) at any one time will be dependent on the level of recursion. This is unlikely to cause problems with memory. Thus, the implementation is a two-way compromise in the end: storing intents globally in a memory efficient data structure for later processing, and at the same time storing intents locally in an operationally efficient data structure to reduce computation time. The optimized code for the In-Close2 algorithm is listed below:

```
1   /*OPTIMIZED IMPLEMENTATION OF INCLOSE2 ALGORITHM */
2   void InClose(int c, int y, unsigned __int64 *Bcurrent)
3   // c: concept number, y: attribute number
4   // Bcurrent: the current intent in Boolean form
5   {
6      /* LOCAL VARIABLES */
7      //attributes where new extents are found
8      int Bchildren[MAX_COLS];
9      //the number of new concepts spawned from current one
10     int numchildren = 0;
11     //the concept no.s of the spawned concepts
12     int Cnums[MAX_COLS];
13     //a child intent in Boolean form
14     unsigned __int64 Bchild[MAX_COLS/64 + 1];
15
16     //calculate the size of current extent
```

```
17    int sizeAc = startA[c+1]-startA[c];
18
19    /********MAIN CYCLE *********************************/
20    //iterate across attribute columns in the context
21    //forming column intersections with current extent
22    for(int j = y; j < n; j++) {
23        /* if j is not an element of B then */
24        if(!(Bcurrent[j>>6] & (1i64 << (j % 64)))){
25            /* C = A intersect {j}downarrow */
26            //point to start of current extent
27            int *Ac = startA[c];
28            //point to start of new extent
29            int *aptr = startA[highc];
30            //NOTE: highc is maintained globally as
31            //next available concept number
32
33            //iterate through objects in current extent
34            for(int i = sizeAc; i > 0; i--){
35                //looking for them in current attribute column
36                if(context[*Ac][j>>6] & (1i64 << (j % 64))){
37                    //if object is found
38                    *aptr = *Ac; //add it to new extent
39                    aptr++;
40                }
41                Ac++;  //next object
42            }
43
44            //calculate size of new extent
45            int size = aptr - startA[highc];
46
47            /* if A = C then */
48            if(size == sizeAc){
49                //add current attribute to current intent
50                *bptr = j; //in the B tree
51                bptr++;
52                sizeBnode[c]++;
53                //and in the Boolean form of intent
54                Bcurrent[j>>6] = Bcurrent[j>>6] | (1i64 << (j % 64));
55            }
56            else { //size < sizeAc so:
57                //if new extent is canonical
58                if(IsCannonical(j,aptr,Bcurrent)){
59                    /* PUT CHILD IN THE QUEUE */
60                    //record the attribute where it was found
61                    Bchildren[numchildren] = j;
62                    //record the new concept number
63                    Cnums[numchildren++] = highc;
64                    //record the parent concept number
65                    nodeParent[highc] = c;
66                    //record the start of the new extent in A
67                    startA[++highc] = aptr;
68                }
69            }
70        }
71    }
72
73    /* GET CHILDREN FROM THE QUEUE */
74    for(int i = numchildren-1; i >= 0 ; i--){
75        /* D = B U {j} */
76        //inherit attributes
77        memcpy(Bchild,Bcurrent,nArray*8);
78        //record the start of the child intent in B tree
79        startB[Cnums[i]] = bptr;
80        //add spawning attribute to B tree
81        *bptr = Bchildren[i];
82        bptr++;
83        sizeBnode[Cnums[i]]++;
84        //and to Boolean form of child intent
```

```
85        Bchild[Bchildren[i]>>6] =
86          Bchild[Bchildren[i]>>6] | (1i64 << (Bchildren[i] % 64));
87
88        //close the child concept from j+1
89        InClose(Cnums[i], Bchildren[i]+1, Bchild);
90      }
91    }
```

7.1 Optimizing the Canonicity Test

Possibly the greatest time savings can be made in the implementation of the canonicity test. The test is, essentially, a search and is the code most frequently executed in the program. Any performance efficiencies made here will have a significant impact on the overal computation time. The task is to find the candidate new extent in an earlier column in the context cross-table. If it can be found, then the extent is not canonical and thus not new. However, the search must avoid looking in columns representing attributes already in the intent of the current concept - as these will, of course, contain the new extent as a subset. The primary source of efficiency here, is the exploitation of the context as a bit array. Using 64-bits, the search becomes a fine-grained parallelization, searching 64 columns of the context simultaneously. To avoid looking in columns representing attributes already in the intent, a bit-mask can be used to mask out the attributes in question. The mask can be created simply by inverting the Boolean form of the current intent, Bcurrent, so that bit positions corresponding to attributes in the current intent become zero and all others are set to 1. The mask is then applied to each object in the new extent (i.e. each corresponding row of the context) using bit-wise 'and'. If the object is present, the corresponding bit in the mask will remain set, if the object is absent the bit will be zeroed.

Further efficiency is possible by stopping the search as soon as the mask becomes completely zeroed - in other words, as soon as it is clear that an object in the extent is not present in any of the columns, it is unnecessary to search for the other objects. The search can then move on the next 64 columns in the context. Conversely, the search can also be stopped as soon as the extent is found: once found it is then not necessary to search any more columns. The combination of fine-grained parallel processing using bit-wise operators and minimizing the amount of searching required, makes the optimized canonicity test extremely efficient. The optimizied canonicity test code is listed below:

```
1    /* OPTIMIZED CANONICITY TEST */
2    bool IsCannonical(int y, int* endAhighc, unsigned __int64 ↵
         Bcurrent[])
3    /* y: attribute number, endAhighc: points to end of the new ↵
         extent */
4    /* Bcurrent: the current intent in Boolean form */
5    {
6        /* CREATE BIT MASK FOR SEARCHING */
7        unsigned __int64 Bmask[MAX_COLS/64 + 1];
8        int p; //counter for 64 bit segments
9        for(p = 0; p < y>>6; p++){
```

```
10        //invert 64 bit segments of current intent
11        Bmask[p]=~Bcurrent[p];
12     }
13     //invert last 64 bits up to current attribute
14     //zeroing any bits after current attribute
15     Bmask[p]= ~Bcurrent[p] & ((1i64 << (y % 64))-1);
16
17     /* SEARCH 64 BIT SEGMENTS OF CONTEXT FOR THE EXTENT */
18     for(p=0; p <= y>>6; p++){
19        int i; //object counter
20        //point to start of extent
21        int* Ahighc = startA[highc];
22        //iterate through objects in new extent
23        for(i = endAhighc - Ahighc; i > 0; i--){
24           //apply mask to context (testing 64 cells at a time)
25           Bmask[p] = Bmask[p] & context[*Ahighc][p];
26           //if an object is not found, stop searching this segment
27           if(!Bmask[p]) break;
28           Ahighc++;        //otherwise, next object
29        }
30        //if extent has been found, it is not canonical
31        if(i==0) return(false);
32     }
33     //if extent has not been found, it is canonical
34     return(true);
35  }
```

8   Evaluation

Evaluation of the optimization was carried out using some standard FCA data sets from the UCI Machine Learning Repository [8] and some artificial data sets. The comparison was between a version of In-Close with and without the optimizations described above, i.e. without a bit-array for the context (an array of type `Bool` is used instead), without the Boolean form of intent being used to skip inherited attributes (the 'tree' of intents is searched instead), and without physical sorting of the context. The difference in performance on the standard data sets, that can be seen in Table 1, is striking, particularly when bearing in mind that the same algorithm is being implemented in both cases - the code optimization is the only difference.

Table 1. UCI data set results (timings in seconds).

Data set	Mushroom	Adult	Internet ads
$|X| \times |Y|$	8124×125	48842×96	3279×1565
Density	17.36%	8.24%	0.77%
#Concepts	226,921	1,436,102	16,570
Optimized	0.16	0.83	0.05
Unoptimized	0.47	2.14	0.39

Artificial data sets were used that, although partly randomized, were constrained by properties of real data sets, such as many valued attributes and a fixed number of possible values. The results of the artificial data set experiments are given in Table 2 and, again, show a significant improvement achieved by the optimized implementation.

Table 2. Artificial data set results (timings in seconds).

Data set	M7X10G120K	M10X30G120K	T10I4D100K
$|X| \times |Y|$	$120,000 \times 70$	$120,000 \times 300$	$100,000 \times 1,000$
Density	10.00%	3.33%	1.01%
#Concepts	1,166,343	4,570,498	2,347,376
Optimized	0.98	8.37	9.10
Unoptimized	2.42	18.65	33.21

9 Conclusions and Further Work

It is clear that certain optimization techniques can make a significant difference to the performance of implementations of CbO-type algorithms. Bit-wise operations and efficient use of cache memory are big factors in this, along with a choice of data structures for storing formal concepts that make a good compromise between size and speed, given the memory typically available and addressable in standard personal computers. Clearly, with more specialized and expensive hardware and with the use of multi-core parallel processing, other significant improvements can be made. However, as far as optimizations are concerned, the ones presented here are probably the most important.

Although space does not permit here, it would be interesting, perhaps in a future, expanded work, to investigate the individual effects of each optimization. It may be that some optimizations are more useful than others. Similarly, it may be interesting to investigate the comparative effectiveness of optimization with respect to varying the number of attributes, number of objects and context density.

The power of 64-bit bit-wise operators naturally leads to the tempting possibility of using even larger bit-strings to further increase the level of fine-grained parallel processing. So-called streaming SIMD extensions (SSEs) and corresponding chip architecture from manufacturers such as Intel and AMD [1,10] provide the opportunity of 128 and even 256 bit-wise operations. However, our early attempts to leverage this power have not shown any significant speed-up. It seems that the overheads of manipulating the 128/256 bit registers and variables are outweighing the increase in parallelism. It may be because we are currently applying the parallelism to the columns of a formal context (the bit-mask in the canonicity test) rather than the rows, that we are not seeing good results from SSEs. Whereas there are typically only tens or perhaps hundreds of columns, there are often tens or even hundreds of *thousands* of rows, particularly if we are applying FCA to data sets. Thus, a 256-bit parallel process is likely to have more impact used column-wise than row-wise. The task will be to work out how to incorporate this approach into an implementation.

It may also be worth exploring how the optimizations presented here could be transferred into other popular programming languages, although interpreted languages, such as Python, are clearly not an ideal choice where speed is of the essence. For Java and C#, there appears to be some debate on efficiency compared to C++. It would be interesting to experiment to obtain some empirical evidence.

In-Close is available free and open source on SourceForge[1].

References

1. AMD: AMD64 Architecture Programmers Manual Volume 6: 128-Bit and 256-Bit XOP, FMA4 and CVT16 Instructions, May 2009
2. Andrews, S.: In-Close, a fast algorithm for computing formal concepts. In: Rudolph, S., Dau, F., Kuznetsov, S.O. (eds.) ICCS 2009, vol. 483. CEUR WS (2009)
3. Andrews, S.: In-Close2, a high performance formal concept miner. In: Andrews, S., Polovina, S., Hill, R., Akhgar, B. (eds.) ICCS 2011. LNCS (LNAI), vol. 6828, pp. 50–62. Springer, Heidelberg (2011). https://doi.org/10.1007/978-3-642-22688-5_4
4. Andrews, S.: A partial-closure canonicity test to increase the efficiency of CbO-type algorithms. In: Hernandez, N., Jäschke, R., Croitoru, M. (eds.) ICCS 2014. LNCS (LNAI), vol. 8577, pp. 37–50. Springer, Cham (2014). https://doi.org/10.1007/978-3-319-08389-6_5
5. Andrews, S.: A best-of-breed approach for designing a fast algorithm for computing fixpoints of Galois connections. Inf. Sci. **295**, 633–649 (2015)
6. Andrews, S.: Making use of empty intersections to improve the performance of CbO-type algorithms. In: Bertet, K., Borchmann, D., Cellier, P., Ferré, S. (eds.) ICFCA 2017. LNCS (LNAI), vol. 10308, pp. 56–71. Springer, Cham (2017). https://doi.org/10.1007/978-3-319-59271-8_4
7. Carpineto, C., Romano, G.: Concept Data Analysis: Theory and Applications. Wiley, Hoboken (2004)
8. Frank, A., Asuncion, A.: UCI machine learning repository (2010). http://archive.ics.uci.edu/ml
9. Ganter, B., Wille, R.: Formal Concept Analysis: Mathematical Foundations. Springer, Heidelberg (1998). https://doi.org/10.1007/978-3-642-59830-2
10. Intel: Intel Developer Zone, ISA Extensions. https://software.intel.com/en-us/isa-extensions. Accessed June 2016
11. Krajca, P., Outrata, J., Vychodil, V.: Parallel recursive algorithm for FCA. In: Belohavlek, R., Kuznetsov, S.O. (eds.) Proceedings of Concept Lattices and their Applications (2008)
12. Krajca, P., Outrata, J., Vychodil, V.: FCbO program (2012). http://fcalgs.sourceforge.net/
13. Krajca, P., Vychodil, V., Outrata, J.: Advances in algorithms based on CbO. In: Kryszkiewicz, M., Obiedkov, S. (eds.) CLA 2010, pp. 325–337. University of Sevilla (2010)

---

[1] In-Close on SourceForge: https://sourceforge.net/projects/inclose/.

14. Kuznetsov, S.O.: A fast algorithm for computing all intersections of objects in a finite semi-lattice. Nauchno-Tekhnicheskaya Informatsiya, ser. 2 **27**(5), 11–21 (1993)
15. Kuznetsov, S.O.: Mathematical aspects of concept analysis. Math. Sci. **80**(2), 1654–1698 (1996)
16. Outrata, J., Vychodil, V.: Fast algorithm for computing fixpoints of Galois connections induced by object-attribute relational data. Inf. Sci. **185**(1), 114–127 (2012)
17. Priss, U.: Formal concept analysis in information science. Ann. Rev. Inf. Sci. Technol. (ASIST) **40** (2008)
18. Wille, R.: Formal concept analysis as mathematical theory of concepts and concept hierarchies. In: Ganter, B., Stumme, G., Wille, R. (eds.) Formal Concept Analysis. LNCS (LNAI), vol. 3626, pp. 1–33. Springer, Heidelberg (2005). https://doi.org/10.1007/11528784_1
19. Wolff, K.E.: A first course in formal concept analysis: how to understand line diagrams. Adv. Stat. Softw. **4**, 429–438 (1993)

Preventing Overlaps in Agglomerative Hierarchical Conceptual Clustering

Quentin Brabant[(✉)], Amira Mouakher, and Aurélie Bertaux

CIAD, Université de Bourgogne, 21000 Dijon, France
{quentin.brabant,amira.mouakher,aurelie.bertaux}@u-bourgogne.fr

Abstract. Hierarchical Clustering is an unsupervised learning task, whi-ch seeks to build a set of clusters ordered by the inclusion relation. It is usually assumed that the result is a tree-like structure with no overlapping clusters, i.e., where clusters are either disjoint or nested. In Hierarchical Conceptual Clustering (HCC), each cluster is provided with a conceptual description which belongs to a predefined set called the *pattern language*. Depending on the application domain, the elements in the pattern language can be of different nature: logical formulas, graphs, tests on the attributes, etc. In this paper, we tackle the issue of overlapping concepts in the agglomerative approach of HCC. We provide a formal characterization of pattern languages that ensures a result without overlaps. Unfortunately, this characterization excludes many pattern languages which may be relevant for agglomerative HCC. Then, we propose two variants of the basic agglomerative HCC approach. Both of them guarantee a result without overlaps; the second one refines the given pattern language so that any two disjoint clusters have mutually exclusive descriptions.

Keywords: Conceptual knowledge acquisition · Conceptual clustering · Hierarchical clustering · Agglomerative clustering · Conceptual structure · Overlap

1 Introduction

Cluster analysis or simply clustering is the unsupervised task of partitioning a set of objects into groups called *clusters*, such that objects belonging to the same cluster are more similar than objects belonging to different clusters. Based on regularities in data, this process is targeted to identify relevant groupings or taxonomies in real-world databases [9]. There are many different clustering methods, and each of them may give a different grouping of a dataset. One of the most important method of clustering analysis is the hierarchical clustering [14]. In fact, in the latter, the set of objects is partitioned at different levels, and the ordering of clusters, w.r.t. inclusion, can be represented as a dendogram.

Traditional clustering methods are usually unable to provide human-readable definitions of the generated clusters. However, conceptual clustering techniques,

© Springer Nature Switzerland AG 2020
M. Alam et al. (Eds.): ICCS 2020, LNAI 12277, pp. 74–89, 2020.
https://doi.org/10.1007/978-3-030-57855-8_6

in addition to the list of objects belonging to the clusters, provide for each cluster a definition, as an explanation of the clusters. This definition belongs to a predefined set called the *pattern language*. The pair of a cluster and its definition is usually called a *concept*.

In this paper, we are paying hand to Hierarchical Conceptual Clustering (HCC), to wit the task of generating concepts that decompose the set of data at different levels. We focus on the agglomerative approach, which is easily adaptable to various application cases. Indeed, its requirements on the pattern language are easy to meet (see Sect. 2).

A particularity of conceptual clustering approaches is that only clusters having a definition in the pattern language can be returned. Quite often, the chosen pattern language does not allow expressing every possible subset of objects in the data. Thus, the pattern language can be seen as a tool for guiding the clustering and avoiding over-fitting. However, this particularity may lead to an issue: naïve agglomerative HCC algorithms outputs are sometimes not, strictly speaking, hierarchical. A structure of this kind cannot be represented by a dendogram. This problem is the main focus of the present paper, which is organized as follows:

The next section recalls the key notions used throughout this paper and reviews the related work. In Sect. 3, we provide a formal characterization of pattern languages ensuring that the result of agglomerative HCC does not contain overlaps. As many relevant pattern languages for the agglomerative HCC are excluded from our proposed characterization, we provide, in Sect. 4, a variant of agglomerative HCC that always outputs a set of non-overlapping clusters. Then, Sect. 5 reports an experimental study and its results. Section 6 concludes the paper and identifies avenues for future work.

2   Preliminaries and Related Work

This section reviews the fundamental notions used in this paper, then briefly surveys the related works in Agglomerative Hierarchical Conceptual Clustering.

2.1   Some Definitions

Pattern Language. We consider a partially ordered set $(\mathcal{L}, \sqsubseteq)$, to which we refer as the *pattern language*. The partial order $\sqsubseteq$ is called a *generality relation*. For any two patterns $p, q \in \mathcal{L}$, the relation $p \sqsubseteq q$ indicates that any object that is described by p is also described by q. We say that q is *more general* than p (or that q *generalizes* p) and that p is *more specific* than q (or that p *specifies* q). The set of most general elements of a set of patterns P is:

$$\widehat{P} = \{p \in P \mid \forall q \in P, \ p \not\sqsubseteq q\}.$$

Example 1. We now describe a pattern language that will be used as an example throughout the paper. This pattern language is composed of all subsets of $\{0, \ldots, 9\}$, i.e., $\mathcal{L} = 2^{\{0,\ldots,9\}}$. The generality relation $\sqsubseteq$ is defined as the inverse of inclusion ($p \sqsubseteq q$ if and only if $q \subseteq p$). In other words, the more elements a pattern contains, the more specific it is; for instance $\{1, 2\} \sqsubseteq \{1\}$. This framework is similar to that of FCA (see, e.g. [8]).

Data Representation. We consider a set of objects X. Each object $x \in X$ is associated to a pattern referred to as its *most specific description* (*MSD*) through a function $\delta : X \to D$, where D is a subset of $\mathcal{L}$ that contains all potential MSD of objects. The MSD $\delta(x)$ can be interpreted as the pattern providing the most information about x.

Example 2. We consider $X = \{x_1, \ldots, x_5\}$, $D = \mathcal{L}$ and $\delta : X \to D$ such that:

x	x_1	x_2	x_3	x_4	x_5
$\delta(x)$	$\{0, 1\}$	$\{1, 2, 3, 4\}$	$\{1, 2, 3, 5\}$	$\{2, 5, 6\}$	$\{2, 5, 7\}$

Clusters and Concepts. For any pattern p, we denote by $\mathrm{cl}(p)$ the cluster of objects that p describes, i.e.:

$$\mathrm{cl}(p) = \{x \in X \mid \delta(x) \sqsubseteq p\}.$$

It follows from this definition that $p \sqsubseteq q$ is equivalent to $\mathrm{cl}(p) \subseteq \mathrm{cl}(q)$. A pair $(\mathrm{cl}(p), p)$ is called a *concept* if there is no pattern $q \in \mathcal{L}$ such that $q \sqsubset p$ and $\mathrm{cl}(q) = \mathrm{cl}(p)$. The pattern p and the cluster $\mathrm{cl}(p)$ are then called the *intension* and the *extension* of $(\mathrm{cl}(p), p)$, respectively. Note that if, for a given cluster $A \subseteq X$, there is no $p \in \mathcal{L}$ such that $A = \mathrm{cl}(p)$, then no concept corresponds to A. A natural order relation of concepts is defined by:

$$(\mathrm{cl}(p), p) \leq (\mathrm{cl}(q), q) \iff p \sqsubseteq q \iff \mathrm{cl}(p) \subseteq \mathrm{cl}(q). \tag{1}$$

Example 3. Let's consider the following patterns: $\{1, 2, 3\}$, $\{2, 5\}$ and $\emptyset$. The corresponding concepts are $(\{x_2, x_3\}, \{1, 2, 3\})$, $(\{x_3, x_4, x_5\}, \{2, 5\})$ and $(X, \emptyset)$. The pattern $\{5\}$ has no corresponding concept, since $\mathrm{cl}(\{5\}) = \{x_3, x_4, x_5\}$ and $\{2, 5\}$ is a more specific pattern that describes the same cluster. The cluster $\{x_4, x_5\}$ has also no corresponding concept, since the most specific pattern that describes x_4 and x_5 (which is $\{2, 5\}$) also describes x_3. As an illustration of (1), notice that $\{1, 2, 3\} \sqsubseteq \emptyset$ and $\{x_2, x_3\} \subseteq X$, and thus $(\{x_2, x_3\}, \{1, 2, 3\}) \leq (X, \emptyset)$.

Agglomerative Clustering. The principle of (non-conceptual) agglomerative clustering is the following:

1. a set of clusters $H = \{\{x\} \mid x \in X\}$ is initialized;
2. while H does not contain the cluster X:
   (a) pick C_1 and C_2 from $\{C \in H \mid \forall C' \in H, \ C \not\subset C'\}$;
   (b) add $C_1 \cup C_2$ to H.

At the end of the process, clusters of H are either nested or disjoint, which allows to represent H by a dendogram. Usually, the chosen clusters C_1 and C_2 are the closest according to some inter-cluster distance, which is itself defined w.r.t. a given inter-object distance.

Generalization Operation. In the case of agglomerative HCC, we substitute clusters with concepts. Merging two concepts $(cl(p), p)$, $(cl(q), q)$ is done by choosing a pattern r that generalises both p and q; the resulting concept is then $(cl(r), r)$. In this paper, we consider a binary operation $\sqcup$ on $\mathcal{L}$ such that $p \sqcup q$ generalizes both p and q. Moreover, we assume that $\sqcup$ is a join semilattice operator [4]. This assumption is not very restrictive, since the properties that characterize join operators are quite natural for the purpose of agglomerative HCC. Indeed, $\sqcup$ begin a join semilattice operation is equivalent to:

- $\sqcup$ being idempotent, commutative and associative;
- $\sqcup$ being idempotent, monotonic and satisfies $p \sqsubseteq p \sqcup q$ for all $p, q \in \mathcal{L}$;
- $p \sqcup q$ being the most specific generalization of p and q for all $p, q \in \mathcal{L}$.

Since $\sqcup$ is associative, it naturally extends into the function $\bigsqcup : 2^{\mathcal{L}} \to \mathcal{L}$, where:

$$\bigsqcup \{p_1, \ldots, p_n\} = p_1 \sqcup \ldots \sqcup p_n \quad \text{for all } n > 0 \text{ and all } p_1, \ldots, p_n \in \mathcal{L}.$$

Example 4. In the pattern language of the previous examples, the most specific generalization of two sets is given by their intersection. Thus, the join operation associated to $\mathcal{L}$ and $\subseteq$ is $\cap$. So, if we want to merge the concepts $(\{x_1\}, \{0, 1\})$ and $(\{x_2\}, \{1, 2, 3, 4\})$, we first compute

$$\{0, 1\} \sqcup \{1, 2, 3, 4\} = \{0, 1\} \cap \{1, 2, 3, 4\} = \{1\},$$

and then

$$cl(\{1\}) = \{x \in X \mid \delta(x) \sqsubseteq \{1\}\} = \{x_1, x_2, x_3\},$$

and we get the concept $(\{x_1, x_2, x_3\}, \{1\})$.

Finally, we assume that $\mathcal{L}$ has a minimal element $\bot$, such that $\bot \notin D$. Since $(\mathcal{L}, \sqsubseteq)$ is a join semi-lattice with a lower bound, it is a lattice. We denote its meet operation by $\sqcap$. Note that $\bot$ cannot describe any object, since $\bot \sqsubset p$ for all $p \in D$. Furthermore, saying that $p \sqcap q = \bot$ is equivalent to say that no object can be described by both p and q.

Example 5. Although $\{1, \ldots, 9\}$ is the least elements of $\mathcal{L}$, we have $\{1, \ldots, 9\} \in D$. Thus, in order to fit our assumptions about $\bot$, we set $\mathcal{L} = 2^{\{0, \ldots, 9\}} \cup \{\bot\}$ such that $\bot \sqsubset \{1, \ldots, 9\}$, and $D = \mathcal{L} \setminus \{\bot\}$. Finally, the reader can check that the meet operation associated to $\mathcal{L}$ is the set union $\cup$.

2.2   Related Work

In the following, we review the few previous works that addressed the agglomerative approach of HCC. For a broader review on conceptual clustering, we refer the reader to [12].

The work that is the most closely related to ours is certainly [6], where an agglomerative HCC algorithm is described. This algorithm takes as parameter a pattern language and a distance over the set of objects. Moreover, the authors define several levels of "agreement" between the chosen pattern language and distance. Those levels of agreement are though as conditions that limit the impact of the pattern language on the outcome of the clustering (when compared to a classical approach relying only on distance). However, the clusters produced by this approach can overlap with each other.

Other papers propose algorithms that make use of a specific pattern language: [13] introduces a method (HICAP) for hierarchical conceptual clustering where patterns are itemsets. Just as the classical UPGMA method, HICAP relies on the average linkage criteria. It seems to perform as well as UPGMA or bisecting k-means, while providing clusters with human-readable definitions.

One of the reason for avoiding overlaps in the result of HCC is readability. However, it is possible to allow some overlaps while preserving readability to some extent. *Pyramids* are cluster structures that can be drawn without crossing edges, while allowing some overlaps. In this context, Brito and Diday proposed a clustering method using the pyramidal model to structure symbolic objects [2]. Their approach is based on an agglomerative algorithm to build the pyramid structure. Each cluster is defined by the set of its elements and a symbolic object, which describes their properties. This approach is used for knowledge representation and leads to a readable graphical representation.

Finally, note that the theoretical notions of this paper are directly inspired from the pattern structure formalism [7], which extends Formal Concept Analysis [8] and provides a useful theoretical framework for thinking about pattern languages.

2.3   An Abstract View of Agglomerative HCC

In this paper, we abstract ourselves from the chosen pattern language and from how the concepts to merge are picked at each step. In this respect, our work can be seen as a continuation of [6]. Algorithm 1 formalizes the general process of agglomerative HCC. It takes as argument the data (X and δ), the join operation $\sqcup$ of the pattern language, and a function f that picks, at each step, the two patterns that are going to be merged. Typically, the selected pair is the closest according to some metric on X.

Example 6. We consider a distance d defined as the complement of the Jaccard index of object MSDs:

$$d(x_i, x_j) = 1 - \frac{|\delta(x_i) \cap \delta(x_j)|}{|\delta(x_i) \cup \delta(x_j)|}.$$

```
1 function AHCC(X, δ, ⊔, f):
2   |   P ← {δ(x) | x ∈ X}
3   |   while |P̂| > 1 do
4   |   |   {p₁, p₂} ← f(P̂, X, δ, ⊔)
5   |   |   P ← P ∪ {p₁ ⊔ p₂}
6   |   end
7   |   return P
```

Algorithm 1: The agglomerative approach of HCC. The function returns a set of patterns where each pattern characterizes a concept.

We define f to return the two concepts whose extents are the closest according to d, following a single linkage strategy, i.e., for any two clusters C_i and C_j:

$$d(C_i, C_j) = \min\{d(x_i, x_j) \mid x_i \in C_i,\ x_j \in C_j\}.$$

The set of patterns returned by AHCC is represented in Fig. 1.

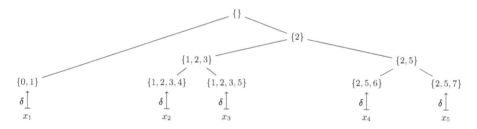

Fig. 1. Result of AHCC in Example 6. The leaves of the tree are created at the initialization of P. The other nodes are created by merging their children, in the following order: $\{1, 2, 3\}$, $\{2, 5\}$, $\{2\}$, $\emptyset$.

2.4 Overlaps

It is usually said that two clusters A, B *overlap* if

$$A \nsubseteq B,\quad B \nsubseteq A,\quad \text{and}\quad A \cap B \neq \emptyset.$$

We define the notion of overlaps for patterns in an analogous manner. We say that two patterns p and q overlap if:

$$p \nsqsubseteq q,\quad q \nsqsubseteq p\quad \text{and}\quad p \sqcap q \neq \bot,$$

This is to say, if one does not generalize the other, and if it can exist an object that is described by both. Note that two patterns p, q necessarily overlap if $cl(p)$ and $cl(q)$ overlap; but the reverse is not true; if p and q overlap, whether $cl(p)$

and $cl(q)$ also overlap depends on the objects in X and there descriptions given by δ. In general, the result of Algorithm 1 can contain both extent overlaps and intent overlaps.

Example 7. In Example 6, we have $cl(\{2,5\}) = \{x_3, x_4, x_5\}$ and $cl(\{1,2,3\}) = \{x_2, x_3\}$. Thus, the clusters described by $\{2,5\}$ and $\{1,2,3\}$ overlap on x_3. Figure 2 is misleading, because it omits the link between the patterns $\{1,2,3,5\}$ and $\{2,5\}$, and it suggests that x_3 does not belong to $cl(\{2,5\})$. Finally, note that, although some pair of patterns describe non-overlapping clusters, any pair of patterns from $2^{\{0,...,9\}}$ is either related by inclusion or overlapping. Indeed, since $\bot \notin 2^{\{0,...,9\}}$, we always have $p \cup q \neq \bot$.

3   Formal Characterization of Pattern Languages Ensuring a Result Without Overlaps

In this section, we present conditions on $\sqcup$ and D that ensure the absence of overlap in $\mathtt{AHCC}(X, \delta, \sqcup, f)$, regardless of X, δ and f. For any pattern p, we say that a set $B \subseteq \mathcal{L}$ is a *base* of p if $\bigsqcup B = p$, and we set

$$\beta(p) = \{B \subseteq D \mid \bigsqcup B = p\}.$$

In other words, $\beta(p)$ is the set of bases of p that are included in D.

Example 8. In our running example, the base of $\{1,2,3\}$ contains all $S \subseteq 2^{\{0,...,9\}}$ such that $\bigcap S = \{1,2,3\}$.

Proposition 1. *The two following propositions are equivalent:*

(a) D contains no overlap and for any overlapping p_1, $p_2 \in \mathcal{L}$ we have

$$\forall G_2 \in \beta(p_2)\ \exists q \in G_2 : q \sqsubseteq p_1 \tag{2}$$

(b) For any X, δ and f, $\mathtt{AHCC}(X, \delta, \sqcup, f)$ contains no overlap.

Proof. In order to make the proof easier to follow, we define, for all $p \in \mathcal{L}$, $\downarrow p = \{q \in \mathcal{L} \mid q \sqsubseteq p\}$. We also reformulate (2) as follows:

$$\forall G_2 \in \beta(p_2) : \quad G_2 \cap \downarrow p_1 \neq \emptyset.$$

We first show by induction that (a) implies (b). Assume that (a) holds, and consider the algorithm of function $\mathtt{AHCC}$.

1. P is initialized with value $\{\delta(x) \mid x \in X\} \subseteq D$, thus without overlaps.
2. Now we consider the k-th iteration of the **while** loop, and assume that P contains no overlap (before line 5 is executed). We will show that $P \cup \{p_1 \sqcup p_2\}$ does not contain overlap either. For any $r \in P$, since $p_1, p_2 \in \widehat{P}$, we have $p_1 \not\sqsubseteq r$ and $p_2 \not\sqsubseteq r$. Then:
    - if $r \sqsubseteq p_1$ or $r \sqsubseteq p_2$ then $r \sqsubseteq p_1 \sqcup p_2$ (thus r and $p_1 \sqcup p_2$ do not overlap);

- if neither $r \sqsubseteq p_1$ nor $r \sqsubseteq p_2$ then, since P contains no overlap, we have:

$$\downarrow p_1 \cap \downarrow r = \downarrow p_2 \cap \downarrow r = \emptyset, \quad \text{and thus} \quad (\downarrow p_1 \cup \downarrow p_2) \cap \downarrow r = \emptyset$$

and therefore for all $B_1 \in \beta(p_1)$ and all $B_2 \in \beta(p_2)$ we have $(B_1 \cup B_2) \cap \downarrow r = \emptyset$. Since

$$\bigsqcup (B_1 \cup B_2) = \left(\bigsqcup B_1 \right) \sqcup \left(\bigsqcup B_2 \right) = p_1 \sqcup p_2$$

we also have $(B_1 \cup B_2) \in \beta(p_1 \sqcup p_2)$. Therefore, there is a base of $p_1 \sqcup p_2$ that is disjoint from $\downarrow r$. Thus, using (a), we can deduce that $p_1 \sqcup p_2$ and r do not overlap.

Hence, $p_1 \sqcup p_2$ does not overlap with any $r \in P$, and thus $P \cup \{p_1 \sqcup p_2\}$ contains no overlap. The proof by induction is then complete.

In order to show that (b) implies (a), we show that if (a) does not hold then (b) does not. Assume that (a) does not hold: we will show that we can define X, δ and f so that $\texttt{AHCC}(X, \delta, \sqcup, f)$ contains at least one overlap.

- If D contains at least two overlapping patterns p_1 and p_2, then $\texttt{AHCC}(X, \delta, \sqcup, f)$ contains overlaps for $X = \{x_1, x_2\}$, $\delta(x_1) = p_1$ and $\delta(x_2) = p_2$.
- If D contains no overlap, then the second part of condition (a) does not hold, i.e., there are overlapping patterns $p_1, p_2 \in \mathcal{L}$ such that

$$\exists\, G_2 \in \beta(p_2) : G_2 \cap \downarrow p_1 = \emptyset.$$

Let $G_2 \in \beta(p_2)$ such that $G_2 \cap \downarrow p_1 = \emptyset$ and let $G_1 \in \beta(p_1)$. We set X and δ so that δ is a bijection from X to $(G_1 \cup G_2)$. The algorithm initializes P to $G_1 \cup G_2$. Since we have not placed any restrictions on the function f, this can be chosen so as to obtain an arbitrary merger order. We choose f such that the order of merging of patterns is as follows: first, the patterns of G_1 are merged with each other until obtaining p_1. When p_1 is added to P, since G_2 is disjoint from $\downarrow p_1$, after p_1 is added to P, we have $\widehat{P} = \{p_1\} \cup G_2$. We then choose the following merging order: the patterns of G_2 are merged with each other until obtaining p_2. Then, we get $p_1, p_2 \in P$, and thus the result of the algorithm is not hierarchical.

$\square$

Remark 1. Condition (a) on D and $\sqcup$ is necessary and sufficient to prevent overlaps in the result of $\texttt{AHCC}$. However, this condition is quite restrictive and is not met by many interesting pattern languages. Some cases are listed below.

- $\mathcal{L}$ is the powerset of a given set and $\sqsubseteq$ is the inverse of the inclusion relation (see Example 1).
- $\mathcal{L}$ is the set of n-tuples whose components are numeric intervals, with $n \geq 3$, and $\sqsubseteq$ is defined as in Subsect. 5.2.

- The pattern language is as defined in [5]. Besides, the paper also presents an example of HCC whose result contains overlaps, although this is not explicitly noted (see Fig. 3, diagrams (c) and (e)).
- The patterns are antichains of a given poset $(X, \leq)$, and $\sqsubseteq$ is defined by:

$$p \sqsubseteq q \quad \Longleftrightarrow \quad \forall a \in q \; \exists b \in p : b \leq a.$$

Note that this includes cases where X contains complex structures (e.g., graphs, trees, sequences, etc) and where $b \leq a$ means "a is the substructure of b". Examples of such pattern languages are given, for instances, in [11] with syntactic trees, and in [10] with graphs representing molecules.

- $\mathcal{L}$ is the set of expressible concepts of a given Description Logic, objects are individuals from an A-Box, and δ maps each individual to its *most specific concept* (see [1], Sect. 6.3). In this case, D equals $\mathcal{L}$ and contains overlaps.

To our current knowledge, languages fulfilling condition (a) are either very expressive or very simple. Some cases of such simple pattern languages are the followings:

- $\mathcal{L}$ contains no overlap (in other words, $\mathcal{L} \setminus \{\bot\}$ can be represented as a tree).
- the elements of $\mathcal{L} \setminus \{\bot\}$ can be seen as interval of some total order, where the join operator is the intersection.

A case of very expressive language is the following: $\mathcal{L}$ is the set of n-ary boolean functions (for some $n > 0$), and $\sqcup$ is the logical OR. For instance, for two functions $b_1, b_2 \in \mathcal{L}$ defined by

$$b_1(x_1, \ldots, x_n) = x_1 \quad \text{and} \quad b_2(x_1, \ldots, x_n) = (x_2 \text{ AND } x_3),$$

the pattern $b_1 \sqcup b_2$ is the function expressed by $(x_1 \text{ OR } (x_2 \text{ AND } x_3))$. Since (a) requires that D does not contain overlap, we define it as the subset of boolean functions that have only one true interpretation, i.e. functions that are of the form:

$$b(x_1, \ldots, x_n) = l_1(x_1) \text{ AND } l_2(x_2) \text{ AND } \ldots \text{ AND } l_n(x_n)$$

with, for each $i \in \{1 \ldots n\}$: either $l_i(x_i) = x_i$, or $l_i(x_i) = \text{NOT } x_i$.

4   Preventing Overlaps in Agglomerative HCC

In this section, we describe a variant of agglomerative HCC where concepts are created agglomeratively but: (i) the pattern merging step is corrected in order to prevent cluster overlaps; (ii) the pattern language is extended with a "pattern negation" and (iii) when a new pattern is created, existing patterns are updated in a top-down fashion for preventing pattern overlaps.

Correcting Pattern Creation. In Algorithm 1, when a new pattern $p_1 \sqcup p_2$ is added to P, it can happen that P already contains some pattern q such that $cl(q)$ and $cl(p_1 \sqcup p_2)$ overlaps. In our variant, we avoid such situation by adding the pattern $p_1 \sqcup p_2 \sqcup q$ to P, instead of $p_1 \sqcup p_2$ (see Algorithm 2).

Refined Pattern Language. We define $\overline{\mathcal{L}}$ as the set of antichains of $\mathcal{L}$, i.e.: $\overline{\mathcal{L}} = \{\widehat{P} \mid P \subseteq \mathcal{L}\}$. We define meet and join operations on $\overline{\mathcal{L}}$ by, respectively:

$$P \sqcap Q = \widehat{P \cup Q} \quad \text{and} \quad P \sqcup Q = \overline{\{p \sqcap q \mid p \in P, \, q \in Q\}}.$$

The set $\overline{\mathcal{L}}$ endowed with $\sqcap$ and $\sqcup$ is a lattice (see [3], Lemma 4.1) whose maximal element is the empty set. Its order relation $\sqsubseteq$ is characterized by:

$$P \sqsubseteq Q \quad \Longleftrightarrow \quad \forall q \in Q \, \exists p \in P : q \sqsubseteq p.$$

Now, we define the lattice $(\mathcal{L}^*, \sqsubseteq^*)$ as the product of $\mathcal{L}$ and $\overline{\mathcal{L}}$. In other words: $\mathcal{L}^* = \mathcal{L} \times \overline{\mathcal{L}}$, the meet and join operations on $\mathcal{L}^*$ are defined by, respectively:

$$(p, N) \sqcap^* (q, M) = (p \sqcap q, P \sqcap Q) \quad \text{and} \quad (p, N) \sqcup^* (q, M) = (p \sqcup q, P \sqcup Q),$$

and the associated order relation $\sqsubseteq^*$ is such that

$$(p, N) \sqsubseteq^* (q, M) \quad \Longleftrightarrow \quad [p \sqsubseteq q \text{ and } P \sqsubseteq Q].$$

We say that $\mathcal{L}^*$ is the *refinement* of $\mathcal{L}$.

Semantic of $\mathcal{L}^*$. Each refined pattern $(p, N) \in \mathcal{L}^*$ can be interpreted as "p minus all patterns in N". A semantic of (p, N) is given by the function $\Psi : \mathcal{L}^* \to 2^{\mathcal{L}}$ such that:

$$\Psi(p, N) = \{q \in \mathcal{L} \mid q \sqsubseteq p \text{ and } \forall r \in N : q \not\sqsubseteq r\}.$$

Notice that, if $(p, N) \sqsubseteq^* (q, M)$, then $\Psi(p, N) \subseteq \Psi(q, M)$ but the reversed implication is not true. We then define the set of objects described by (p, N) by:

$$\mathrm{cl}^*(p, N) = \{x \in X \mid \delta(x) \in \Psi(p, N)\}.$$

Example 9. Following Example 5: the elements of $\overline{\mathcal{L}}$ are antichains from $2^{\{0,\dots,9\}}$. For instance, $\{\{0, 5\}, \{2\}\} \in \overline{\mathcal{L}}$. The pattern $(\{1\}, \{\{0, 5\}, \{2\}\}) \in \mathcal{L}^*$ describes all objects that are described by $\{1\}$, but are not described by $\{0, 5\}$ nor $\{2\}$.

The Algorithm. Algorithm 2 describes our variant `AHCC-Tree` of agglomerative HCC. The result of `AHCC-Tree` is a couple (P, neg), where $P \subseteq \mathcal{L}$ and neg is a map from P to $\overline{\mathcal{L}}$. The couple (P, neg) describes the set of refined patterns

$$P^* = \{(p, neg(p)) \mid p \in P\} \subseteq \mathcal{L}^*.$$

Provided that there are no $x_1, x_2 \in X$ such that $\delta(x_1) \sqsubseteq \delta(x_2)$, the set of clusters $\{\mathrm{cl}(p) \mid p \in P\}$ does not contain overlaps. Provided that $\{\delta(x) \mid x \in X\}$ has no overlap: patterns of P may overlap, but the set of patterns P^* has no overlap.

Example 10. We consider the same $\mathcal{L}, \sqcup, X, \delta$ and f as in Example 7. Throughout the iterations of `AHCC-Tree`, $\widehat{P}$ and neg evolve as follows:

1. Initialization: $\widehat{P} = \{\{0,1\}, \{1,2,3,4\}, \{1,2,3,5\}, \{2,5,6\}, \{2,5,7\}\}$;
   for $p \in P : neg(p) = \emptyset$
2. $\{1,2,3,4\}$ and $\{1,2,3,5\}$ are merged into $\{1,2,3\}$;
   $\widehat{P} = \{\{0,1\}, \{1,2,3\}, \{2,5,6\}, \{2,5,7\}\}$;
   for $p \in \{\{0,1\}, \{2,5,6\}, \{2,5,7\}\} : neg(p) = \{\{1,2,3\}\}$
3. $\{2,5,6\} \sqcup \{2,5,7\}$ gives $\{2,5\}$, but $cl(\{2,5\})$ overlaps with $cl(\{1,2,3\})$, thus
   $\{2,5\}$ and $\{1,2,3\}$ are merged into $\{2\}$, which is added to P;
   $\widehat{P} = \{\{0,1\}, \{2\}\}$;
   $neg(\{0,1\}) = \{\{1,2,3\}\} \mathbin{\square} \{\{2\}\} = \{\{2\}\}$
4. $\{0,1\}$ and $\{2\}$ are merged into $\emptyset$;
   $\widehat{P} = \{\emptyset\}$.

The result is represented in Fig. 2.

```
1  function AHCC-Tree(X, δ, ⊔, f):
2  │    P ← {δ(x) | x ∈ X}
3  │    ∀p ∈ P : [neg(p) ← ∅]
4  │    while |P̂| > 1 do
5  │    │    q ← ⊔f(P̂, X, δ, ⊔)
6  │    │    while ∃p ∈ P̂ : [cl(p) and cl(q) overlap] do
7  │    │    │    q ← q ⊔ p
8  │    │    end
9  │    │    P ← P ∪ {q}
10 │    │    for p ∈ P such that p and q overlap. do
11 │    │    │    neg(p) ← neg(p) ⊓ {q}
12 │    │    end
13 │    end
14 │    return P, neg
```

Algorithm 2: The corrected agglomerative approach of HCC.

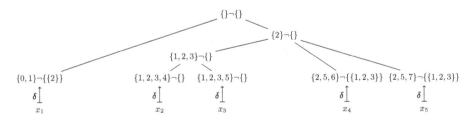

Fig. 2. Set of patterns P^* corresponding to the result of Example 10. Patterns of P^* are written in the form "$p \neg neg(p)$".

5   Empirical Study

In the following experiments, we perform agglomerative HCC on widely used datasets from the UCI repository[1]. We try to quantify the presence of overlaps in the result of agglomerative HCC. Then, we test the corrected version of AHCC and compare it to the basic AHCC in terms of how well results fit with data. The code and datasets used for the experiments are available on GitHub[2].

5.1   Datasets

We ran experiments on 6 datasets form the UCI repository. The characteristics of those datasets are summarized in Table 1. These datasets are 2-dimensional tables where rows can be seen as objects and columns as attributes. An attribute can be numerical or categorical. In some datasets, a target attribute is specified for the purpose of supervised learning; we treat target attributes just as normal ones.

Table 1. Datasets' characteristics.

Id.	Name	# objects	# numerical att.	# categorical att.
1	Glass	214	9	1
2	Wine	178	13	0
3	Yeast	1484	8	1
4	Breast cancer wisconsin	699	10	0
5	Seeds	210	7	1
6	Travel reviews	980	10	0

5.2   Definition of a Pattern Language

The pattern language is defined as follows. Firstly, categorical attributes are translated into numerical ones using a one-hot encoding. We denote by n the number of attributes after this transformation. We define $\mathcal{L}$ as the set of n-tuples of the form $([a_1; b_1], \ldots, [a_n; b_n])$ where each $[a_i; b_i]$ is an interval on $\mathbb{R}$, and we define $\sqcup$ by:

$$([a_1; b_1], \ldots, [a_n; b_n]) \sqcup ([c_1; d_1], \ldots, [c_n; d_n]) =$$
$$([\min(a_1, c_1); \max(b_1, d_1)], \ldots, [\min(a_n, c_n); \max(b_n, d_n)]).$$

Each row corresponds to an object $x \in X$. Let us denote the values in the row by $a_1, \ldots, a_n$. The description of x is then $\delta(x) = ([a_1; a_1], \ldots, [a_n; a_n])$. Finally, we define f as the function that returns the two clusters whose centroïds are closest according to the Euclidean distance.

---

[1] Available at UC Irvine Machine Learning Database http://archive.ics.uci.edu/ml/.
[2] https://github.com/QGBrabant/ACC.

5.3 Basic Agglomerative HCC Experiment

We applied Algorithm 1 on the different dataset presented in Table 1. For each dataset, we ran 10 tenfold cross-validations (except for yeast and travel reviews, which have many rows, and for which we ran 10 twofold cross-validations); a set of patterns P was learned on each training set using the method specified above.

Then, we estimate the number of overlaps contained, on average, in P. This estimation relied on two measures: for all pattern p, we call *covering rate* of p the rate of objects that are described by p, and we call *overlapping rate* of p the rate of objects that are described by p and (at least) another pattern $q \in P$ that is incomparable with p. Measuring one of these two rates can yield different values depending on whether the measure is done the training or test set. We will simply refer to the covering rate of a cluster on the training set as its size. In order to assess the relevance of a cluster, we can compare its size to its covering rate on the test set (a significantly smaller rate on the test set is a sign of overfitting). Here, however, we are mostly interested in the overlapping rate of clusters, depending on their size. The results are depicted by Fig. 3.

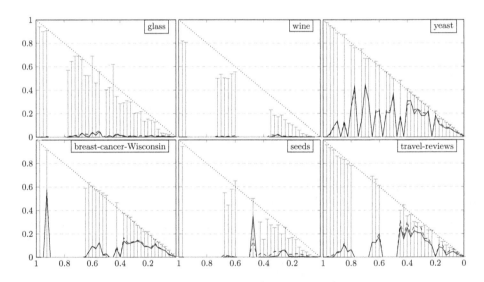

Fig. 3. The abscissa represents the interval of possible cluster sizes (which is $[0; 1]$). This interval is divided into 40 sub-intervals of length 0.025. For each sub-interval $]a; a + 0.025]$, we consider all clusters whose sizes belong to $]a; a + 0.025]$, and we plot their average value for the following rates: covering rate on the test set (vertical line); overlapping rate on the learning set (plain line); overlapping rate on the test set (dashed line). Note that, when no cluster has a size belonging to a given interval, no vertical line is displayed.

We observe that the covering rates on the test sets tend to be close to the size of the clusters. Moreover, the overlapping rates on the test sets are very similar to those obtained on the training sets. Determining which characteristics of the dataset determine the overlapping rate would require and empirical study using more diverse datasets. However, our study allows to conclude that high overlapping rates can occur in practice when performing agglomerative HCC.

5.4   Corrected Agglomerative HCC Experiment

In order to compare how well `AHCC` and `AHCC-Tree` fit to the data, we applied Algorithm 2 on the same data, with the same cross-validation setting.

One way to asses the quality of fit of a pattern set P on a test set X_{test} would be to measure the distance of each $x \in X_{\text{test}}$ to the centroïd of the most specific concept of P it belongs to. However, such a measure could fail to account for the quality of fit of concepts that are "higher in the tree". In order to have a more comprehensive view, we introduce a parameter $k \in [0; 1]$ and define $P(x, k)$ as the set of most specific patterns $p \in P$ such that $\delta(x) \sqsubseteq p$ and $\frac{|\text{cl}(p)|}{|X_{\text{train}}|} \geq k$. Then we define an error function e by:

$$e(P, X_{\text{test}}, k) = \frac{1}{|X_{\text{test}}|} \sum_{x \in X_{\text{test}}} \frac{1}{|P(x, k)|} \sum_{C \in P(x,k)} d(x, C),$$

where $d(x, C)$ is the Euclidean distance between x and the centroïd of C. We rely on e to evaluate both `AHCC` and `AHCC-Tree` on each dataset. The results are reported in Fig. 4.   Although the reported values are consistently in favor of `AHCC`, the difference between both algorithms is very slight. Thus, the proposed method `AHCC-Tree` seems to be a viable alternative to `AHCC` in term of fitting.

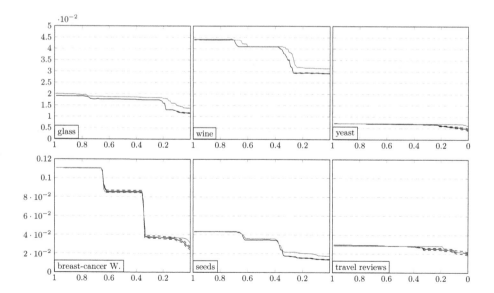

Fig. 4. Mean value of e as a function of k, for `AHCC` (black) and `AHCC-Tree` (red). (Color figure online)

6   Conclusion and Future Work

In this paper, we were interested in Agglomerative Hierarchical Conceptual Clustering. We presented a formal characterization of pattern languages in order to guarantee the hierarchical aspect of the resulting clusters. Unfortunately, this characterization is too restrictive and excludes many relevant pattern languages for HCC. So, we proposed two variants of the basic agglomerative HCC approach preventing overlaps. The second variant also refines the given pattern language so that any two disjoint clusters have mutually exclusive descriptions.

Although more thorough experiments have to be conducted to confirm the empirical results, our study suggests that the proposed `AHCC-Tree` function is a viable alternative to basic agglomerative HCC.

Acknowledgments. This research was supported by the QAPE company under the research project Kover.

References

1. Baader, F., Calvanese, D., McGuinness, D.L., Nardi, D., Patel-Schneider, P.F. (eds.): The Description Logic Handbook: Theory, Implementation, and Applications. Cambridge University Press, New York (2003)

2. Brito, P., Diday, E.: Pyramidal representation of symbolic objects. In: Schader, M., Gaul, W. (eds.) Knowledge, Data and Computer-Assisted Decision. ATO ASI Series, pp. 3–16. Springer, Heidelberg (1990). https://doi.org/10.1007/978-3-642-84218-4_1

3. Crampton, J., Loizou, G.: The completion of a poset in a lattice of antichains. Int. Math. J. **1**(3), 223–238 (2001)

4. Davey, B.A., Priestly, H.A.: Introduction to Lattices and Order. Cambridge University Press, Cambridge (2002)

5. Funes, A., Ferri, C., Hernández-Orallo, J., Ramírez-Quintana, M.J.: An instantiation of hierarchical distance-based conceptual clustering for propositional learning. In: Theeramunkong, T., Kijsirikul, B., Cercone, N., Ho, T.-B. (eds.) PAKDD 2009. LNCS (LNAI), vol. 5476, pp. 637–646. Springer, Heidelberg (2009). https://doi.org/10.1007/978-3-642-01307-2_63

6. Funes, A.M., Ferri, C., Hernández-Orallo, J., Ramírez-Quintana, M.J.: Hierarchical distance-based conceptual clustering. In: Daelemans, W., Goethals, B., Morik, K. (eds.) ECML PKDD 2008. LNCS (LNAI), vol. 5211, pp. 349–364. Springer, Heidelberg (2008). https://doi.org/10.1007/978-3-540-87479-9_41

7. Ganter, B., Kuznetsov, S.O.: Pattern structures and their projections. In: Delugach, H.S., Stumme, G. (eds.) ICCS-ConceptStruct 2001. LNCS (LNAI), vol. 2120, pp. 129–142. Springer, Heidelberg (2001). https://doi.org/10.1007/3-540-44583-8_10

8. Ganter, B., Wille, R.: Formal Concept Analysis: Mathematical Foundations. Springer, Heidelberg (2012). https://doi.org/10.1007/978-3-642-59830-2

9. Jonyer, I., Holder, L.B., Cook, D.J.: Graph-based hierarchical conceptual clustering. Int. J. Artif. Intell. Tools **10**(1–2), 107–135 (2001). https://doi.org/10.1142/S0218213001000441

10. Kuznetsov, S.O.: Machine learning and formal concept analysis. In: Eklund, P. (ed.) ICFCA 2004. LNCS (LNAI), vol. 2961, pp. 287–312. Springer, Heidelberg (2004). https://doi.org/10.1007/978-3-540-24651-0_25

11. Leeuwenberg, A., Buzmakov, A., Toussaint, Y., Napoli, A.: Exploring pattern structures of syntactic trees for relation extraction. In: Baixeries, J., Sacarea, C., Ojeda-Aciego, M. (eds.) ICFCA 2015. LNCS (LNAI), vol. 9113, pp. 153–168. Springer, Cham (2015). https://doi.org/10.1007/978-3-319-19545-2_10

12. Pérez-Suárez, A., Martínez-Trinidad, J.F., Carrasco-Ochoa, J.A.: A review of conceptual clustering algorithms. Artif. Intell. Rev. **52**(2), 1267–1296 (2018). https://doi.org/10.1007/s10462-018-9627-1

13. Xiong, H., Steinbach, M.S., Tan, P., Kumar, V.: HICAP: hierarchical clustering with pattern preservation. In: Proceedings of the Fourth SIAM International Conference on Data Mining, Lake Buena Vista, Florida, USA, 22–24 April 2004, pp. 279–290 (2004)

14. Zhou, B., Wang, H., Wang, C.: A hierarchical clustering algorithm based on GiST. In: Huang, D.-S., Heutte, L., Loog, M. (eds.) ICIC 2007. CCIS, vol. 2, pp. 125–134. Springer, Heidelberg (2007). https://doi.org/10.1007/978-3-540-74282-1_15

Interpretable Concept-Based Classification with Shapley Values

Dmitry I. Ignatov[2,3(✉)] and Léonard Kwuida[1]

[1] Bern University of Applied Sciences, Bern, Switzerland
`leonard.kwuida@bfh.ch`
[2] National Research University Higher School of Economics,
Moscow, Russian Federation
`dignatov@hse.ru`
[3] St. Petersburg Department of Steklov Mathematical Institute of Russian Academy
of Sciences, Saint Petersburg, Russia

Abstract. Among the family of rule-based classification models, there are classifiers based on conjunctions of binary attributes. For example, JSM-method of automatic reasoning (named after John Stuart Mill) was formulated as a classification technique in terms of intents of formal concepts as classification hypotheses. These JSM-hypotheses already represent interpretable model since the respective conjunctions of attributes can be easily read by decision makers and thus provide plausible reasons for model prediction. However, from the interpretable machine learning viewpoint, it is advisable to provide decision makers with importance (or contribution) of individual attributes to classification of a particular object, which may facilitate explanations by experts in various domains with high-cost errors like medicine or finance. To this end, we use the notion of Shapley value from cooperative game theory, also popular in machine learning. We provide the reader with theoretical results, basic examples and attribution of JSM-hypotheses by means of Shapley value on real data.

Keywords: Interpretable Machine Learning · JSM hypotheses · formal concepts · Shapley values

1 Introduction

In this paper we consider the JSM method of inductive reasoning in terms of Formal Concept Analysis for classification problems [6, 8, 19] from Interpretable Machine Learning viewpoint [24]. Briefly, this is a rule-based classification technique [7], i.e. it relies on rules in the form "if an object satisfies a certain subset of attributes, then it belongs to a certain class". Under some conditions these subsets of attributes are called JSM-hypotheses or classification hypotheses (see Sect. 2).

© Springer Nature Switzerland AG 2020
M. Alam et al. (Eds.): ICCS 2020, LNAI 12277, pp. 90–102, 2020.
https://doi.org/10.1007/978-3-030-57855-8_7

In Interpretable Machine Learning (IML) we want to build from our training data a classification model, that is capable not only to infer the class of undetermined examples (not seen in the training data), but also to explain, to some extent, the possible reasons why a particular classification has been performed in terms of separate attributes and their values [24]. From this point of view, classification based on JSM-hypotheses belongs to interpretable machine learning techniques since combination of attributes provides clear interpretation. To have further insights and rely on statistically stable hypotheses under examples deletion, the notion of stability of hypotheses was proposed [16,18]. It enables ranking of hypotheses to sort out the most stable ones for classification purposes.

However, in modern machine learning, especially for the so-called black-box models like deep neural nets, the analyst would like to receive plausible interpretation of particular classification cases (why to approve (or disapprove) a certain money loan, why a certain diagnosis may (or not) take place) even on the level of ranking of individual attributes by their importance for classification [24].

To further enrich the JSM-based methodology not only by ranking single hypotheses, but also by ranking individual attributes, we adopt Shapley value notion from Cooperative Game Theory [25], which has already been proven to be useful in supervised machine learning [21,26]. Following this approach, we play a game on subsets of attributes of a single classification example, also called coalitions, so each player is a single attribute. If a coalition contains any positive hypothesis (or negative one, in case of binary classification problem), then it is called a winning coalition and it receives a value 1 as a pay-off (or -1, in case of negative hypothesis). If we fix a certain attribute m belonging to the chosen classification example, the total pay-off across all the winning coalitions containing m is aggregated into a weighed sum, which takes values in $[0,1]$. This aggregation rule enjoys certain theoretical properties, which guarantee fair division of the total pay-off between players [25], i.e. attributes in our case.

In what follows, we explain the details of this methodology for JSM method in FCA terms with illustrative classification examples and attribute ranking for classic real datasets used in machine learning community.

The paper is organised as follows: Sect. 2 introduces mathematical formalisation of binary classification problem by hypotheses induction based on formal concepts. In Sect. 3, related work on interpretable machine learning and Shapley values from Game Theory is summarised. Section 4 describes one of the possible applications of Shapley values in Formal Concept Analysis setting. Section 5 is devoted to machine experiments with real machine learning data. Finally, Sect. 6 concludes the paper.

2   JSM-Hypotheses and Formal Concepts

The JSM-method of hypothesis generation proposed by Viktor K. Finn in late 1970s was introduced as an attempt to describe induction in purely deductive form, and thus to give at least partial justification of induction [6]. JSM is an acronym after the philosopher John Stuart Mill, who proposed several schemes of inductive reasoning in the 19th century. For example, his Method of Agreement, is formulated as follows: "If two or more instances of the phenomenon under investigation have only one circumstance in common, ... [it] is the cause (or effect) of the given phenomenon."

In FCA community, the JSM-method is known as concept learning from examples in terms of inductive logic related to Galois connection [15]. Thus, in [8,19] this technique was formulated in terms of minimal hypotheses, i.e. minimal intents(see Definition 1) that are not contained in any negative example.

The method proved its ability to enable learning from positive and negative examples in various domains [18], e.g., in life sciences [1].

In what follows, we rely on the definition of a hypothesis ("no counter-example-hypothesis" to be more precise) in FCA terms that was given in [8] for binary classification[1].

There is a well-studied connection of the JSM-method in FCA terms with other concept learning techniques like Version Spaces [10,23]. Among interesting venues of concept learning by means of indiscernibility relation one may find feature selection based on ideas from Rough Set Theory and JSM-reasoning [11] and Rough Version Spaces; the latter allows handling noisy or inconsistent data [3].

Let $\mathbb{K} = (G, M, I)$ be a formal context; that is a set G of objects (to be classified), a set M of attributes (use to describe the objects) and a binary relation $I \subseteq G \times M$ (to indicate if an object satisfies an attribute). Let $w \notin M$ be our *target attribute*. The goal is to classify the objects in G with respect to w. The target attribute w partitions G into three subsets:

- *positive examples*, i.e. the set $G_+ \subseteq G$ of objects known to satisfy w,
- *negative examples*, i.e. the set $G_- \subseteq G$ of objects known not to have w,
- *undetermined examples*, i.e. the set $G_\tau \subseteq G$ of objects for which it remains unknown whether they have the target attribute or do not have it.

This partition induces three subcontexts $\mathbb{K}_\varepsilon := (G_\varepsilon, M, I_\varepsilon)$, $\varepsilon \in \{-, +, \tau\}$ of $\mathbb{K} = (G, M, I)$. The first two of them, the *positive context* $\mathbb{K}_+$ and the *negative context* $\mathbb{K}_-$, form the training set, and are used to build the *learning context* $\mathbb{K}_\pm = (G_+ \cup G_-, M \cup \{w\}, I_+ \cup I_- \cup G_+ \times \{w\})$. The subcontext $\mathbb{K}_\tau$ is called the undetermined context and is used to predict the class of not yet classified objects. The context $\mathbb{K}_c = (G_+ \cup G_- \cup G_\tau, M \cup \{w\}, I_+ \cup I_- \cup I_\tau \cup G_+ \times \{w\})$ is called a *classification context*.

Definition 1. *For a formal context* $\mathbb{K} = (G, M, I)$ *a derivation is defined as follows, on subsets* $A \subseteq G$ *and* $B \subseteq M$*:*

$$A' = \{m \in M \mid aIm, \ \forall a \in A\} \qquad and \qquad B' = \{g \in G \mid gIb, \ \forall b \in B\}.$$

An intent *is a subset* B *of attributes such that* $B'' = B$*.*

---

[1] Basic FCA notions needed for this contribution can be found in one of these books [12,13].

In the subcontexts $\mathbb{K}_\varepsilon := (G_\varepsilon, M, I_\varepsilon)$, $\varepsilon \in \{-, +, \tau\}$ the derivation operators are denoted by $(\cdot)^+$, $(\cdot)^-$, and $(\cdot)^\tau$ respectively. We can now define positive and negative hypotheses.

Definition 2. *A* positive hypothesis $H \subseteq M$ *is an intent of* $\mathbb{K}_+$ *that is not contained in the intent of a negative example. i.e.* $H^{++} = H$ *and* $H \not\subseteq g^-$ *for any* $g \in G_-$. *Equivalently,*

$$H^{++} = H \ \text{and} \ H' \subseteq G_+ \cup G_\tau.$$

Similarly, a negative hypothesis $H \subseteq M$ *is an intent of* $\mathbb{K}_-$ *that is not contained in the intent of a positive example. i.e.* $H^{--} = H$ *and* $H \not\subseteq g^+$ *for any* $g \in G_+$. *Equivalently,*

$$H^{--} = H \ \text{and} \ H' \subseteq G_- \cup G_\tau.$$

An intent of $\mathbb{K}_+$ that is contained in the intent of a negative example is called a *falsified (+)-generalisation*.

Example 1. Table 1 shows a many-valued context representing credit scoring data. The sets of positive and of negative examples are $G_+ = \{1, 2, 3, 4\}$ and $G_- = \{5, 6, 7, 8\}$. The undetermined examples are in $G_\tau = \{9, 10, 11, 12\}$ and should be classified with respect to the target attribute which takes values $+$ and $-$, meaning "low risk" and "high risk" client, respectively.

Table 1. Many-valued classification context for credit scoring

G/M	Gender	Age	Education	Salary	Target
1	Ma	Young	Higher	High	$+$
2	F	Middle	Special	High	$+$
3	F	Middle	Higher	Average	$+$
4	Ma	Old	Higher	High	$+$
5	Ma	Young	Higher	Low	$-$
6	F	Middle	Secondary	Average	$-$
7	F	Old	Special	Average	$-$
8	Ma	Old	Secondary	Low	$-$
9	F	Young	Special	High	τ
10	F	Old	Higher	Average	τ
11	Ma	Middle	Secondary	Low	τ
12	Ma	Old	Secondary	High	τ

To apply JSM-method in FCA terms we need to scale the given data. The context $\mathbb{K}$ below is obtained by nominal scaling the attributes in Table 1. It shows the first eight objects whose class is known (either positive or negative) together with the last four objects which are still to be classified.

$\mathbb{K}$	Ma	F	Y	Mi	O	HE	Sp	Se	HS	A	L	w	$\bar{w}$
g_1	×		×						×			×	
g_2		×		×			×		×			×	
g_3		×		×		×				×		×	
g_4	×				×	×						×	
g_5	×		×			×					×		×
g_6		×		×	×					×			×
g_7		×					×			×			×
g_8	×							×			×		×
g_9		×	×					×	×				
g_{10}		×		×	×				×				
g_{11}	×			×			×			×			
g_{12}	×			×			×	×					

We need to find positive and negative non-falsified hypotheses. Figure 1 shows the lattices of positive and negative examples for the input context, respectively. The intents of the nodes form the hypotheses. Note that the intent of a given node is obtained by collecting all attributes in the order filter of this node[2]. For example the hypothesis given by the intent of the red node, labelled by A, is $\{A, Mi, F, HE\}$.

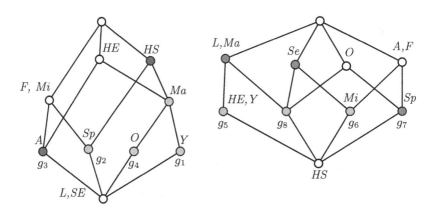

Fig. 1. The line diagrams of the lattice of positive hypotheses (left) and the lattice of negative hypotheses (right).

Shaded nodes correspond to maximal non-falsified hypotheses, i.e. they have no upper neighbours being non-falsified hypotheses. For $\mathbb{K}_+$ the hypothesis $\{HE\}$ is falsified by the object g_5, since $\{HE\} \subseteq g_5^- = \{Ma, Y, HE, L\}$. For $\mathbb{K}_-$ the hypothesis $\{A, F\}$ is falsified by the object g_3, since $\{A, F\} \subseteq g_3^+ = \{F, Mi, HE, A\}$. □

---

[2] This concise way of representation is called reduced labelling [13].

The undetermined examples g_τ from G_τ will be classified as follows:

- If g_τ^τ contains a positive, but no negative hypothesis, then g_τ is *classified positively* (presence of the target attribute w predicted).
- If g_τ^τ contains a negative, but no positive hypothesis, then g_τ *classified negatively* (absence of the target attribute w predicted).
- If g_τ^τ contains both negative and positive hypotheses, or if g_τ^τ does not contain any hypothesis, then this object classification is *contradictory* or *undetermined*, respectively. In both cases g_τ is not classified.

For performing classification it is enough to have only minimal hypotheses (w.r.t. $\subseteq$), negative and positive ones.

There is a strong connection between hypotheses and implications. An implication in a context $\mathbb{K} := (G, M, I)$ is a pair of attribute sets (B_1, B_2), also denoted by $B_1 \rightarrow B_2$. The implication $B_1 \rightarrow B_2$ holds in $\mathbb{K}$ if each object having all attributes in B_1 also has all attributes in B_2. We call B_1 premiss and B_2 conclusion.

Proposition 1 ([16]). *A positive hypothesis H corresponds to an implication $H \rightarrow \{w\}$ in the context $K_+ = (G_+, M \cup \{w\}, I_+ \cup G_+ \times \{w\})$. Similarly, a negative hypothesis H corresponds to an implication $H \rightarrow \{\bar{w}\}$ in the context $K_- = (G_-, M \cup \{\bar{w}\}, I_- \cup G_- \times \{\bar{w}\})$. Hypotheses are implications which premises are closed (in K_+ or in K_-).*

A detailed yet retrospective survey on JSM-method (in FCA-based and original formulation) and its applications can be found in [15]. A further extension of JSM-method to triadic data with target attribute in FCA-based formulation can be found in [14]; there, the triadic extension of JSM-method used CbO-like algorithm for classification in Bibsonomy data.

Input data are often numeric or categorical and need scaling, however, it might not be evident what to do in case of learning with labelled graphs [17]. Motivated by the search of a possible extensions of original FCA to analyse data with complex structure, the so called Pattern Structures were proposed [9].

3 Interpretable Machine Learning and Shapley Values

3.1 Interpretable Machine Learning

In early 90ies, the discipline of Data Mining emerged a step of Knowledge Discovery in Databases (KDD) process, which was defined as follows: "KDD is the nontrivial process of identifying valid, novel, potentially useful, and ultimately understandable patterns in data" [5]. In [5], the primary goals of data mining were also identified as prediction and description, where the latter focuses on finding human-interpretable patterns describing the data. The authors also noted that the boundaries between prediction and description are not sharp. So, from the very beginning, Data Mining is geared towards understandable or human-interpretable patterns, while Machine Learning and Deep Learning, in particular, do not share this constraint.

However, recently machine learning researchers realised the necessity of interpretation for a wide variety of black-box models[3] and even for ensemble rule-based methods when many attributes are involved [20].

Among the family of approaches, the book [24] on interpretable machine learning poses global versus local interpretations. Thus, the global interpretability "is about understanding how the model makes decisions, based on a holistic view of its features and each of the learned components such as weights, other parameters and structures", while the local interpretability focuses on "a single instance and examines what the model predicts for this input, and explains why" [24]. From this point of view, the JSM-method provides local interpretations when we deal with a particular classification example. According to the other taxonomic criteria, the JSM-method is intrinsic but not a post-hoc model since interpretability is introduced already on the level of hypotheses generation and their application (inference phase), and provides model-specific but not model-agnostic interpretations since it is based on a concrete rule-based model.

Shapley value is a model-agnostic method and produces a ranking of individual attributes by their importance for the classification of a particular example, i.e. it provides a decision maker with local interpretations. This attribution methodology is equivalent to the Shapely value solution to value distribution in Cooperative Game Theory [25]. Štrumbelj and Kononenko [26] consistently show that Shapley value is the only solution for the problem of single attribute importance (or attribution problem) measured as the difference between model's prediction with and without this particular attribute across all possible subsets of attributes. Lundberg and Lee [21] extend this approach further to align it with several other additive attribution approaches like LIME and DeepLift under the name SHAP (Shapley Additive explanation) values [21].

To compute SHAP value for an example x and an attribute m the authors define $f_x(S)$, the expected value of the model prediction conditioned on a subset S of the input attributes, which can be approximated by integrating over samples from the training dataset. SHAP values combine these conditional expectations with the classic Shapley values from game theory to assign a value ϕ_m to each attribute m:

$$\phi_m = \sum_{S \subseteq M \setminus \{m\}} \frac{|S|!(|M| - |S| - 1)!}{|M|!} \left(f_x(S \cup \{m\}) - f_x(S) \right), \qquad (1)$$

where M is the set of all input attributes and S a certain coalition of players, i.e. set of attributes. In our exposition of this problem, we will follow classical definition of Shapley value [25], where a Boolean function is used instead of the expected value $f_x(S)$.

---

[3] The workshops on Interpretable Machine Learning: https://sites.google.com/view/whi2018 and https://sites.google.com/view/hill2019.

3.2   Shapley Values in FCA Community

In [4], the authors introduced cooperative games on concept lattices, where a concept is a pair (S, S'), S is a subset of players or objects, and S' is a subset of attributes. In its turn, any game of this type induces a game on the set of objects, and a game on the set of attributes. In these games, the notion of Shapley value naturally arises as a rational solution for distributing the total worth of the cooperation among the players. The authors of [22] continued the development of the topic by studying algorithms to compute the Shapley value for a cooperative game on a lattice of closed sets given by an implication system; the main computational advantage of the proposed algorithms is based on maximal chains and product of chains of fixed length.

Even though these approaches considering games on lattices of closed sets and implication systems are related to hypotheses families, they do not use Shapley values for interpretation or ranking attributes in classification setting.

4   Shapley Values as Means of Attribute Importance for a Given Example

Let $\mathbb{K}_c = (G_+ \cup G_- \cup G_\tau, M \cup \{w\}, I_+ \cup I_- \cup I_\tau \cup G_+ \times \{w\})$ be our learning context. The set of all minimal positive and all minimal negative hypotheses of $\mathbb{K}_c$ are denoted by $\mathcal{H}_+$ and $\mathcal{H}_-$, respectively. For a given object $g \in G$, the Shapley value of an attribute $m \in g'$ is defined as follows:

$$\varphi_m(g) = \sum_{S \subseteq g' \setminus \{m\}} \frac{|S|!(|g'| - |S| - 1)!}{|g'|!} \left(v(S \cup \{m\}) - v(S)\right), \qquad (2)$$

where

$$v(S) = \begin{cases} 1, & \exists H_+ \in \mathcal{H}_+ : H_+ \subseteq S \text{ and } \forall H_- \in \mathcal{H}_- : H_- \not\subseteq S \\ 0, & (\forall H_+ \in \mathcal{H}_+ : H_+ \not\subseteq S \text{ and } \forall H_- \in \mathcal{H}_- : H_- \not\subseteq S) \\ & \text{or } (\exists H_+ \in \mathcal{H}_+ : H_+ \subseteq S \text{ and } \exists H_- \in \mathcal{H}_- : H_- \subseteq S) \\ -1, & \forall H_+ \in \mathcal{H}_+ : H_+ \not\subseteq S \text{ and } \exists H_- \in \mathcal{H}_- : H_- \subseteq S. \end{cases}$$

The Shapley value $\varphi_{\tilde{m}}(g)$ is set to 0 for every $\tilde{m} \in M \setminus g'$. In other words, if we consider an undetermined object g_S such $g'_S = S$, then $v(S) = 1$ when g_S is classified positively, $v(S) = 0$ when g_S is classified contradictory or remains undetermined, and $v(S) = -1$ if g_S is classified negatively. Note that $v(\emptyset) = 0$.

Let us consider the example from Sect. 2. The set of positive hypotheses, $\mathcal{H}_+$ consists of $\{F, Mi, HE, A\}$ and $\{HS\}$, while $\mathcal{H}_-$ contains three negative hypotheses $\{F, O, Sp, A\}$, $\{Se\}$, and $\{M, L\}$.

Now, let us classify every undetermined example and find the Shapley value of each attribute, i.e. the corresponding Shapley vector denoted $\Phi(g)$. The example g_9 is classified positively since it does not contain any negative hypothesis, while $\{HS\} \subseteq g'_9 = \{F, Y, Sp, HS\}$. The corresponding Shapley vector is

$$\Phi(g_9) = (0, 0.0, 0.0, 0, 0, 0, 0.0, 0, 1.0, 0, 0).$$

The decimal point for some zero values of $\varphi_m(g)$, i.e. 0.0, means that these values have been computed, while 0 (without decimal point) means that the corresponding attribute m is not in g'. For the example g_9, only one attribute has non-zero Shapley value, $\varphi_{HS}(g_9) = 1$. The example g_{10} remains undetermined, since $g'_{10} = \{F, O, HE, A\}$ does not contain positive or negative hypotheses. This results in zero Shapley vector:

$$\Phi(g_{10}) = (0, 0.0, 0, 0, 0.0, 0.0, 0, 0, 0, 0.0, 0).$$

When an undetermined example is classified negatively, the Shapley vector contains negative values that add up to -1. For example, two negative hypotheses are contained in g_{11}, namely $\{Se\} \subseteq g'_{11} = \{M, Mi, Se, L\}$ and $\{M, L\} \subseteq g'_{11}$. Only the attributes of these two negative hypotheses have non-zero Shapley values:

$$\Phi(g_{11}) = (-1/6, 0, 0, 0.0, 0, 0, 0, -2/3, 0, 0, -1/6).$$

In case an undetermined example is classified contradictory, at least two hypotheses of both signs are contained in it and the sum of Shapley values for all its attributes is equal to zero. The positive hypothesis $\{HS\}$ is contained in $g'_{12} = \{M, O, Se, HS\}$, which also contains the negative hypothesis $\{Se\}$. Two components of the Shapley vector are non-zero, namely $\varphi_{Se}(g_{12}) = -1$ and $\varphi_{HS}(g_{12}) = 1$. Thus,

$$\Phi(g_{12}) = (0.0, 0, 0, 0, 0.0, 0, 0, -1.0, 1.0, 0, 0).$$

Having Shapley values of undetermined examples, we are able to not only determine the result of classification but also to rank individual attributes by their importance for the outcome of the classification. In case of the example g_{11}, the attribute Se denoting secondary education has two times higher value in magnitude than the two remaining attributes Ma and L, expressing male gender and low income, respectively; Their signs show negative classification. In case of the example g_{12}, both attributes Se and HS are equally important, but being of opposite signs cancels classification to one of the two classes.

Proposition 2. *The Shapley value of an attribute m for an object g of $\varphi_m(g)$ fulfils the following properties:*

1. *$\varphi_m(g) = 0$ for every $m \in g'$ that does not belong to at least one positive or negative hypothesis contained in g';*
2. *$\sum_{m \in g'} \varphi_m(g) = 1$ if g is classified positively;*
3. *$\sum_{m \in g'} \varphi_m(g) = 0$ if g is classified contradictory or remains undetermined;*
4. *$\sum_{m \in g'} \varphi_m(g) = -1$ if g is classified negatively.*

An attribute m such that $\varphi_m(g) = 0$ is known as the dummy player [25] since its contribution for every formed coalition is zero.

5   Machine Experiments Demo

To provide the reader with examples of Shapley vectors on real data, we take the Zoo dataset from UCI Machine Learning Repository[4]. It has 101 examples of different animals along with their 16 attributes; the target attribute, *type*, has seven values. One attribute expresses the number of legs with values 0, 2, 4, 5, 6 and 8. We transform it into a binary attribute using nominal scale. The resulting input context has 101 objects and 21 attributes in total.

Since this dataset supposes a solution to a multi-class problem, we consider one of possible associated binary classification problems where the major class, mammals, is our positive class, while all the remaining compose the negative class. We could also consider the remaining six classes as positive classes using the scheme one-versus-the-rest.

There are 41 examples for the positive class and 60 examples for the negative class[5]. After generating the hypotheses, we get only one positive hypothesis,

$$\mathcal{H}_+ = \big\{\{milk, backbone, breathes\}\big\}$$

and nine negative hypotheses:

$$\mathcal{H}_- = \big\{\{feathers, eggs, backbone, breathes, legs_2, tail\}, \{predator, legs_8\},$$
$$\{eggs, airborne, breathes\}, \{eggs, aquatic, predator, legs_5\}, \{eggs, legs_0\},$$
$$\{eggs, toothed, backbone\}, \{eggs, legs_6\}, \{venomous\}, \{eggs, domestic\}\big\}.$$

If we apply the trained JSM classifier to all the examples of positive class, we obtain the same Shapley vector for all of them since they classified positively by the only one positive hypothesis (in the absence of negative hypotheses):

$$(0.0, 0, 0, 1/3, 0, 0, 0.0, 0.0, 1/3, 1/3, 0, 0, 0.0, 0, 0, 0, 0, 0, 0, 0, 0.0).$$

Note that in the Shapley vector above, we display zero components in two different ways as it was explained previously. Thus, values 0.0 are shown for non-contributing attributes of example 1, i.e. aardvark with attributes

$$\{hair, milk, predator, toothed, backbone, breathes, legs_4, tail, catsize\}.$$

All the attributes from the unique positive hypothesis, i.e. *milk, backbone* and *breathes* contribute equally by 1/3.

However, not every negative example is classified negatively. Two negative examples crab and tortoise remain undetermined:

$$crab' = \{eggs, aquatic, predator, legs_4\}$$

---

[4] https://archive.ics.uci.edu/ml/datasets/zoo.

[5] There are no undetermined examples here since we would like to test decision explainability by means of Shapley values rather than to test prediction accuracy of the JSM-method.

and

$$tortoise' = \{eggs, backbone, breathes, legs_4, tail, catsize\}.$$

Let us have a look at the correctly classified negative examples. For example, $duck' = \{feathers, eggs, airborne, aquatic, backbone, breathes, legs_2, tail\}$ contains two negative hypotheses $\{feathers, eggs, backbone, breathes, legs_2, tail\}$ and $\{eggs, airborne, breathes\}$. The Shapley vector for the duck example is[6]:

$$-(0, 0.024, 0.357, 0, 0.190, 0.0, 0, 0, 0.024, 0.357, 0, 0, 0, 0, 0.024, 0, 0, 0, 0.024, 0, 0).$$

Eggs, breathes, and airborne are the most important attributes with Shapley values -0.357, -0.357, and -0.19, respectively, while the attribute aquatic has zero importance in terms of Shapley value.

A useful interpretation of classification results could be an explanation for true positive or true negative cases. Thus, one can see which attributes has largest contribution to the wrong classification, i.e. possible reason of the classifier's mistake.

The executable iPython scripts for the synthetic context on credit scoring and the scaled zoo context, can be found at http://bit.ly/ShapDemo2020[7].

6   Conclusion

In this paper we have introduced usage of Shapley value from Cooperative Game Theory to rank attributes of objects while performing binary classification with the JSM-method within FCA setting. It helps a decision maker to not only see the hypotheses contained in the corresponding example's description but to also take into account the constituent attributes contribution. Thus, it is also possible to explain mistakes of the classifiers known as false positive and false negative examples.

As the forthcoming work, we would like to address scalability issues, which are due to subset enumeration and suitable visual display for showing attribute importance. Note that all the subsets of attributes from g' that do not contain any positive or negative hypothesis can be omitted during summation in (2). Therefore, we need to explore only order filters (w.r.t. the Boolean lattice $(2^{g'}, \subseteq)$) of hypotheses contained in g'. Histograms of importance vectors can be implemented and used for better differentiation between small and high importance values of vectors like XGBoost feature importance diagrams [2].

The considered variant of JSM-method might be rather crisp and cautious in the sense that it prohibits classification in case of hypotheses of both signs, so its variants with voting are important. Another interesting venue is the prospective extension of the proposed approach for multi-class classification problems via

---

[6] All the non-zero values are given with precision up to the third significant sign after decimal point.

[7] The full version of this script along with the used datasets will be available at https://github.com/dimachine/Shap4JSM.

one-versus-the-rest and one-versus-one schemes for reduction to binary classification problems.

The comparison with SHAP [21] is also desirable. However, it is not possible in a direct way since SHAP relies on probabilistic interpretation of Shapley values in terms of conditional probability to belong to a certain class given an input example $\mathbf{x}$, e.g. $P(Class = +1|\mathbf{x})$, and designed for classifiers with such a probabilistic output.

Acknowledgements. The study was implemented in the framework of the Basic Research Program at the National Research University Higher School of Economics, and funded by the Russian Academic Excellence Project '5-100'. The first author was also supported by Russian Science Foundation under grant 17-11-01276 at St. Petersburg Department of Steklov Mathematical Institute of Russian Academy of Sciences, Russia. The first author would like to thank Prof. Fuad Aleskerov for the inspirational lectures on Collective Choice and Alexey Dral' from BigData Team for pointing to Shapley values as an explainable Machine Learning tool.

References

1. Blinova, V.G., Dobrynin, D.A., Finn, V.K., Kuznetsov, S.O., Pankratova, E.S.: Toxicology analysis by means of the JSM-method. Bioinformatics **19**(10), 1201–1207 (2003)

2. Chen, T., Guestrin, C.: XGBoost: a scalable tree boosting system. In: Proceedings of the 22nd ACM SIGKDD International Conference on Knowledge Discovery and Data Mining, 2016, pp. 785–794 (2016)

3. Dubois, V., Quafafou, M.: Concept learning with approximation: rough version spaces. In: Alpigini, J.J., Peters, J.F., Skowron, A., Zhong, N. (eds.) RSCTC 2002. LNCS (LNAI), vol. 2475, pp. 239–246. Springer, Heidelberg (2002). https://doi.org/10.1007/3-540-45813-1_31

4. Faigle, U., Grabisch, M., Jiménez-Losada, A., Ordóñez, M.: Games on concept lattices: Shapley value and core. Discrete Appl. Math. **198**, 29–47 (2016)

5. Fayyad, U.M., Piatetsky-Shapiro, G., Smyth, P.: From data mining to knowledge discovery in databases. AI Mag. **17**(3), 37–54 (1996)

6. Finn, V.: On machine-oriented formalization of plausible reasoning in F. Bacon-J.S.Mill Style. Semiotika i Informatika **20**, 35–101 (1983). (in Russian)

7. Fürnkranz, J., Gamberger, D., Lavrac, N.: Foundations of Rule Learning. Cognitive Technologies. Springer, Heidelberg (2012). https://doi.org/10.1007/978-3-540-75197-7

8. Harras, G.: Concepts in linguistics – concepts in natural language. In: Ganter, B., Mineau, G.W. (eds.) ICCS-ConceptStruct 2000. LNCS (LNAI), vol. 1867, pp. 13–26. Springer, Heidelberg (2000). https://doi.org/10.1007/10722280_2

9. Ganter, B., Kuznetsov, S.O.: Pattern structures and their projections. In: Delugach, H.S., Stumme, G. (eds.) ICCS-ConceptStruct 2001. LNCS (LNAI), vol. 2120, pp. 129–142. Springer, Heidelberg (2001). https://doi.org/10.1007/3-540-44583-8_10

10. Ganter, B., Kuznetsov, S.O.: Hypotheses and version spaces. In: Ganter, B., de Moor, A., Lex, W. (eds.) ICCS-ConceptStruct 2003. LNCS (LNAI), vol. 2746, pp. 83–95. Springer, Heidelberg (2003). https://doi.org/10.1007/978-3-540-45091-7_6

11. Ganter, B., Kuznetsov, S.O.: Scale coarsening as feature selection. In: Medina, R., Obiedkov, S. (eds.) ICFCA 2008. LNCS (LNAI), vol. 4933, pp. 217–228. Springer, Heidelberg (2008). https://doi.org/10.1007/978-3-540-78137-0_16

12. Ganter, B., Obiedkov, S.A.: Conceptual Exploration. Springer, Heidelberg (2016). https://doi.org/10.1007/978-3-662-49291-8

13. Ganter, B., Wille, R.: Formal Concept Analysis - Mathematical Foundations. Springer, Heidelberg (1999). https://doi.org/10.1007/978-3-642-59830-2

14. Ignatov, D.I., Zhuk, R., Konstantinova, N.: Learning hypotheses from triadic labeled data. In: 2014 IEEE/WIC/ACM International Joint Conference on Web Intelligence (WI) and Intelligent Agent Technologies (IAT), 2014, vol. I, pp. 474–480 (2014)

15. Kuznetsov, S.O.: Galois connections in data analysis: contributions from the Soviet era and modern Russian research. In: Ganter, B., Stumme, G., Wille, R. (eds.) Formal Concept Analysis. LNCS (LNAI), vol. 3626, pp. 196–225. Springer, Heidelberg (2005). https://doi.org/10.1007/11528784_11

16. Kuznetsov, S.O.: On stability of a formal concept. Ann. Math. Artif. Intell. **49**(1–4), 101–115 (2007)

17. Kuznetsov, S.O., Samokhin, M.V.: Learning closed sets of labeled graphs for chemical applications. In: Kramer, S., Pfahringer, B. (eds.) ILP 2005. LNCS (LNAI), vol. 3625, pp. 190–208. Springer, Heidelberg (2005). https://doi.org/10.1007/11536314_12

18. Kuznetsov, S.: JSM-method as a machine learning method. Itogi Nauki i Tekhniki, ser. Informatika **15**, 17–53 (1991). (in Russian)

19. Kuznetsov, S.: Mathematical aspects of concept analysis. J. Math. Sci. **80**(2), 1654–1698 (1996)

20. Lipton, Z.C.: The mythos of model interpretability. Commun. ACM **61**(10), 36–43 (2018)

21. Lundberg, S.M., Lee, S.I.: A unified approach to interpreting model predictions. In: I.G., et al. (ed.) Advances in Neural Information Processing Systems, vol. 30, pp. 4765–4774. Curran Associates, Inc. (2017)

22. Maafa, K., Nourine, L., Radjef, M.S.: Algorithms for computing the Shapley value of cooperative games on lattices. Discrete Appl. Math. **249**, 91–105 (2018)

23. Mitchell, T.M.: Version spaces: a candidate elimination approach to rule learning. In: Reddy, R. (ed.) Proceedings of the 5th International Joint Conference on Artificial Intelligence, 1977, pp. 305–310. William Kaufmann (1977)

24. Molnar, C.: Interpretable Machine Learning (2019). https://christophm.github.io/interpretable-ml-book/

25. Shapley, L.S.: A value for n-person games. In: Contributions to the Theory of Games, vol. 2, no. 28, pp. 307–317 (1953)

26. Štrumbelj, E., Kononenko, I.: Explaining prediction models and individual predictions with feature contributions. Knowl. Inf. Syst. **41**(3), 647–665 (2013). https://doi.org/10.1007/s10115-013-0679-x

Pruning in Map-Reduce Style CbO Algorithms

Jan Konecny[ID] and Petr Krajča[✉][ID]

Department of Computer Science, Palacký University Olomouc,
17. listopadu 12, 77146 Olomouc, Czech Republic
{jan.konecny,petr.krajca}@upol.cz

Abstract. Enumeration of formal concepts is crucial in formal concept analysis. Particularly efficient for this task are algorithms from the Close-by-One family (shortly, CbO-based algorithms). State-of-the-art CbO-based algorithms, e.g. FCbO, In-Close4, and In-Close5, employ several techniques, which we call pruning, to avoid some unnecessary computations. However, the number of the formal concepts can be exponential w.r.t. dimension of the input data. Therefore, the algorithms do not scale well and large datasets become intractable. To resolve this weakness, several parallel and distributed algorithms were proposed. We propose new CbO-based algorithms intended for Apache Spark or a similar programming model and show how the pruning can be incorporated into them. We experimentally evaluate the impact of the pruning and demonstrate the scalability of the new algorithm.

Keywords: Formal concept analysis · Closed sets · Map-reduce model · Close-by-One · Distributed computing

1 Introduction

Formal concept analysis (FCA) [10] is a well-established method of data analysis, having numerous applications, including, for instance, mining of non-redundant association rules [19], factorization of Boolean matrices [7], text mining [16], or recommendation systems [1]. The central notion of FCA is a formal concept and many applications of FCA depend on enumeration of formal concepts.

Kuznetsov [14] proposed a tree-recursive algorithm called Close-by-One (CbO) which enumerates formal concepts in lexicographical order. The tree-recursive nature of CbO allows for more efficient implementation and further enhancements. These enhancements include parallel execution [11,12], partial closure computation [2–6], pruning [4–6,15], or execution using the map-reduce framework [13]. The CbO-based algorithms are among the fastest algorithms for enumerating formal concepts.

Supported by the grant JG 2019 of Palacký University Olomouc, No. JG_2019_008.

M. Alam et al. (Eds.): ICCS 2020, LNAI 12277, pp. 103–116, 2020.
https://doi.org/10.1007/978-3-030-57855-8_8

One of the most recognized problems of FCA is the large amount of formal concepts present in the data. Typically, with growing sizes of data, the number of formal concepts grows substantially: even adding one column can double the number of formal concepts. Due to this exponential nature, large datasets become intractable.

To resolve this weakness, several parallel [11,12] and distributed [8,13,17] algorithms have been proposed. However, parallel or distributed programming may be challenging even for experienced developers. To simplify the development of distributed programs, Google proposed a restricted programming model called map-reduce [9]. This model allows the user to describe algorithms solely by simple transformation functions and leave tasks related to distributed computing to the underlying framework. This approach has been the subject of enhancements and currently is superseded by a framework called Apache Spark – a state-of-the-art approach to large datasets processing. This framework transforms data similarly, but provides a less restricted interface for data processing than map-reduce and, most importantly, is by more than an order of magnitude faster [18].

The main contribution of the paper are new CbO-based algorithms for enumerating formal concepts intended for Apache Spark or a similar programming model. Furthermore, we show how the pruning utilized in [5] can be incorporated into them. We experimentally evaluate the impact of the pruning and demonstrate the scalability of the new algorithm.

This paper is organized as follows. In Sect. 2, we introduce basic notions of FCA along with the programming model we use. In Sect. 3, we describe the basic CbO algorithm, its enhanced variants, and reformulation of these algorithms for an Apache Spark programming model. The performance of these algorithms is evaluated in Sect. 4. Section 5 sumarizes and concludes the paper.

2   Preliminaries

We introduce basic notions of FCA and the programming model we use to describe proposed algorithms.

2.1   Formal Concept Analysis

The input for FCA is a *formal context*—a triplet $\langle X, Y, I \rangle$ where X is a finite non-empty set of objects, Y is a finite non-empty set of attributes, and $I \subseteq X \times Y$ is a relation of incidence between objects and attributes; incidence $\langle x, y \rangle \in I$ means that the object $x \in X$ has the attribute $y \in Y$.

Every formal context $\langle X, Y, I \rangle$ induces two so called *concept-forming operators* $\uparrow: 2^X \rightarrow 2^Y$ and $\downarrow: 2^Y \rightarrow 2^X$ defined, for each $A \subseteq X$ and $B \subseteq Y$, by

$$A^\uparrow = \{y \in Y \,|\, \text{for each } x \in A \colon \langle x, y \rangle \in I\}, \tag{1}$$

$$B^\downarrow = \{x \in X \,|\, \text{for each } y \in B \colon \langle x, y \rangle \in I\}. \tag{2}$$

In words, $A^\uparrow$ is the set of all attributes shared by all objects from A and $B^\downarrow$ is the set of all objects sharing all attributes from B. For singletons $\{i\}$, we use the simplified notation $i^\uparrow$ and $i^\downarrow$.

A *formal concept* in $\langle X, Y, I \rangle$ is a pair $\langle A, B \rangle$ such that $A^\uparrow = B$ and $B^\downarrow = A$, where $^\uparrow$ and $^\downarrow$ are concept-forming operators induced by $\langle X, Y, I \rangle$. The sets A and B are called the *extent* and the *intent*, respectively.

Throughout the paper, we assume that the set of attributes is $Y = \{1, 2, \ldots, n\}$.

We have introduced only the notions from FCA that are necessary for the rest of the paper. The interested reader can find more detailed description of FCA in [10].

2.2   Map-Reduce Style Data Processing

In seminal work [9], Google revealed the architecture of its internal system which allows them to process large datasets with commodity hardware. In short, the proposed system and its programming model represents all data as key-value pairs which are transformed with two operations, *map* and *reduce*. This is why the data processing system based on this model is called the map-reduce framework. The main advantage of this approach is that the programmer has to provide transformation functions and the framework takes care of all necessary tasks related to distributed computation, for instance, workload distribution, failure detection and recovery, etc.

Several independent implementations of the map-reduce framework [9] are available. The most prominent is Apache Hadoop[1]. Beyond this, the map-reduce data processing model is used, for instance, in Infinispan, Twister, or Apache CouchDB.

Remark 1. It has been shown that many algorithms can be represented only with these two operations. Algorithms for enumeration of formal concepts are not an exception. Variants of CbO [13], Ganter's NextClosure [17], and UpperNeighbor [8] were proposed for map-reduce framework. In the cases of [17] and [8], to handle iterative algorithms, specialized map-reduce frameworks are used.

Nowadays, the original map-reduce approach was superseded by more general techniques, namely by Resilient Distributed Datasets (RDDs) [18] as implemented in Apache Spark[2]. RDDs allow us to work with general tuples and provide a more convenient interface for data processing. This interface is not limited to the two elementary operations, *map* and *reduce*. More convenient operations, like *map*, *flatMap*, *filter*, *groupBy*, or *join*, are available. Even though the underlying technology is different, the approach to data processing is similar to map-reduce. Likewise, the program is also represented as a sequence of transformations and the framework takes care of workload distribution, etc.

---

[1] https://hadoop.apache.org/.
[2] https://spark.apache.org/.

Remark 2. Throughout the paper, to describe the proposed algorithms, we use operations which are close to those provided by Apache Spark. However, all of these operations can be transformed to *map* and *reduce* operations as used in the map-reduce framework [9]. Therefore, we term the proposed algorithms *map-reduce style*.

We shall introduce the most important Apache Spark operations we use in this paper:

(i) Operation **map**(X, f) takes a collection of tuples X and function f, and applies f on each tuple in X.

(ii) Operation **filter**(X, p) takes a collection of tuples X and predicate p, and keeps only tuples satisfying the predicate p.

(iii) Operation **flatMap**(X, f) takes a collection of tuples X and function f that for every tuple returns a collection of tuples, and applies the function f on every tuple. It then merges all the collections into a single collection.

Other operations we introduce where necessary. Furthermore, we shall use $x \Rightarrow y$ to denote transformation functions. Namely:

(i) $\langle x_1, \ldots, x_n \rangle \Rightarrow \langle y_1, \ldots, y_m \rangle$ denotes a function transforming a tuple $\langle x_1, \ldots, x_n \rangle$ into a tuple $\langle y_1, \ldots, y_m \rangle$,

(ii) $\langle x_1, \ldots, x_n \rangle \Rightarrow \{\langle y_1, \ldots, y_m \rangle \mid cond\}$ is a function transforming a tuple $\langle x_1, \ldots, x_n \rangle$ into a set of tuples $\langle y_1, \ldots, y_m \rangle$ satisfying condition *cond*,

(iii) $\langle x_1, \ldots, x_n \rangle \Rightarrow condition$ represents a predicate.

For example, for a set $X = \{\langle a, 1 \rangle, \langle b, -2 \rangle, \langle c, 3 \rangle\} \subseteq \{a, b, c\} \times \mathbb{Z}$:

$$
\begin{aligned}
\mathbf{map}(X, \langle x, y \rangle \Rightarrow \langle x, y, y^2 \rangle) &= \{\langle a, 1, 1 \rangle, \langle b, -2, 4 \rangle, \langle c, 3, 9 \rangle\}, \\
\mathbf{filter}(X, \langle x, y \rangle \Rightarrow y > 0) &= \{\langle a, 1 \rangle, \langle c, 3 \rangle\}, \\
\mathbf{flatMap}(X, \langle x, y \rangle \Rightarrow \{\langle x, z \rangle \mid z > 0 \text{ and } z \leq y\}) &= \{\langle a, 1 \rangle, \langle c, 1 \rangle, \langle c, 2 \rangle, \langle c, 3 \rangle\}.
\end{aligned}
$$

3   Close-by-One Algorithm

We describe the basic CbO algorithm and its two reformulations for the map-reduce style programming model. Then we discuss pruning techniques improving efficiency of CbO. We show how one of these techniques can be incorporated into the map-reduce style CbO algorithms. The two new map-reduce style CbO algorithms with pruning are the main contribution of the paper.

3.1   Basic Close-by-One

The CbO algorithm belongs to a family of algorithms that enumerate formal concepts in lexicographical (or similar) order and use this order to ensure that every formal concept is listed exactly once. Note that intent B is lexicographically smaller than D, if $B \subset D$, or $B \not\subset D$ and $\min((B \cup D) \setminus (B \cap D)) \in B$.

For instance, a set $\{1\}$ is lexicographically smaller than $\{1, 2\}$ and the set $\{1, 2\}$ is lexicographically smaller than $\{1, 3\}$.

The CbO algorithm can be described as a tree recursive procedure, GENERATEFROM, which has three parameters (see Algorithm 1)—extent A, intent B, and attribute y, indicating the last attribute included into the intent. The algorithm starts (line 9) with the topmost formal concept, i.e. $\langle X, X^{\uparrow} \rangle$ and 0 (indicating no attribute has been included yet).

The GENERATEFROM procedure prints the given concept $\langle A, B \rangle$ out (line 2) and extends the intent B with all attributes i such that $i \notin B$ and $i > y$ (line 3 and 4). Subsequently, a new extent $(B \cup \{i\})^{\downarrow}$ is obtained. Note that $(B \cup \{i\})^{\downarrow} = A \cap i^{\downarrow}$. This fact allows us to eliminate the time consuming operation $^{\downarrow}$ and replace it with an intersection which is significantly faster (line 5). Afterwards, a new intent $(B \cup \{i\})^{\downarrow\uparrow}$ is computed (line 6) and its canonicity is checked (line 7). A formal concept is canonical if its intent D is not lexicographically smaller than B. That is, if $D \cap \{1, \ldots, i-1\} = B \cap \{1, \ldots, i-1\}$. For convenience, we use the shorter notation $D_i = D \cap \{1, \ldots, i-1\}$. If the concept is canonical, it is recursively passed to GENERATEFROM, along with the attribute that was inserted into the intent (line 8).

Algorithm 1: Close-by-One

---

1 **proc** GENERATEFROM(A, B, y):
　　input : A is extent, B is intent, y is the last added attribute

2　　**print**($\langle A, B \rangle$)
3　　**for** $i \leftarrow y + 1$ **to** n **do**
4　　　**if** $i \notin B$ **then**
5　　　　$C \leftarrow A \cap i^{\downarrow}$
6　　　　$D \leftarrow C^{\uparrow}$
7　　　　**if** $D_i = B_i$ **then**
8　　　　　GENERATEFROM(C, D, i)

9 GENERATEFROM(X, $X^{\uparrow}$, 0)

3.2 Map-Reduce Style Close-by-One

We use a depth first search (DFS) strategy to describe CbO since this strategy is natural for the algorithm. However, other search strategies are possible. One may use also breadth-first search (BFS) [13] and even a combination of BFS and DFS [3–6,15]. No matter which strategy is used, CbO always enumerates the same set of formal concepts, but in different order. This feature is essential since it allows us to express CbO by means of distributed and parallel frameworks. Note that algorithms for map-reduce frameworks often demand BFS.

The map-reduce style CbO algorithm is an iterative algorithm, see Algorithm 2 for pseudo-codes. Each of its iterations represents the processing of a single layer of the CbO's search tree. Note that each step has to be expressed in transformations provided by the given framework.

Algorithm 2: Close-by-One

1 **proc** CBOPASS($\mathcal{L}_i$):

    input : $\mathcal{L}_i$ is a collection of tuples $\langle A, B, y \rangle$ where A is extent, B is intent, y is the last added attribute

2    $\mathcal{L}_i^{\text{att}} \leftarrow \textbf{flatMap}(\mathcal{L}_i, \langle A, B, y \rangle \Rightarrow \{\langle A, B, y, i \rangle \mid i \in Y \text{ and } i > y \text{ and } i \notin B\})$

3    $\mathcal{L}_i^{\text{ext}} \leftarrow \textbf{map}(\mathcal{L}_i^{\text{att}}, \langle A, B, y, i \rangle \Rightarrow \langle B, y, i, A \cap i^{\downarrow} \rangle)$

4    $\mathcal{L}_i^{\text{int}} \leftarrow \textbf{map}(\mathcal{L}_i^{\text{ext}}, \langle B, y, i, C \rangle \Rightarrow \langle B, y, i, C, C^{\uparrow} \rangle)$

5    $\mathcal{L}_i^{\text{can}} \leftarrow \textbf{filter}(\mathcal{L}_i^{\text{int}}, \langle B, y, i, C, D \rangle \Rightarrow (B_i = D_i))$

6    $\mathcal{L}_{i+1} \leftarrow \textbf{map}(\mathcal{L}_i^{\text{can}}, \langle B, y, i, C, D \rangle \Rightarrow \langle C, D, i \rangle)$

7   **return** $\mathcal{L}_{i+1}$

8 $\mathcal{L}_0 \leftarrow \{\langle X, X^{\uparrow}, 0 \rangle\}$

9 $i \leftarrow 0$

10 **while** $|L_i| > 0$ **do**

11    $\mathcal{L}_{i+1} \leftarrow$ CBOPASS($\mathcal{L}_i$)

12    $i \leftarrow i + 1$

13 **return** $\bigcup_{j=0}^{i} \mathcal{L}_j$

The algorithm starts (line 8) with the first layer $\mathcal{L}_0$ containing a single tuple $\langle X, X^{\uparrow}, 0 \rangle$ describing the topmost formal concept, along with attribute 0, indicating that no attribute has been included yet to build this formal concept. This layer is passed to the CBOPASS procedure, which uses a sequence of transformations to obtain a new layer of formal concepts.

The first transformation (line 2) for each formal concept generates a set of tuples consisting of a given concept along with an attribute that will extend the given concept in the next step. Subsequently, these tuples are used to compute the extents of the new concepts (line 3). Notice that the original extent is no longer necessary, thus is omitted from the tuple. Afterwards, the intents are obtained (line 4). At this point, the new formal concepts are fully available and all that remains is to filter those passing the canonicity test (line 5) and keep only the new extent and the intent along with the attribute that was added (line 6).

The outcome of the CBOPASS is then used as an input for the next iteration of the algorithm. The algorithm stops when no new concept is generated (lines 10 to 12).

All transformations used in Algorithm 2 are obviously parallelizable. However, the first transformation (line 2) is not associated with a computationally heavy task, hence the workload distribution may cause an unnecessary overhead.

Thus, it may be reasonable to combine lines 2 and 3 into a single transformation as follows:

$$\mathcal{L}_i^{\text{ext}} \leftarrow \textbf{flatMap}(\mathcal{L}_i, \langle A, B, y \rangle \Rightarrow \{\langle B, y, A \cap i^{\downarrow} \rangle \mid i \in Y \text{ and } i > y \text{ and } i \notin B\}).$$

This gives two variants of map-reduce style CbO: (i) the first one as described in Algorithm 2 and (ii) the latter, where the first two transformations are combined together. To distinguish these variants, we denote them (i) fine-grained and (ii) coarse-grained, since the first variant provides more fine-grained parallelism and the second one more coarse-grained parallelism.

3.3   Close-by-One with Pruning

The most fundamental challenge which all algorithms for enumerating formal concepts are facing is the fact that some concepts are computed multiple times. Due to the canonicity test, each concept is returned only once. However, the canonicity test does not prevent redundant computations. Therefore, several strategies to reduce redundant computations were proposed.

In FCbO [15], a history of failed canonicity tests is kept during the tree descent and is used to skip particular attributes for which it is clear that the canonicity test fails. To maintain this history, FCbO uses an indexed set of sets of attributes. This means, each invocation of FCbO's GENERATEFROM requires passing a data structure of size $O(|Y|^2)$. This space requirement makes FCbO unsuitable for map-reduce style frameworks.

In-Close4 [5] keeps a set of attributes during the descent for which intersection $A \cap i^{\downarrow}$ is empty. This allows us to skip some unnecessary steps. Furthermore, In-Close5 [6] extends In-Close4 with a new method for passing information about failed canonicity tests. Unlike FCbO, In-Close4 and In-Close5 require the passing of only a single set of attributes for which the canonicity test failed. This makes them more suitable for distributed programming.

3.4   Using Empty Intersections for Pruning

The In-Close4 algorithm is based on two observations. (i) If the intersection $C = A \cap i^{\downarrow}$ (Algorithm 1, line 5) is empty, then the corresponding intent $C^{\uparrow}$ is Y. Note that the concept with the intent Y is the lexicographically largest concept which always exists and is always listed as the last one. Thus, the canonicity test fails for all such concepts with the exception of the last one. (ii) Further, from the properties of concept-forming operators, it follows that for every two intents $B, D \subseteq Y$ and attribute $i \in Y$ such that $B \subset D$, $i \notin B$, and $i \notin D$ holds that $(B \cup \{i\})^{\downarrow} \supseteq (D \cup \{i\})^{\downarrow}$. Particularly, if $(B \cup \{i\})^{\downarrow} = \emptyset$, then $(D \cup \{i\})^{\downarrow} = \emptyset$.

In fact, observations (i) and (ii) provide information on certain canonicity test failures and their propagation. Not considering the last concept $\langle Y^{\downarrow}, Y \rangle$, we may use a simplified assumption that an empty extent implies canonicity failure. Furthermore, if adding an attribute i to the intent B leads to an empty extent, then adding i into any of its supersets D leads to an empty extent as well. Subsequently, this leads to a canonicity test failure, unless it is the last concept. Note that concept $\langle Y^{\downarrow}, Y \rangle$ has to be treated separately.

Algorithm 3: Close-by-One with In-Close4 pruning

```
1  proc GENERATEFROM(A, B, y, N):
       input : A is extent, B is intent, y is the last added attribute,
                N is a set of attributes to skip

2      print(⟨A, B⟩)
3      M ← N
4      for i ← y + 1 to n do
5          if i ∉ B and i ∉ N then
6              C ← A ∩ i↓
7              if C = ∅ then
8                  M ← M ∪ {i}
9              else
10                 D ← C↑
11                 if Dᵢ = Bᵢ then
12                     PUTINQUEUE(⟨C, D, i⟩)

13     while GETFROMQUEUE(⟨C, D, i⟩) do
14         GENERATEFROM(C, D, i, M)

15 GENERATEFROM(X, X↑, 0, ∅)
```

Algorithm 3 shows how these observations can be incorporated into CbO. First, there is an additional argument N, a set of attributes that can be skipped (line 5) since their inclusion into an intent of a newly formed concept would lead to an empty extent. Additionally, a set M which is a copy of N is created (line 3). If the newly formed extent (line 6) is empty, the attribute i is inserted into the set M and algorithm proceeds with the next attribute.

To collect information on canonicity test failures, Algorithm 3 uses a combined DFS and BFS. The combination of DFS and BFS means that the recursive call is not performed immediately, but rather is postponed until all attributes are processed (line 12). All recursive calls are then processed in a single loop (lines 13 and 14).

Remark 3. Algorithm 3 is similar to In-Close4 [5], it uses empty intersections for pruning and a combined depth-first and breadth-first search, however, it does not compute formal concepts incrementally.

In the same way as CbO is transformed into an iterative BFS map-reduce style algorithm, one may transform Algorithm 3 as well. However, handling information on empty intersections requires additional steps. All steps of the algorithm are described in Algorithm 4.

We highlight only the main differences w.r.t. Algorithm 2. Namely, tuples processed in Algorithm 4 contain the additional set N with attributes to skip.

Algorithm 4: Close-by-One with In-Close4 pruning (fine-grained)

---

1 **proc** CBO4PASSFINE($\mathcal{L}_i$):

    input : $\mathcal{L}_i$ is a collection of tuples $\langle A, B, y, N \rangle$ where A is extent, B is intent, y is the last added attribute, N is a set of attributes to skip

2   $\mathcal{L}_i^{\text{att}} \leftarrow \textbf{flatMap}(\mathcal{L}_i, \langle A, B, y, N \rangle \Rightarrow \{\langle A, B, y, i, N \rangle \mid i \in Y \text{ and } i > y \text{ and } i \notin B \text{ and } i \notin N\})$

3   $\mathcal{L}_i^{\text{ex0}} \leftarrow \textbf{map}(\mathcal{L}_i^{\text{att}}, \langle A, B, y, i, N \rangle \Rightarrow \langle B, y, i, N, A \cap i^{\downarrow} \rangle)$

4   $\mathcal{L}_i^{\text{ext}} \leftarrow \textbf{filter}(\mathcal{L}_i^{\text{ex0}}, \langle A, B, y, i, N, C \rangle \Rightarrow |C| > 0)$

5   $\mathcal{L}_i^{\text{int}} \leftarrow \textbf{map}(\mathcal{L}_i^{\text{ext}}, \langle B, y, i, N, C \rangle \Rightarrow \langle B, y, i, N, C, C^{\uparrow} \rangle)$

6   $\mathcal{L}_i^{\text{can}} \leftarrow \textbf{filter}(\mathcal{L}_i^{\text{int}}, \langle B, y, i, N, C, D \rangle \Rightarrow (B_i = D_i))$

7   $\mathcal{L}_i^{\text{em0}} \leftarrow \textbf{filter}(\mathcal{L}_i^{\text{ex0}}, \langle A, B, y, i, N, C \rangle \Rightarrow |C| = 0)$

8   $\mathcal{L}_i^{\text{emp}} \leftarrow \textbf{map}(\mathcal{L}_i^{\text{em0}}, \langle A, B, y, i, N, C \rangle \Rightarrow \langle \langle B, y \rangle, i \rangle)$

9   $\mathcal{L}_i^{\text{fails}} \leftarrow \textbf{groupByKey}(\mathcal{L}_i^{\text{emp}})$

10   $\mathcal{L}_i^{\text{join}} \leftarrow \textbf{leftOutterJoin}(\mathcal{L}_i^{\text{can}}, \mathcal{L}_i^{\text{fails}})$ **on** B, y

11   $\mathcal{L}_{i+1} \leftarrow \textbf{map}(\mathcal{L}_i^{\text{join}}, \langle B, y, i, N, C, D, M \rangle \Rightarrow \langle C, D, i, M \cup N \rangle)$

12   **return** $\mathcal{L}_{i+1}$

13 $\mathcal{L}_0 \leftarrow \{\langle X, X^{\uparrow}, 0, \emptyset \rangle\}$

14 $i \leftarrow 0$

15 **while** $|L_i| > 0$ **do**

16   $\mathcal{L}_{i+1} \leftarrow$ CBO4PASSFINE($\mathcal{L}_i$)

17   $i \leftarrow i + 1$

18 **return** $\bigcup_{j=0}^{i} \mathcal{L}_j$

The condition in line 2 contains additional check whether $i \notin N$. Extents are computed (line 3) and non-empty extents (line 4) are used to obtain intents (line 5) which are tested for canonicity (line 6).

Beside this, information on empty extents is collected (lines 7 to 9). First, empty extents are selected (line 7) and transformed to key-value pairs $\langle \langle B, y \rangle, i \rangle$ (line 8). Then, operation **groupByKey** is used to group these pairs by their keys (line 9) to form new pairs $\langle \langle B, y \rangle, M \rangle$, where M denotes a set of attributes which led to an empty extent.

It only remains to join together the valid concepts and information on attributes implying canonicity test failures (line 10). This subtask is achieved with the **leftOutterJoin** operation. This operation for each tuple $\langle B, Y, i, N, C, D \rangle$ in a set $\mathcal{L}_i^{\text{can}}$ finds a matching pair $\langle \langle B, y \rangle, M \rangle$ in $\mathcal{L}_i^{\text{fails}}$ (i.e. values B and y of both tuples are equal) and forms a new tuple $\langle B, Y, i, N, C, D, M \rangle$. In the case that there is no matching pair in $\mathcal{L}_i^{\text{fails}}$, an empty set is used instead of M. Afterwards, every tuple is transformed into a form suitable for the next iteration (line 11). Namely, values related to the current iteration are stripped out and sets M and N are merged into a single set.

Algorithm 5: Computing extents

---

1 **proc** COARSEEXTENTS(A, B, y, N):

    input : A is extent, B is intent, y is last added attribute,
                 N is set of attributes to skip

2     $M \leftarrow N$

3     $E \leftarrow \emptyset$

4   **for** $i \leftarrow y + 1$ **to** n **do**

5   **if** $i \notin B$ **and** $i \notin N$ **then**

6           $C \leftarrow A \cap i^{\downarrow}$

7   **if** $C = \emptyset$ **then**

8              $M \leftarrow M \cup \{i\}$

9   **else**

10              $E \leftarrow E \cup \{C\}$

11     $E' \leftarrow \emptyset$

12   **foreach** $C \in E$ **do**

13        $E' \leftarrow E' \cup \{\langle B, y, i, M, C \rangle\}$

14   **return** E'

In Sect. 3.2, two variants of map-reduce style CbO are proposed—fine-grained and coarse-grained. Algorithm 4 corresponds to the fine-grained variant. Analogously, the coarse-grained variant can also be considered. To simplify the description of the coarse-grained variant, we introduce the auxiliary procedure COARSE-EXTENTS (see Algorithm 5), which for a given formal concept $\langle A, B \rangle$, attribute y, and a set N returns set of tuples $\langle B, y, i, M, A \cap i^{\downarrow} \rangle$ such that i is newly added attribute, $A \cap i^{\downarrow}$ is a non-empty extent and M is a set of attributes which implies empty intersections for the given intent B.

Algorithm 6: Close-by-One pass with In-Close4 pruning (coarse-grained)

---

1 **proc** CBO4PASSCOARSE($\mathcal{L}_i$):

    input : $\mathcal{L}_i$ is a collection of tuples $\langle A, B, y, N \rangle$ where A is extent, B is
              intent, y is the last added attribute, N is a set of attributes to
              skip

2     $\mathcal{L}_i^{\text{ext}} \leftarrow \textbf{flatMap}(\mathcal{L}_i, \langle A, B, y, N \rangle \Rightarrow \text{COARSEEXTENTS}(A, B, y, N))$

3     $\mathcal{L}_i^{\text{int}} \leftarrow \textbf{map}(\mathcal{L}_i^{\text{ext}}, \langle B, y, i, M, C \rangle \Rightarrow \langle B, y, i, M, C, C^{\uparrow} \rangle)$

4     $\mathcal{L}_i^{\text{can}} \leftarrow \textbf{filter}(\mathcal{L}_i^{\text{int}}, \langle B, y, i, M, C, D \rangle \Rightarrow (B_i = D_i))$

5     $\mathcal{L}_{i+1} \leftarrow \textbf{map}(\mathcal{L}_i^{\text{can}}, \langle B, y, i, M, C, D \rangle \Rightarrow \langle C, D, i, M \rangle)$

6   **return** $\mathcal{L}_{i+1}$

The coarse-grained variant of the algorithm is presented in Algorithm 6. One can see that it requires fewer steps than Algorithm 4, since all steps related to empty intersections are processed in the CoarseExtents procedure. Notice that the coarse-grained variant is similar to Algorithm 2 – both consist of four steps: (i) computation of extents, (ii) computations of intents, (iii) application of canonicity test, and (iv) transformation for the next pass. Steps collecting information on empty intersections are omitted in Algorithm 6.

4 Evaluation

We implemented all described algorithms as Apache Spark jobs to evaluate their performance and scalability. A cluster of three virtual computers (nodes) equipped with 40 cores of Intel Xeon E5-2660 (at 2.2 GHz) and 374 GiB of RAM, each interconnected with 1 Gbps network was used. All nodes were running Debian 10.2, OpenJDK 1.8.0, and Apache Spark 2.4.4. All source codes were compiled with Scala 2.12. One node was selected as a master, and all nodes served as workers. To improve data locality, we limited each worker to 20 GiB RAM. To distribute the workload equally, after each iteration, we repartitioned the data into a number of partitions equal to twice the number of cores.

We focus on overall performance and scalability of proposed algorithms first. We have selected three datasets from the UCI Machine Learning Repository (mushrooms, anonymous web, T10I4D100K) and our own dataset (debian tags) and measured time taken to enumerate all formal concepts using 1, 20, 40, and 80 cores. The results are presented in Table 1. According to these results, map-reduce style CbO without pruning is significantly slower than the novel algorithms we propose. Furthermore, coarse-grained variants of both algorithms seem to be in many cases slightly faster, but it is not a general rule.

Properties of the datasets and results of measurements in Table 1 suggest that the map-reduce approach is more suited for large datasets. To confirm this, we prepared a second set of experiments. We created artificial datasets[3] that simulate transactional data and focused on how the number of object and attributes affects scalability. Scalability is a ratio $S_T(n) = \frac{T_1}{T_n}$ where T_1 and T_n are times necessary to complete the task with one and with n CPU cores, respectively. In other words, scalability provides information on how efficiently an algorithm can utilize multiple CPU cores.

Results of this experiment are presented in Figs. 1 and 2 which show scalability CbO with the In-Close4 pruning for datasets having 500 attributes, 2 % density, and varying numbers of objects (Fig. 1), and scalability for datasets consisting of 10,000 objects, 2 % density, and varying numbers of attributes (Fig. 2). These results confirm that scalability depends on the size of the data and that mainly large datasets can benefit from distributed data processing. Notice that fine-grained variants appear to scale better than coarse-grained variants. This is partially due to the fact that the fine-grained variants tend to be slower when running on a single CPU core. When multiple cores are used, the differences between fine-grained and coarse-grained variants become negligible.

---

[3] *IBM Quest Synthetic Data Generator* was used.

Table 1. Running times for selected datasets (cbo—algorithm without pruning; cbo4—algorithm with pruning from In-Close4)

Data	Cores	cbo/fine	cbo/coarse	cbo4/fine	cbo4/coarse
Debian-tags	1	475.2 s	431.4 s	34.0 s	**17.2 s**
Size: 8124 × 119	20	104.3 s	83.7 s	14.8 s	**11.7 s**
Density: 19 %	40	41.9 s	47.1 s	14.8 s	**11.0 s**
	80	40.5 s	53.1 s	17.7 s	**12.8 s**
An. web	1	711.6 s	603.6 s	101.5 s	**61.7 s**
Size: 32710 × 296	20	102.8 s	74.3 s	23.9 s	**21.3 s**
Density: 1 %	40	60.7 s	68.3 s	21.1 s	**19.4 s**
	80	70.0 s	56.5 s	24.7 s	**21.9 s**
Mushrooms	1	64.4 s	60.4 s	47.4 s	**33.6 s**
Size: 8124 × 119	20	22.2 s	22.7 s	**18.1 s**	18.5 s
Density: 19 %	40	18.3 s	17.2 s	**17.1 s**	19.2 s
	80	31.7 s	30.8 s	**21.6 s**	32.0 s
T10I4D100K	1	3+ h	3+ h	79.5 min	**40.7 min**
Size: 100000 × 1000	20	49.5 min	54.3 min	4.8 min	**3.2 min**
Density: 1 %	40	39.3 min	37.9 min	3.5 min	**2.4 min**
	80	35.9 min	34.1 min	3.2 min	**2.5 min**

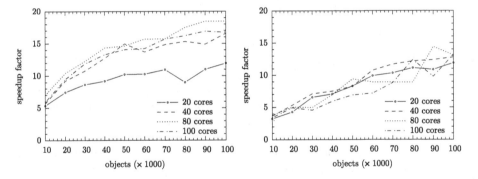

Fig. 1. Scalability of CbO with the In-Close4 pruning w.r.t. number of objects—fine-grained (left), coarse-grained (right)

Remark 4. Besides the CbO-based algorithms with In-Close4 pruning, we also implemented algorithms with:

– FCbO pruning [15]. The performance of the resulting algorithm was very unsatisfactory. As expected, the algorithm was slow and memory demanding due to the quadratic nature of information on failed canonicity tests.

– In-Close5 pruning [6]: The performance of the resulting algorithm did not show any significant improvements. We will present detailed results in the full version of this paper.

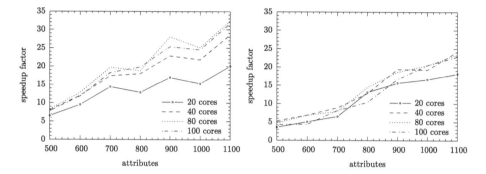

Fig. 2. Scalability of CbO with the In-Close4 pruning w.r.t. number of attributes—fine-grained (left), coarse-grained (right)

5 Conclusions

We designed and implemented a CbO-based algorithm with pruning intended for Apache Spark. While a few FCA algorithms were adapted to map-reduce framework (see Remark 1), to our best knowledge, this is the first map-reduce style algorithm for enumeration of formal concepts which utilizes pruning techniques. Our experimental evaluation indicates promising performance results.

References

1. Akhmatnurov, M., Ignatov, D.I.: Context-aware recommender system based on Boolean matrix factorisation. In: Yahia, S.B., Konecny, J. (eds.) Proceedings of the Twelfth International Conference on Concept Lattices and Their Applications, Clermont-Ferrand, France, 13–16 October 2015, CEUR Workshop Proceedings, vol. 1466, pp. 99–110 (2015). CEUR-WS.org
2. Andrews, S.: In-Close, a fast algorithm for computing formal concepts. In: 17th International Conference on Conceptual Structures, ICCS 2009. Springer (2009)
3. Andrews, S.: In-Close2, a high performance formal concept miner. In: Andrews, S., Polovina, S., Hill, R., Akhgar, B. (eds.) ICCS 2011. LNCS (LNAI), vol. 6828, pp. 50–62. Springer, Heidelberg (2011). https://doi.org/10.1007/978-3-642-22688-5_4
4. Andrews, S.: A 'best-of-breed' approach for designing a fast algorithm for computing fixpoints of Galois connections. Inf. Sci. **295**, 633–649 (2015)
5. Andrews, S.: Making use of empty intersections to improve the performance of CbO-type algorithms. In: Bertet, K., Borchmann, D., Cellier, P., Ferré, S. (eds.) ICFCA 2017. LNCS (LNAI), vol. 10308, pp. 56–71. Springer, Cham (2017). https://doi.org/10.1007/978-3-319-59271-8_4

6. Andrews, S.: A new method for inheriting canonicity test failures in Close-by-One type algorithms. In: Ignatov, D.I., Nourine, L. (eds.) Proceedings of the Fourteenth International Conference on Concept Lattices and Their Applications, CLA 2018, Olomouc, Czech Republic, 12–14 June 2018, CEUR Workshop Proceedings, vol. 2123, pp. 255–266 (2018). CEUR-WS.org
7. Belohlavek, R., Vychodil, V.: Discovery of optimal factors in binary data via a novel method of matrix decomposition. J. Comput. Syst. Sci. **76**(1), 3–20 (2010)
8. Chunduri, R.K., Cherukuri, A.K.: Haloop approach for concept generation in formal concept analysis. JIKM **17**(3), 1850029 (2018)
9. Dean, J., Ghemawat, S.: MapReduce: simplified data processing on large clusters. In: Brewer, E.A., Chen, P. (eds.) 6th Symposium on Operating System Design and Implementation (OSDI 2004), San Francisco, California, USA, 6–8 December 2004, pp. 137–150. USENIX Association (2004)
10. Ganter, B., Wille, R.: Formal Concept Analysis Mathematical Foundations. Springer, Heidelberg (1999). https://doi.org/10.1007/978-3-642-59830-2
11. Krajca, P., Outrata, J., Vychodil, V.: Advances in algorithms based on CbO. In: Proceedings of the 7th International Conference on Concept Lattices and Their Applications, Sevilla, Spain, 19–21 October 2010, pp. 325–337 (2010)
12. Krajca, P., Outrata, J., Vychodil, V.: Parallel algorithm for computing fixpoints of Galois connections. Ann. Math. Artif. Intell. **59**(2), 257–272 (2010)
13. Krajca, P., Vychodil, V.: Distributed algorithm for computing formal concepts using map-reduce framework. In: Adams, N.M., Robardet, C., Siebes, A., Boulicaut, J.-F. (eds.) IDA 2009. LNCS, vol. 5772, pp. 333–344. Springer, Heidelberg (2009). https://doi.org/10.1007/978-3-642-03915-7_29
14. Kuznetsov, S.O.: A fast algorithm for computing all intersections of objects from an arbitrary semilattice. Nauchno-Tekhnicheskaya Informatsiya Seriya 2-Informatsionnye Protsessy i Sistemy **27**(1), 17–20 (1993). https://www.researchgate.net/publication/273759395_SOKuznetsov_A_fast_algorithm_for_computing_all_intersections_of_objects_from_an_arbitrary_semilattice_Nauchno-Tekhnicheskaya_Informatsiya_Seriya_2_-_Informatsionnye_protsessy_i_sistemy_No_1_pp17-20_19
15. Outrata, J., Vychodil, V.: Fast algorithm for computing fixpoints of Galois connections induced by object-attribute relational data. Inf. Sci. **185**(1), 114–127 (2012)
16. Poelmans, J., Ignatov, D.I., Viaene, S., Dedene, G., Kuznetsov, S.O.: Text mining scientific papers: a survey on FCA-based information retrieval research. In: Perner, P. (ed.) ICDM 2012. LNCS (LNAI), vol. 7377, pp. 273–287. Springer, Heidelberg (2012). https://doi.org/10.1007/978-3-642-31488-9_22
17. Xu, B., de Fréin, R., Robson, E., Ó Foghlú, M.: Distributed formal concept analysis algorithms based on an iterative MapReduce framework. In: Domenach, F., Ignatov, D.I., Poelmans, J. (eds.) ICFCA 2012. LNCS (LNAI), vol. 7278, pp. 292–308. Springer, Heidelberg (2012). https://doi.org/10.1007/978-3-642-29892-9_26
18. Zaharia, M., Das, T., Li, H., Shenker, S., Stoica, I.: Discretized streams: an efficient and fault-tolerant model for stream processing on large clusters. In: Fonseca, R., Maltz, D.A. (eds.) 4th USENIX Workshop on Hot Topics in Cloud Computing, HotCloud 2012, Boston, MA, USA, 12–13 June 2012. USENIX Association (2012)
19. Zaki, M.J.: Mining non-redundant association rules. Data Min. Knowl. Discov. **9**(3), 223–248 (2004)

Pattern Discovery in Triadic Contexts

Rokia Missaoui[1(✉)], Pedro H. B. Ruas[2], Léonard Kwuida[3],
and Mark A. J. Song[2]

[1] Université du Québec en Outaouais, Gatineau, Canada
`rokia.missaoui@uqo.ca`
[2] Pontifical Catholic University of Minas Gerais, Belo Horizonte, Brazil
`pedrohbruas@gmail.com, song@pucminas.br`
[3] Bern University of Applied Sciences, Bern, Switzerland
`leonard.kwuida@bfh.ch`

Abstract. Many real-life applications are best represented as ternary and more generally n-ary relations. In this paper, we use Triadic Concept Analysis as a framework to mainly discover implications. Indeed, our contributions are as follows. First, we adapt the *iPred* algorithm for precedence link computation in concept lattices to the triadic framework. Then, new algorithms are proposed to compute triadic generators by extending the notion of faces and blockers to further calculate implications.

Keywords: Triadic concepts · Triadic generators · Implication rules

1 Introduction

Multidimensional data are ubiquitous in many real-life applications and Web resources. This is the case of multidimensional social networks, social resource sharing systems, and security policies. For instance, in the latter application, a user is authorized to use resources with given privileges under constrained conditions. A folksonomy is a resource sharing system where users assign tags to resources. Finding homogeneous groups of users and associations among their features can be useful for decision making and recommendation purposes.

The contributions of this paper are as follows: (i) we adapt the *iPred* algorithm for precedence link computation in concept lattices [1] to the triadic framework, and (ii) we propose new algorithms for computing triadic generators and implications. Our research work is implemented in a mostly Python coded platform whose architecture includes the following modules, as presented in Fig. 1:

1. The call of *Data-Peeler* procedure [4] to get triadic concepts
2. The computation of the precedence links by adapting *iPred* to the triadic setting
3. The calculation of two kinds of generators, namely feature-based and extent-based generators

This study was financed in part by the NSERC (Natural Sciences and Engineering Research Council of Canada) and by the Coordenação de Aperfeiçoamento de Pessoal de Nível Superior - Brazil (CAPES) - Finance Code 001.

© Springer Nature Switzerland AG 2020
M. Alam et al. (Eds.): ICCS 2020, LNAI 12277, pp. 117–131, 2020.
https://doi.org/10.1007/978-3-030-57855-8_9

4. The generation of three kinds of triadic implications as well as two kinds of association rules
5. The adaptation of stability and separation indices to the triadic framework.

In this paper, we will focus on presenting our work on Module 2 and parts of Modules 3 and 4 only.

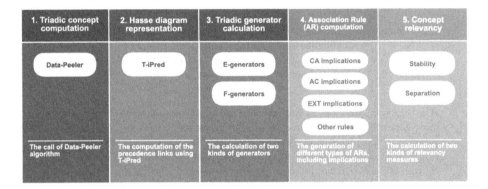

Fig. 1. The architecture modules of our proposed solution.

Our findings consider the initial triadic context without any transformation such as context flattening used in [7,9], and extend notions and algorithms initially defined in Formal Concept Analysis to its triadic counterpart.

The paper is organized as follows: in Sect. 2 we provide a background on Triadic Concept Analysis while in Sect. 3 we propose an adapted version of the *iPred* algorithm to link triadic concepts (TCs) according to the quasi-order based on extents. In a similar way, one can build a Hasse diagram with respect to either the intent or the modus. The identification of links allows us not only to produce a *poset* of triadic concepts, but also to compute generators using the notion of faces and blockers as defined by [10]. Section 4 describes algorithms for computing triadic generators while Sect. 5 provides a procedure to generate implications. Section 6 describes a preliminary empirical study, and Sect. 7 concludes the paper and identifies the future work.

2   Background

In this section we first recall the main notions related to Triadic Concept Analysis such as triadic concepts and implications. Then, we recall other notions related to the border and the faces of a given concept.

2.1   Triadic Concept Analysis

Triadic Concept Analysis (TCA) was originally introduced by Lehmann and Wille [8,12] as an extension to Formal Concept Analysis [6], to analyze data described by three sets K_1 (objects), K_2 (attributes) and K_3 (conditions) together with a ternary relation $Y \subseteq K_1 \times K_2 \times K_3$. We call $\mathbb{K} := (K_1, K_2, K_3, Y)$ a *triadic context* as illustrated. by Table 1 borrowed from [5] and its adaptation in [9]. It represents the purchase of customers in $K_1 := \{1, 2, 3, 4, 5\}$ from suppliers in $K_2 := \{\textbf{P}eter, \textbf{N}elson, \textbf{R}ick, \textbf{K}evin, \textbf{S}imon\}$ of products in $K_3 := \{\textbf{a}ccessories, \textbf{b}ooks, \textbf{c}omputers, \textbf{d}igital\ cameras\}$.

With $(a_1, a_2, a_3) \in Y$, we mean that the object a_1 possesses the attribute a_2 under the condition a_3. For example, the value ac at the cross of Row 1 and Column R means that Customer 1 orders from Supplier R the products a and c. We will often use simplified notations for sets: e.g. $1\,2\,5$ (or simply 125) stands for $\{1, 2, 5\}$ and $a\,b$ (or simply ab) means $\{a, b\}$.

A *triadic concept* or *closed tri-set* of a triadic context $\mathbb{K}$ is a triple (A_1, A_2, A_3) (also denoted by $A_1 \times A_2 \times A_3$) with $A_1 \subseteq K_1$, $A_2 \subseteq K_2$, $A_3 \subseteq K_3$ and $A_1 \times A_2 \times A_3 \subseteq Y$ is maximal with respect to inclusion in Y. For example, the tri-set $135 \times PN \times d \subseteq Y$ is not closed since $135 \times PN \times d \subseteq Y \subsetneq 12345 \times PN \times d \subseteq Y$.

Let (A_1, A_2, A_3) be a triadic concept; We will refer to A_1 as its *extent*, A_2 as its *intent*, A_3 as its *modus*, and (A_2, A_3) as its *feature*. From Table 1, we can extract three triadic concepts with the same extent $2\,5$, namely $25 \times PNR \times d$, $25 \times PR \times ad$ and $25 \times R \times abd$.

To compute triadic concepts, three derivation operators are introduced. Let $\mathbb{K} := (K_1, K_2, K_3, Y)$ be a triadic context and $\{i, j, k\} = \{1, 2, 3\}$ with $j < k$. Let $X_i \subseteq K_i$ and $(X_j, X_k) \subseteq K_j \times K_k$[1]. The $^{(i)}$-derivation [8] is defined by:

$$X_i^{(i)} := \{(a_j, a_k) \in K_j \times K_k \mid (a_i, a_j, a_k) \in Y\ \forall a_i \in X_i\} \tag{1}$$

$$(X_j, X_k)^{(i)} := \{a_i \in K_i \mid (a_i, a_j, a_k) \in Y\ \text{for all}\ (a_j, a_k) \in X_j \times X_k\}. \tag{2}$$

For example, the $^{(2)}$-derivation in $\mathbb{K}$ is the derivation in the dyadic context $\mathbb{K}^{(2)} := (K_2, K_1 \times K_3, Y^{(2)})$ with $(y, (x, z)) \in Y^{(2)} : \Longleftrightarrow (x, y, z) \in Y$.

Table 1. A triadic context.

	P	N	R	K	S
1	abd	abd	ac	ab	a
2	ad	bcd	abd	ad	d
3	abd	d	ab	ab	a
4	abd	bd	ab	ab	d
5	ad	ad	abd	abc	a

The set of triadic concepts can be ordered and forms a complete trilattice with a tridimensional representation [3,8]. For each $i \in \{1, 2, 3\}$, the relation

---

[1] We write $(X_j, X_k) \subseteq K_j \times K_k$ to mean that $X_j \subseteq K_j$ and $X_k \subseteq K_k$.

$(A_1, A_2, A_3) \lesssim_i (B_1, B_2, B_3) \Leftrightarrow A_i \subseteq B_i$ is a quasi-order whose equivalence relation $\sim_i$ is given by: $(A_1, A_2, A_3) \sim_i (B_1, B_2, B_3) \Leftrightarrow A_i = B_i$. These three quasi-orders satisfy the following *antiordinal dependencies*:

$$\left. \begin{array}{l} (A_1, A_2, A_3) \lesssim_i (B_1, B_2, B_3) \\ (A_1, A_2, A_3) \lesssim_j (B_1, B_2, B_3) \end{array} \right\} \implies (B_1, B_2, B_3) \lesssim_k (A_1, A_2, A_3)$$

for $\{i, j, k\} = \{1, 2, 3\}$ and for all triadic concepts (A_1, A_2, A_3) and (B_1, B_2, B_3).

Biedermann [3] was the first to investigate implications in triadic contexts. A *triadic implication* has the form $(A \to D)_C$ and holds *if* A occurs under conditions in C as a whole, *then* D also occurs under the same set of conditions. Later on, Ganter and Obiedkov [5] extended Biedermann's work and defined three types of implications: *attribute × condition* implications (AxCIs), *conditional attribute* implications (CAIs), and *attributional condition* implications (ACIs). In this paper we focus on implications "à la Biedermann", and we borrow the following definitions from [9] for *conditional attribute* and *attributional condition* implications.

A *Biedermann conditional attribute* implication (BCAI) has the form $(A \to D)_C$ (s), and means that whenever A occurs under the conditions in C, then D also occurs under the same condition set with a support s. A *Biedermann attributional condition* implication (BACI) has the form $(A \to D)_C$ (s), and means that whenever the conditions in A occur for all the attributes in C, then the conditions in D also occur for the same attribute set with a support s.

2.2 Border and Faces

Let $(P, \leq)$ be a poset. If $x \leq y$ (resp. $x < y$) we state that x is below (resp. strictly below) y. If $x < y$ and there is no element between x and y, we call x a lower cover of y, and y an upper cover of x, and write $x \prec y$. The upper cover of x is $uc(x) = \{y \mid x \prec y\}$, and its lower cover is $lc(x) = \{y \mid y \prec x\}$ [2].

Let $\mathcal{L} = (\mathcal{C}, \leq_1)$ be a poset such that each node represents all the triadic concepts associated with the same extent, and $\leq_1$ the order relation induced by the quasi-order $\lesssim_1$. This poset is not a complete lattice since the intersection of extents is not necessarily an extent in the triadic setting. The goal is to construct the Hasse diagram of $\mathcal{L}$. Thus we need the covering relation $\prec_1$ of $\leq_1$. The elements will be processed in a linear ordering $<_p$ on $\mathrm{Ext}(\mathcal{C})$ according to an increasing size of the extents. To each current node/extent x, we associate its border $B(x)$, which consists of maximal elements w.r.t. $\leq_1$ among the elements already processed. Therefore:

$$y \in B(x) \iff \mathrm{ext}(y) <_p \mathrm{ext}(x) \text{ and } y \text{ is maximal w.r.t.} \leq_1.$$

This definition of border is different from the one proposed in [2] but identical to the one stated in [1]. It is important to note that in our definition, the value of $B(x)$ depends on the ordering of the extents with the same size in $\mathrm{Ext}(\mathcal{C})$.

Using the notion of face in [1,10], we define the *extent-based face* of a node $n \in \mathcal{L}$ with respect to an *immediate predecessor* $\tilde{n}$, denoted by $\mathrm{Face}_E(n \succ \tilde{n})$, as the difference between their extents. In a similar way, we define the *feature-based face* of a node $n \in \mathcal{L}$ with respect to an *immediate successor* $\tilde{n}$, denoted by $\text{Face}_F(n \prec \tilde{n})$, as the difference between the union of the features associated with n and the union of those attached to $\tilde{n}$.

$$\text{Face}_F(n \prec \tilde{n}) = \left\{ \bigcup Features(n) \setminus \bigcup Features(\tilde{n}) \right\} \tag{3}$$

These two face variants will be useful for precedence link computation and feature-based generator identification respectively.

If we consider the extents 1 4 and 1 3 4 and their associated features computed using *Data-Peeler*, we get:

$\text{Face}_F(1\,4 \prec 1\,3\,4) = (KNP \times b \cup NP \times bd) \setminus (P \times abd \cup KP \times ab) = N \times bd.$

$\text{Face}_E(1\,3\,4 \succ 1\,4) = 3.$

3   The Hasse Diagram Representation

To the best of our knowledge, the unique work about trilattice representation is due to [12]. However, the authors in [11] highlight the difficulty to read and navigate through such structure, and hence suggest new visualization, navigation and exploration mechanisms based either on reachability relation among formal concepts or membership constraints.

In order to visualize and navigate through triadic concepts together with their quasi-order with respect to the extents, we build a Hasse diagram in which each node represents a set of triadic concepts with the same extent, and the precedence link is defined as an adaptation of *iPred* algorithm [1].

Such adaptation that we call *T-iPred* considers concepts according to an increasing order of their extent size rather than their intent size, and hence builds the diagram from the bottom to the top. Since the obtained poset is not closed under the intersection of either the extent, intent or modus, we had to modify the initial *iPred* procedure to first discard some extent intersections that do no represent actual extents of existing TCs. Therefore, a link is created between two nodes in two cases: i) when the intersection of the accumulated - union of - extent-based faces of a candidate node together with the extent of the current node is empty, ii) or when the union of this intersection together with the candidate extent represents a discarded intersection of actual extents. An intersection B_1 of extents is discarded whenever all its associated features describe a superset of B_1. In our example, this is the case of the object subsets 3, 1 3 and 3 5. Indeed, although 3 has five features, the associated actual extents are either 3 4, 1 3 4, 1 3 5 or 1 2 3 4 5. For example, $KPRS \times a$ is already attached to 1 3 5.

3.1   T-iPred Algorithm

Starting from a set of extents, Algorithm 1 computes borders, candidates and links between two nodes w.r.t. to their extent. In Line 1, the extents of triadic concepts are sorted in an ascending order of their size while in Line 2, the variable which will store all the created links is initialized with the empty set. In Lines 3 to 5, a hash structure (denoted by $\triangle$) is created using the extents presented in the set $\mathcal{E}$ as a key and the empty set as the initial value associated with each key (extent). The first element in the border is the element with the smallest extent size (Line 6). In Lines 7 to 19, all remaining elements in the input sequence are processed in the order in which they appear in the enumeration. The *Candidate* set is computed by intersecting the current element $\mathcal{E}[i]$ with all elements present in the border (Line 8). Since some intersections of extents are not extents of existing triadic concepts, Lines 9 to 10 aim to discard them from the *Candidate* set. If *Discarded* is equal to the empty set, it means that all the candidates represent valid extents. The *Discarded* set is then removed from the current *Candidate* set.

Algorithm 1: *T-iPred* algorithm.

    Input   : $E = \{e_1, ..., e_l\}$ the set of the existing extents.
    Output: $(\mathcal{E}, \lesssim_1)$
1 $\mathcal{E} \leftarrow Sort(E)$
2 $\lesssim_1 \leftarrow \emptyset$
3 **foreach** $i = 2 \dots l$ **do**
4 | $\triangle[\mathcal{E}[i]] \leftarrow \emptyset$
5 **end**
6 $Border \leftarrow \mathcal{E}[1]$
7 **foreach** $i \in \{2, l\}$ **do**
8 | $Candidate \leftarrow \{\mathcal{E}[i] \cap \tilde{e} \mid \tilde{e} \in Border\}$
9 | $Discarded \leftarrow Candidate \setminus \mathcal{E}$
10 | $Candidate \leftarrow Candidate \setminus Discarded$
11 | **foreach** $\tilde{e} \in Candidate$ **do**
12 | | $e = \triangle[\tilde{e}] \cap e_i$
13 | | **if** $e = \emptyset$ *or* $e \cup \tilde{e} \in Discarded$ **then**
14 | | | $\lesssim_1 \leftarrow \lesssim_1 \cup (\mathcal{E}[i], \tilde{e})$
15 | | | $\triangle[\tilde{e}] = \triangle[\tilde{e}] \cup (\mathcal{E}[i] - \tilde{e})$
16 | | | $Border \leftarrow Border - \tilde{e}$
17 | **end**
18 | $Border \leftarrow Border \cup \mathcal{E}[i]$
19 **end**

In Lines 11 to 17 we check if the current extent belongs to the lower set of the elements in the candidate set. If the intersection of the accumulated faces of a candidate node together with the extent of the current node is empty, or if the union of this intersection together with the candidate extent represents a discarded extent, a link is added to the output set (Line 14). Then, the current extent is inserted into the set of accumulated faces of $\tilde{e}$ while the current candidate $\tilde{e}$ is removed from that set and from the *Border* set (Line 16). Finally, in Line 18, before processing the next extent, the current extent is added to the *Border* set.

Let us assume that one of the possible orderings for the $\mathcal{E}$ is:

$$\mathcal{E} = [\emptyset, 5, 2, 1, 4, 2\,4, 3\,4, 1\,4, 2\,5, 1\,5, \cdots\cdots, 1\,2\,3\,4\,5].$$

In Table 2 we present a running example with only the first nine triadic concepts for the *T-iPred* algorithm based on the triadic context given in Table 1. To illustrate how the algorithm works for a given extent, let us see the processing of $e_i = 24$ with its border equal to $\{5, 2, 1, 4\}^2$. Line 6 of Algorithm 1 returns the candidate set $\{\emptyset, 2, 4\}$. In Lines 7 to 8, no element is discarded from the candidate set. If we consider the candidate $\tilde{e} = 2$ in Line 9, then $e = \triangle[2] \cap 2\,4 = \emptyset$. Since the condition in Line 11 is true, a link is then created between $e_i = 24$ and $\tilde{e} = 2$ and the accumulated face $\triangle[2]$ changes from $\emptyset$ to $\{4\}$ (Line 13), and $\tilde{e} = 2$ is removed from the border (Line 14). After processing all the candidates, a second link is created between $e_i = 24$ and $\tilde{e} = 4$, and the border takes the value $(\{5, 2, 1, 4\} \setminus \{2, 4\}) \cup \{24\} = \{5, 1, 24\}$.

Table 2. A part of the *T-iPred* trace. We used a simplified notation for sets. For example $\{5, 1, 2\,4\}$ stands for the set of sets $\{\{5\}, \{1\}, \{2, 4\}\}$.

e_i	Candidate set	$\triangle[\tilde{e}] \cap e_i$	$\succ_{\mathcal{L}}$	$\triangle[\tilde{e}]$	Border
					$\emptyset$
5	$5 \cap \emptyset = \emptyset$	$\triangle[\emptyset] \cap 5 = \emptyset$	$(5, \emptyset)$	$\triangle[\emptyset] = \{5\}$	$\{5\}$
2	$2 \cap \{5\} = \emptyset$	$\triangle[\emptyset] \cap 2 = \emptyset$	$(2, \emptyset)$	$\triangle[\emptyset] = \{5, 2\}$	$\{5,2\}$
1	$1 \cap \{5, 2\} = \emptyset$	$\triangle[\emptyset] \cap 1 = \emptyset$	$(1, \emptyset)$	$\triangle[\emptyset] = \{5, 2, 1\}$	$\{5,2,1\}$
4	$4 \cap \{5, 2, 1\} = \emptyset$	$\triangle[\emptyset] \cap 4 = \emptyset$	$(4, \emptyset)$	$\triangle[\emptyset] = \{5, 2, 1, 4\}$	$\{5,2,1,4\}$
2 4	$2\,4 \cap \{5, 2, 1, 4\} = \{\emptyset, 2, 4\}$	$\triangle[\emptyset] \cap 2\,4 = \{\emptyset, 2, 4\}$	⊢	$\triangle[\emptyset] = \{5, 2, 1, 4\}$	
	$2\,4 \cap \{5, 2, 1, 4\} = \{\emptyset, \mathbf{2}, 4\}$	$\triangle[2] \cap 2\,4 = \emptyset$	$(2\,4, 2)$	$\triangle[2] = \{4\}$	$\{5,1,4\}$
	$2\,4 \cap \{5, 2, 1, 4\} = \{\emptyset, 2, \mathbf{4}\}$	$\triangle[4] \cap 2\,4 = \emptyset$	$(2\,4, 4)$	$\triangle[4] = \{2\}$	$\{5,1,2\,4\}$
3 4	$3\,4 \cap \{5, 1, 2\,4\} = \{\emptyset, 4\}$	$\triangle[\emptyset] \cap 3\,4 = \{\emptyset, 4\}$	⊢	$\triangle[\emptyset] = \{5, 2, 1, 4\}$	
	$3\,4 \cap \{5, 1, 2\,4\} = \{\emptyset, \mathbf{4}\}$	$\triangle[4] \cap 3\,4 = \emptyset$	$(3\,4, 4)$	$\triangle[4] = \{2, 3\}$	$\{5,1,2\,4,3\,4\}$
1 4	$1\,4 \cap \{5, 1, 2\,4, 3\,4\} = \{\emptyset, 1, 4\}$	$\triangle[\emptyset] \cap 1\,4 = \{\emptyset, 1, 4\}$	⊢	$\triangle[\emptyset] = \{5, 2, 1, 4\}$	
	$1\,4 \cap \{5, 1, 2\,4, 3\,4\} = \{\emptyset, \mathbf{1}, 4\}$	$\triangle[1] \cap 1\,4 = \emptyset$	$(1\,4, 1)$	$\triangle[1] = \{4\}$	$\{5, 2\,4, 3\,4\}$
	$1\,4 \cap \{5, 1, 2\,4, 3\,4\} = \{\emptyset, 1, \mathbf{4}\}$	$\triangle[4] \cap 1\,4 = \emptyset$	$(1\,4, 4)$	$\triangle[4] = \{2, 3, 1\}$	$\{5, 2\,4, 3\,4, 1\,4\}$
2 5	$2\,5 \cap \{5, 2\,4, 3\,4, 1\,4\} = \{\mathbf{5}, 2, \emptyset\}$	$\triangle[5] \cap 2\,5 = \emptyset$	$(2\,5, 5)$	$\triangle[5] = \{2\}$	$\{2\,4, 3\,4, 1\,4\}$
	$2\,5 \cap \{5, 2\,4, 3\,4, 1\,4\} = \{5, \mathbf{2}, \emptyset\}$	$\triangle[2] \cap 2\,5 = \emptyset$	$(2\,5, 2)$	$\triangle[2] = \{4, 5\}$	$\{2\,4, 3\,4, 1\,4\}$
	$2\,5 \cap \{5, 2\,4, 3\,4, 1\,4\} = \{5, 2, \mathbf{\emptyset}\}$	$\triangle[\emptyset] \cap 2\,5 = \{5, 2, \emptyset\}$	⊢	$\triangle[\emptyset] = \{5, 2, 1, 4\}$	$\{2\,4, 3\,4, 1\,4, 2\,5\}$
1 5	$1\,5 \cap \{2\,4, 3\,4, 1\,4, 2\,5\} = \{\emptyset, 1, 5\}$	$\triangle[\emptyset] \cap 1\,5 = \{5, 1, \emptyset\}$	⊢	$\triangle[\emptyset] = \{5, 2, 1, 4\}$	
	$1\,5 \cap \{2\,4, 3\,4, 1\,4, 2\,5\} = \{\emptyset, 1, 5\}$	$\triangle[\emptyset] \cap 1\,5 = \emptyset$	$(15,1)$	$\triangle[1] = \{4, 5\}$	$\{2\,4, 3\,4, 1\,4, 2\,5\}$
	$1\,5 \cap \{2\,4, 3\,4, 1\,4, 2\,5\} = \{\emptyset, 1, \mathbf{5}\}$	$\triangle[5] \cap 1\,5 = \emptyset$	$(15,5)$	$\triangle[5] = \{2, 1\}$	$\{2\,4, 3\,4, 1\,4, 2\,5, 1\,5\}$

Once we process the element whose extent is 15, we obtain the lower part of the Hasse diagram presented in Fig. 2.

---

[2] The border of a node (extent) at the beginning of an extent processing appears in the immediately upper line of Table 2.

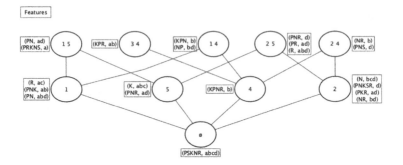

Fig. 2. Lower part of the Hasse diagram after computing the element 15.

At the end, once all the elements in $\mathcal{E}$ are processed, we get the Hasse diagram of triadic concepts presented in Fig. 3 where the value inside each node represents an extent while the pairs of values are the corresponding features. For example, the node with the label 25 represents the extent of the TCs $(25, NPR, d)$, $(25, PR, ad)$ and $(25, R, abd)$.

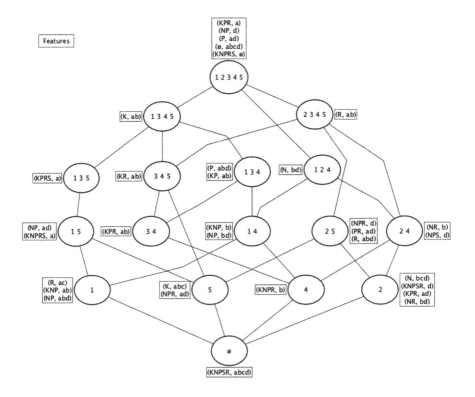

Fig. 3. Final Hass diagram of triadic concepts obtained with T-$iPred$.

The complexity of *T-iPred* algorithm can be estimated by $|E| \times w(\mathcal{L}) \times |K_1|$ as an adaptation of the complexity of *iPred* where E, $w(\mathcal{L})$ and K_1 are the set of extents, the width of the diagram $\mathcal{L}$ and the whole object set.

4 Triadic Generators Computation

In this section we define a triadic feature-based generator and propose new algorithms to compute it.

4.1 Definition

Definition 1. *Let* (A_1, A_2, A_3) *be a triadic concept.* (B_2, B_3) *is a triadic feature-based generator (F-generator for short) of* (A_2, A_3) *if* $A_2 \times A_3 \subseteq (B_2, B_3)^{(1)(1)}$.

As a generator, (B_2, B_3) needs to be minimal and have a non empty intersection with each face of the node with the extent A_1.

4.2 Algorithms

Algorithm 2: Computing Feature-based generators

Input : A formal context $C = (K_2^c, K_3^c, I^c)$ that represents all the features associated
with the node c whose extent is E in the lattice.
A triadic context $K = (K_1, K_2, K_3, Y)$.
The s formal contexts $C_k = (K_2^k, K_3^k, I_k)$, $k = 1, \ldots, s$ as the successors of c.
Output: A set T_G of triadic generators of the current node c

1 $n \leftarrow |K_2^c| \qquad m \leftarrow |K_3^c|$
2 $G \leftarrow \emptyset \qquad V_A(n) := Attrib(K_2^c) \qquad V_M(m) := Cond(K_3^c)$
3 **for** $k = 1, s$ **do**
4 $\qquad$ $F_k \leftarrow I^c \setminus I^k$
5 $\qquad$ **if** $k=1$ **then**
6 $\qquad\qquad$ **for** $i=1, n$ **do**
7 $\qquad\qquad\qquad$ **for** $j=1, m$ **do**
8 $\qquad\qquad\qquad\qquad$ **if** $F_k(i,j) = 1$ **then** $G \leftarrow G \cup \{V_A(i), V_M(j)\}$;
9 $\qquad\qquad\qquad$ **end**
10 $\qquad\qquad$ **end**
11 $\qquad$ **else**
12 $\qquad\qquad$ $F \leftarrow Face(c_k)$
13 $\qquad\qquad$ $Update(G, F)$
14 **end**
15 $T_G \leftarrow \emptyset$
16 **for** e *in* G **do**
17 $\qquad$ **if** $Derive(e) = E$ **then** $T_G \leftarrow T_G \cup e$;
18 **end**
19 **return** $MinSet(T_G)$

In Lines 1 and 2, a few variables are initialized. The set G of generators is initialized to the empty set while V_A and V_M are global variables that store the n attributes and the m conditions found in the features of node c. In Lines 3 to 14, each successor c_k of c is used to compute the feature-based face of node

c with respect to its successor c_k to further compute the set G of potential generators. Line 4 computes the k-th face of c named F_k as the matrix of size $n \times m$ representing the difference between the two binary relations I^c and I^k. If $k = 1$ (Lines 5 to 10), the first face F_1 is decomposed into a set of elementary pairs (b_2, b_3) as cells in F_1 with $b_2 \in K_2^c$ and $b_3 \in K_3^c$. The set of these pairs serves as the preliminary value of G. Lines 12 to 13 compute the subsequent faces and update the set G. $Update(G, F)$ aims to check if each potential generator g in G has a non empty intersection with the current face. If not, g needs to be augmented in its intent and/or its modus parts with elements from the current face as indicated in Algorithm 3. Since the latter set may contain elements whose corresponding extent is possibly larger that the current extent E, Lines 16 to 18 use the derivation operation to discard such elements. Finally, the set of minimal F-generators is returned.

Algorithm 3: FACE - Computing the components of the k-th face when $k > 1$

> **Input** : A formal context $C_k = (K_2^k, K_3^k, I^k)$ of the k-th successor of $C = (K_2^c, K_3^c, I^c)$.
> $n = |K_2^c|$
> $m = |K_3^c|$
> **Output:** The component set F of the face F_k
> 1 $F_k \leftarrow I^c \setminus I^k \qquad U_3 \leftarrow \emptyset \qquad F \leftarrow \emptyset$
> 2 **for** $i=1, n$ **do**
> 3 $\quad$ **for** $j = 1, m$ **do**
> 4 $\quad\quad$ | **if** $F_k(i, j) = 1$ **then** $U_3 \leftarrow U_3 \cup V_M(j)$;
> 5 $\quad$ **end**
> 6 $\quad$ $F \leftarrow F \cup (V_A(i), U_3)$
> 7 **end**
> 8 **return** F

Algorithm 4: UPDATE - Updating the set of feature-based generators

> **Input** : The temporary set of G of T-generator.
> The set F of Face components.
> **Output:** The updated set G of the $T - generators$.
> 1 $G_1 \leftarrow G$
> 2 **for** g in G **do**
> 3 $\quad$ $i \leftarrow 0$
> 4 $\quad$ **switch** $\exists f \in F$ **do**
> 5 $\quad\quad$ **case** $(\text{Int}(f) \cap \text{Int}(g) \neq \emptyset$ & $\text{Modus}(f) \cap \text{Modus}(g) \neq \emptyset)$ **do**
> 6 $\quad\quad\quad$ | $i \leftarrow 2$
> 7 $\quad\quad$ **case** $(\text{Int}(f) \cap \text{Int}(g) = \emptyset$ & $\text{Modus}(f) \cap \text{Modus}(g) = \emptyset)$ **do**
> 8 $\quad\quad\quad$ $i \leftarrow 1$
> 9 $\quad\quad\quad$ **for** e in $\text{Int}(f)$ **do** $G_1 \leftarrow G_1 \cup (\text{Int}(g) \cup e, \text{Modus}(g))$;
> 10 $\quad\quad\quad$ **for** e in $\text{Modus}(f)$ **do** $G_1 \leftarrow G_1 \cup (\text{Int}(g), \text{Modus}(g) \cup e)$;
> 11 $\quad\quad$ **case** $(\text{Int}(f) \cap \text{Int}(g) = \emptyset$ & $\text{Modus}(f) \cap \text{Modus}(g) \neq \emptyset)$ **do**
> 12 $\quad\quad\quad$ $i \leftarrow 1$
> 13 $\quad\quad\quad$ **for** e in $\text{Int}(f)$ **do** $G_1 \leftarrow G_1 \cup (\text{Int}(g) \cup e, \text{Modus}(g))$;
> 14 $\quad\quad$ **case** $(\text{Int}(f) \cap \text{Int}(g) \neq \emptyset$ & $\text{Modus}(f) \cap \text{Modus}(g) = \emptyset)$ **do**
> 15 $\quad\quad\quad$ $i \leftarrow 1$
> 16 $\quad\quad\quad$ **for** e in $\text{Modus}(f)$ **do** $G_1 \leftarrow G_1 \cup (\text{Int}(g), \text{Modus}(g) \cup e)$;
> 17 $\quad$ **end**
> 18 $\quad$ **if** $i = 1$ **then** $G_1 \leftarrow G_1 \setminus g$;
> 19 **end**
> 20 **return** G_1

4.3   Example

As an example, let us consider the feature-based generators for the triadic concepts associated with the extent 14. The first step is to compute the feature-based face of the node labelled by this extent and each one of its successors, which are 134 and 124.

To do so, we create a dyadic context representing all the features - $KNP \times b$ and $NP \times bd$ - associated with the current node whose extent is 14, and then we remove the features - $P \times abd$ and $KP \times ab$ - which belong to its first successor 134. Then, the second face F_2 is computed by considering the following feature associated with the successor node 124: $N, \times bd$, as shown in Tables 3 and 4.

Table 3. Face F_1 covering the non highlighted crosses

	b	d
K	**x**	
N	x	x
P	**x**	**x**

Table 4. Face F_2

	b	d
K	x	
N	**x**	**x**
P	x	x

Since $F_1 = N \times bd$ is the first computed face, the set G is assigned the value $\{N \times b, N \times d\}$ obtained by a combination of an element of the intent part with an element of the modus part of F_1. The second face is $F_2 = \{K \times b, P \times bd\}$. Next, it is necessary to update the set G by checking if each element of the current generator set has a non empty intersection with F_2. This is illustrated as follows:

- The first element g in G is (N, b) and has no intersection with F_2. Then we proceed as follows:
  - $Int(K, b) \cap Int(N, b) = \emptyset$ (3rd case of Algorithm 4)
    - Then, $G = \{(\mathbf{NK,b}), (N, d)\}$
  - $Int(P, bd) \cap Int(N, b) = \emptyset$ (3rd case of Algorithm 4)
    - Then, $G = \{(NK, b), (\mathbf{NP,b}), (N, d)\}$
- The second element (N, d) in G does not have an intersection with F_2:
  - $Int(K, b) \cap Int(N, d) = \emptyset$ and $Modus(K, b) \cap Modus(N, d) = \emptyset$ (2nd case of Algorithm 4)
    - Then, $G = \{(NK, b), (NP, b), (\mathbf{NK,\ bd})\}$
  - $Int(P, bd) \cap Int(N, d) = \emptyset$ (3rd case of Algorithm 4)
    - Then, $G = \{(NK, b), (NP, b), (NK, bd), (\mathbf{NP,\ d})\}$.

Now, we need to check if all the elements in G are actually F-generators of the features associated with the node whose extent is 14. The pairs (NK, bd) and (NP, d) will be removed from G because the former is not minimal while the extent associated with the latter is actually 12345. The final set of F-generators of the features associated with the node whose extent is 14 is $G = \{(NK, b), (NP, b)\}$.

Once all the features associated with the distinct extents in E are processed, we get the lattice annotated with the F-generators as presented in Fig. 4.

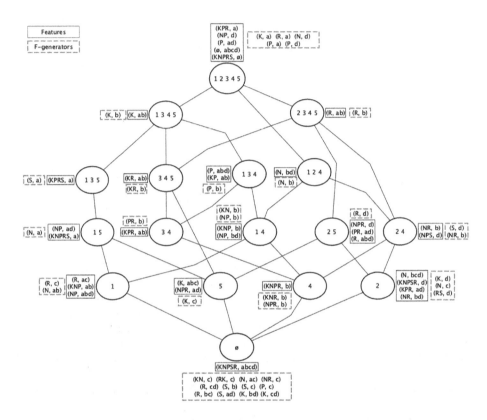

Fig. 4. Triadic lattice annotated with features and F-generators.

5   Implication Computation

In the following, we propose a more precise definition than the one given in [9] for two types of implications using feature-based generators.

5.1   Feature-Based Implications

Proposition 1. *Let (A_1, A_2, A_3) be a triadic concept and (B_2, B_3) a feature-based generator of (A_2, A_3). Then, the BCAI-implication $(B_2 \rightarrow A_2 \setminus B_2)_{B_3}$ holds with a support equal to $|A_1|/|K_1|$ if $B_2 \subset A_2$ and $B_3 \subseteq A_3$, where K_1 stands for the set of objects. Dually, the BACI-implication $(B_3 \rightarrow A_3 \setminus B_3)_{B_2}$ holds with a support equal to $|A_1|/|K_1|$ if $B_3 \subset A_3$ and $B_2 \subseteq A_2$.*

Proof. The implication $(B_2 \rightarrow A_2 \setminus B_2)_{B_3}$ is valid iff $(B_2, B_3)^{(1)} \subseteq (A_2 \setminus B_2, A_3 \setminus B_3)^{(1)}$, i.e., all the objects having the attributes in the premise B_2 own necessarily the attributes in the conclusion $A_2 \setminus B_2$ under the conditions in B_3. This is equivalent to the condition $A_2 \times A_3 \subseteq (B_2, B_3)^{(1)(1)}$ in the definition of F-generators (see Definition 1).

For example, we can extract the following implications from the node whose extent is 14 in Fig. 4: $(KN \rightarrow P)_b$, $(NP \rightarrow K)_b$ and $(b \rightarrow d)_{NP}$. The first one means that whenever N and K supply the item b, then the supplier P does so. The last implication means that if the product b is supplied jointly by P and N, then product d is also jointly supplied by these suppliers.

5.2   Algorithm

Algorithm 5: Computing feature-based implications.

Input   : The set $C = \{(A_i^1, A_i^2, A_i^3)\}$ of triadic concepts
                    A hash structure FG of F-generators associated with the concepts in C
Output: The set AC and CA of implications.

1 $AC \leftarrow \emptyset$; $CA \leftarrow \emptyset$;
2 **foreach** $c \in C$ **do**
3 $\quad$ $A_1 \leftarrow Ext(c)$ $\qquad$ $A_2 \leftarrow Int(c)$ $\qquad$ $A_3 \leftarrow Modus(c)$
4 $\quad$ **for** $f \in FG(A_1)$ **do**
5 $\quad\quad$ $B_2 \leftarrow Int(f)$ $\qquad$ $B_3 \leftarrow Modus(f)$
6 $\quad\quad$ **if** $(B_2 \subset A_2)$ *and* $(B_3 \subseteq A_3)$ **then**
7 $\quad\quad\quad$ $AC \leftarrow AC \cup (B_2 \rightarrow A_2 \setminus B_2, B_3, \frac{|A_1|}{|K_1|})$
8 $\quad\quad$ **if** $(B_3 \subset A_3)$ *and* $B_2 \subseteq A_2$ **then**
9 $\quad\quad\quad$ $CA \leftarrow CA \cup (B_3 \rightarrow A_3 \setminus B_3, B_2, \frac{|A_1|}{|K_1|})$
10 $\quad$ **end**
11 **end**

In Line 1 of Algorithm 5, the two sets AC and CA for storing the implications BACIs and BCAIs respectively are initialized to the empty set. Each element in the set CA is a triple that represents an association between attribute subsets, the condition part and the implication support. For the set AC, the triple contains an association between condition subsets, the attribute part and the support.

The *outer loop* in Lines 2 to 11 explores each triadic concept to get its extent, its intent and its modus. The *inner loop* in Lines 4 to 10 looks for each F-generator in the hash structure FG to extract the implications BCAIs and BACIs as defined in Proposition 1.

6   Experimental Results

The objective of this section is to conduct preliminary tests and empirically provide the execution time of each module of our software solution that produces the Hasse diagram of TCs, F-generators, and implications.

All the empirical tests were executed on a Ubuntu 19.10 based system with 32 GB of RAM memory and an Intel i7-4790 3.6 GHz 8-core processor. Regarding the data sets used in our experiments, a random selection on both objects and attributes of *The Mushroom Data Set*[3] was performed. Indeed, we took four subsets (100, 250, 500 and 1000) of the mushroom set and split a subset of the initial attribute set into a set of ten attributes and a set of four corresponding conditions. In Table 5 we present the execution time of each module and the amount of Implication rules (BCAIs and BACIs) computed for each data set.

Table 5. Execution time in seconds for each module.

Subsets of the mushroom data set				
Objects	100	250	500	1000
Attributes	10	10	10	10
Conditions	4	4	4	4
Context density	31.3%	32.6%	33.2%	32.7%
Triadic concepts	28	34	34	63
Links	20	24	24	84
Number of implications	90	92	92	125
Data peeler	0.0036	0.0084	0.0146	0.0413
T-iPred	0.0006	0.0010	0.0014	0.0086
F-Generators	0.4154	1.5039	5.6808	109.4080
Implications	0.0009	0.0009	0.0009	0.0013
Total time	0.4205	1.5142	5.6977	109.4592

One can see from Table 5 that the execution time is dominated by the computation of the F-generators. Such a preliminary result is stimulating us to improve the underlying procedures and exploit parallel processing in the near future.

7   Conclusion

In this paper we described a set of algorithms in Triadic Concept Analysis to construct the Hasse diagram of triadic concepts, compute generators and implications. The objective of having a Hasse diagram that represents the set of triadic concepts partially ordered according to their extent is to allow (i) the computation of feature-based generators to further identify implications and more generally association rules, and (ii) the browsing and the querying of this structure. While the former objective is detailed in the paper, the latter is a research topic that we are about to complete in order to either retrieve a triadic concept or compute the approximation of a triple (A_1, A_2, A_3). The query against the

---

[3] Available at: https://archive.ics.uci.edu/ml/datasets/mushroom.

diagram can concern the three dimensions: objects, attributes and conditions, or any subset of them. Moreover, the implementation of the T-iPred algorithm allows us to order concepts according to anyone of the three dimensions.

To the best of our knowledge, there are neither implementations nor algorithms that compute *in a same way* the type of patterns (generators and implications) that we considered in this paper.

We are presently working on the following topics: (i) the design of procedures for both computing feature-based association rules and a new kind of extent-based implications, (ii) the investigation of new relevancy measures for triadic concepts, and (iii) finally the implementation of our algorithms to analyze large triadic contexts using Apache Spark.

References

1. Baixeries, J., Szathmary, L., Valtchev, P., Godin, R.: Yet a faster algorithm for building the hasse diagram of a concept lattice. In: ICFCA 2009, pp. 162–177 (2009)
2. Balcázar, J.L., Tîrnăucă, C.: Border algorithms for computing hasse diagrams of arbitrary lattices. In: Valtchev, P., Jäschke, R. (eds.) ICFCA 2011. LNCS (LNAI), vol. 6628, pp. 49–64. Springer, Heidelberg (2011). https://doi.org/10.1007/978-3-642-20514-9_6
3. Biedermann, K.: How triadic diagrams represent conceptual structures. In: ICCS, pp. 304–317 (1997)
4. Cerf, L., Besson, J., Robardet, C., Boulicaut, J.F.: Data-peeler: constraint-based closed pattern mining in n-ary relations. In: ICDM 2008, pp. 37–48 (2008)
5. Ganter, B., Obiedkov, S.A.: Implications in triadic formal contexts. In: ICCS, pp. 186–195 (2004)
6. Ganter, B., Wille, R.: Formal Concept Analysis. Springer, Heidelberg (1999). https://doi.org/10.1007/978-3-642-59830-2. translator-C. Franzke
7. Jaschke, R., Hotho, A., Schmitz, C., Ganter, B., Stumme, G.: TRIAS - an algorithm for mining iceberg tri-lattices. In: ICDM 2006, pp. 907–911 (2006)
8. Lehmann, F., Wille, R.: A triadic approach to formal concept analysis. In: ICCS, pp. 32–43 (1995)
9. Missaoui, R., Kwuida, L.: Mining triadic association rules from ternary relations. In: Valtchev, P., Jäschke, R. (eds.) ICFCA 2011. LNCS (LNAI), vol. 6628, pp. 204–218. Springer, Heidelberg (2011). https://doi.org/10.1007/978-3-642-20514-9_16
10. Pfaltz, J.L., Taylor, C.M.: Closed set mining of biological data. In: BIOKDD 2002, pp. 43–48 (2002)
11. Rudolph, S., Sacarea, C., Troanca, D.: Towards a navigation paradigm for triadic concepts. In: ICFCA 2015, pp. 252–267 (2015)
12. Wille, R.: The basic theorem of triadic concept analysis. Order **12**(2), 149–158 (1995)

Characterizing Movie Genres Using Formal Concept Analysis

Raji Ghawi$^{(\boxtimes)}$ and Jürgen Pfeffer

Bavarian School of Public Policy, Technical University of Munich, Munich, Germany
{raji.ghawi,juergen.pfeffer}@tum.de

Abstract. We propose to use Formal Concept Analysis to conceptualize movies and their associated genres. We construct a formal context in which movies are objects and genres are attribute. The context is then used to find formal concepts organized in a concept lattice. This conceptual structure is useful to measure semantic genre-based similarity of movies, which is important for content-based recommender systems.

Keywords: Formal Concept Analysis · Genre · Semantic similarity

1 Introduction

The term "genre" was used to organize films according to type since the earliest days of cinema. Genre is a class, type or category, associated with any form of art or entertainment (literature, music, film, etc.) based on some set of stylistic criteria, such as science fiction, musical, horror, comedy, and thriller. Films are rarely purely from one genre, rather, many films cross into multiple genres. For example, spy films often cross genre boundaries with thriller films [7].

Genre is an important feature of movies, where it can be effectively used in measuring movie-similarity, along with other features, such as actors, director, location, etc. Hwang et al. [8] proposed an algorithm for movie recommendation that exploits the genre of the movie to enhance the accuracy of rating predictions.

In order to understand the relatedness among different film genres, we need a data-driven analysis, not only at statistical level, but at structural level as well. In this paper, we are interested in studying the inter-relatedness of genres, based on the movies that cross multiple genres. For this purpose, we use Formal Concept Analysis (FCA), which is a mathematical framework mainly used for classification and knowledge discovery [5]. FCA has been used in many practical applications in various fields [9], including: data mining [4], text mining [3], machine learning [10], knowledge management [11], and semantic web [1].

Central to FCA is the notion of a *formal context*, which is a structure that comprises a set of objects, described through a set of attributes, via a binary relation, called *incidence*, that expresses which objects have which attributes. Another central notion in FCA is *formal concept*, which associates a set of objects A (called the extent) with a set of attributes B (called the intent), where the

© Springer Nature Switzerland AG 2020
M. Alam et al. (Eds.): ICCS 2020, LNAI 12277, pp. 132–141, 2020.
https://doi.org/10.1007/978-3-030-57855-8_10

extent A consists of all objects that share the attributes in B, and the intent B consists of all attributes shared by the objects in A. The formal concepts of a given context can be ordered in a hierarchy called the context's *concept lattice*.

Organizing movies and genres in a concept lattice provides many advantages. Among others, a promising application is the ability to measure semantic genre-based similarity between movies. Semantic similarity can be measured using several approaches based on the edges in a concept lattice, or based on the nodes (information content). The contributions of the paper are the following:

- We propose to use FCA methods to characterize movie genres.
- We construct a formal context, such that movies are the objects, and genres are the attributes, and use this context to find formal concepts and organize them into a concept lattice.
- We demonstrate how to use the concept lattice in order to measure semantic similarity of movies using several approaches.

The paper is organized as follows. Section 2 provides a preliminary introduction about Formal Concept Analysis, while Sect. 3 gives an overview about the used dataset. In Sect. 4, we address how to construct a formal context for movies and genres; and the concept lattice derived from it. Finally, Sect. 5 discusses how the concept lattice can be used to measure the semantic similarity between movies, and Sect. 6 concludes the paper.

2   Formal Concept Analysis

Formal Concept Analysis (FCA) [5] starts with a *formal context*, which is a triple $\mathbb{K} = \langle G, M, I \rangle$ where $G = \{g_1, \cdots, g_n\}$ is a set of objects, $M = \{m_1, \cdots, m_k\}$ a set of attributes, and $I \subseteq G \times M$ is a binary relation, called *incidence relation*, with $(g, m) \in I$ (denoted gIm) meaning that object g has attribute m. Two dual derivation operators, denoted by $(.)'$, are defined as follows:

$$A' = \{m \in M \mid \forall g \in A, gIm\} \text{ for } A \subseteq G$$
$$B' = \{g \in G \mid \forall m \in B, gIm\} \text{ for } B \subseteq M$$

A' is the set of attributes common to all objects of A; and B' is the set of objects sharing all attributes of B. The two compositions of both derivation operators, denoted by $(.)''$, are closure operators. In particular, for $A \subseteq G$ and $B \subseteq M$, we have $A \subseteq A''$ and $B \subseteq B''$. Then A and B are closed sets when $A = A''$ and $B = B''$ respectively. A *formal concept* is a pair (A, B), where $A \subseteq G$, $B \subseteq M$, whenever $A' = B$ and $B' = A$, where A is closed and called the "extent" of the concept (A, B), and B is closed and called the "intent" of the concept (A, B). The set of all concepts is denoted by $\mathfrak{B}(\mathbb{K})$.

The formal concepts of a given context are partially ordered by the sub-concept - superconcept relation as defined by the inclusion of their extents or (which is equivalent) inverse inclusion of their intent. An order $\leqslant$ on the concepts is defined as follows: for any two concepts (A_1, B_1) and (A_2, B_2) of $\mathbb{K}$, we say that

$(A_1, B_1) \leqslant (A_2, B_2)$ precisely when $A_1 \subseteq A_2$. Equivalently, $(A_1, B_1) \leqslant (A_2, B_2)$ whenever $B_1 \supseteq B_2$. The set of all formal concepts of a context $\mathbb{K}$ together with the order relation $\leqslant$ forms the *concept lattice* of $\mathbb{K}$, denoted $\mathfrak{B}(\mathbb{K})$. Every set of formal concepts has a *greatest common subconcept*. Its extent consists of those objects that are common to all extents of the set. Dually, every set of formal concepts has a *least common superconcept*, the intent of which comprises all attributes which all objects of that set of concepts have.

3   Data

We used the MovieLens 20M movie ratings dataset[1] [6] which includes a *movies* table, that comprises movie information. In this table, each entry represents one movie, and has the following format: $(movieId, title, genres)$. This table comprises 27,278 movies. Genres are a pipe-separated list, and are selected from the following set of 20 genres: Action, Adventure, Animation, Children, Comedy, Crime, Documentary, Drama, Fantasy, Film-Noir, Horror, IMAX, Musical, Mystery, Romance, Sci-Fi, Thriller, War, Western and (no genres listed).

The distribution of genres (number of movies of each genre) is shown in Fig. 1-a, where we can observe that the most frequent genre is Drama (about 13,000 movies), followed by Comedy (about 8,000 movies). Figure 1-b shows the distribution of number of genres per movies. For instance, about 10,800 movies have one genre only, while about 8,800 movies have two genres. Very few movies have more than 5 genres. On average, a movie has 2 genres.

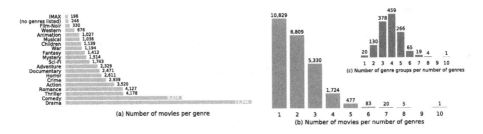

Fig. 1. Genres distribution

In the dataset, there are 1,342 different combinations (groups) of genres. Figure 1-c shows how many of these combinations exist per number of genres. For instance, there are 20 groups of size 1 (corresponding to the 20 genres); whereas there are 130 groups of 2 genres, and 378 groups of 3 genres, etc. Table 1 shows the largest genres groups along with the number of movies in each group. For instance, the largest 2-genres group is {Comedy, Drama} (1,264 movies), whereas the largest 3-genres group is {Comedy, Drama, Romance} (605 movies).

---

[1] https://grouplens.org/datasets/movielens/20m/.

Table 1. Largest genre groups

	Genres group	# movies		Genres group	# movies
1	{Drama}	4,520	3	{Comedy, Drama, Romance}	605
	{Comedy}	2,294		{Crime, Drama, Thriller}	304
	{Documentary}	1,942		{Action, Crime, Thriller}	127
	{Horror}	565		{Horror, Mystery, Thriller}	115
	{Thriller}	268		{Action, Crime, Drama}	114
2	{Comedy, Drama}	1,264	4	{Action, Crime, Drama, Thriller}	109
	{Drama, Romance}	1,075		{Crime, Drama, Mystery, Thriller}	71
	{Comedy, Romance}	757		{Drama, Horror, Mystery, Thriller}	38
	{Crime, Drama}	448		{Adventure, Animation, Children, Comedy}	36
	{Drama, Thriller}	426		{Action, Adventure, Drama, War}	36

4 Movie Genres Formal Context and Concept Lattice

The objective of this paper is to use FCA in order to characterize movie genres. The first step is to construct a *formal context* describing the relation between movies and their genres. In this context, the objects are the movies, and the attributes are the genres. We draw an incidence between a movie and a genre whenever that movie has (belongs to) that genre.

To illustrate the construction of the formal context, we use a toy example as shown in Table 2, where we have seven well known movies, that are the objects of the formal context (the rows). Each movie belongs to one or more genres. The genres are the attributes, and hence shown in the columns of the context. For example, the movie *The Matrix* has three genres: Action, Thriller, and Sci-Fi; whereas the movie *Braveheart* has the three genres: Action, War, and Drama.

Table 2. Example formal context

	Crime	Action	War	Drama	Adventure	Thriller	Sci-Fi
The Matrix		×				×	×
Jurassic Park		×			×	×	×
Independence Day		×			×	×	×
Gladiator		×		×	×		
Braveheart		×	×	×			
The Godfather	×				×		
Batman	×	×				×	

The formal context constructed from our movie-genres dataset (Sect. 3) consists of 20 attributes corresponding to the 20 genres, and 27,278 objects corresponding to all the movies in the dataset. It consists of 54,406 incidences, each of which corresponds to an association of a movie and a genre.

In order to reduce the complexity of the formal context, we perform context *clarification*. A formal context is called *clarified* if the corresponding table does neither contain identical rows nor identical columns. Clarification can therefore be performed by removing identical rows and columns (only one of several identical rows/columns is left). In our case, many movies share the same set of genres; i.e., genres groups, as we can see in Table 1. The concept lattice derived from a clarified context is isomorphic to that one of the original formal context. In our example formal context (Table 2), the movies *Jurassic Park* and *Independence Day* have both the same set of genres, namely: Action, Adventure, Thriller, and Sci-Fi. Hence, it is possible to remove one of them and retain the other.

After performing clarification on the complete movie-genres formal context, the resulting clarified context consists of: 20 attributes, 1,342 objects (4.9%), and 5,145 incidences (9.5%). Since no two genres have the same set of movies, the clarified context has the same set of attributes (genres) as the original one. The next step is to use the clarified formal context in order to find all formal concepts, which can be then organised in a concept lattice.

Figure 2 shows the concept lattice corresponding to our formal context example (Table 2). For instance, under the top concept, we can see three concepts corresponding to the attributes/genres: Action, Drama and Crime. The concept corresponding to the Crime genre has two sub-concepts which correspond to the movies: *Batman* and *The Godfather*.

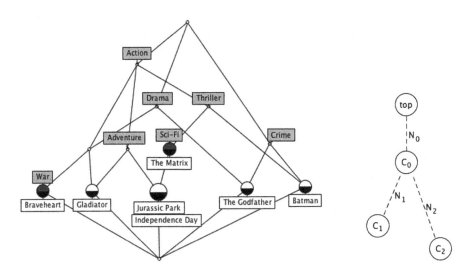

Fig. 2. Concept lattice of the example   **Fig. 3.** Edge distance

The actual concept lattice corresponding to the complete clarified formal context consists of 1,773 formal concepts. After the construction of this concept lattice, we re-populate each concept with its original set of objects/movies. Trivially, the top concept consists of all movies/objects (27,278) and has no attributes/genres. The immediate sub-concepts of the top concept are 20 concepts that correspond to the 20 attributes/genres. Also, the bottom concept has all the 20 attributes/genres, and has no objects. It has 265 immediate super-concepts.

5   Semantic Similarity of Movies

Recommender systems are tools which attempt to predict a user's interest towards an item, such as movies to watch, books to read, or products to buy. Recommender systems are popular in both commercial and research settings, and they are applied in a variety of applications such as movies, music, books, social connections and venues. In particular, movie recommender systems (such as Netflix) provide the customers with personal recommendations of movies they might like. Recommender systems usually make use of either or both collaborative filtering and content-based filtering. Content-based filtering methods are based on a description of the item and a profile of the user's preferences. They try to recommend items that are similar to those that a user liked in the past. Similarity between items is based on the content of the item, i.e., known data about the item. For instance, similarity between movies can be modeled using the properties of movies, such as title, description, actors, director, genres, etc.

To measure the similarity of two movies based on their sets of genres, one can use some set-based similarity measure, such as the Jaccard index: $S_{Jac}(x, y) = \frac{|x \cap y|}{|x \cup y|}$ or Sorensen coefficient: $S_{Sor}(x, y) = \frac{2|x \cap y|}{|x| + |y|}$.

One of the advantages of the movie-genre concept lattice that we constructed is the ability to compute semantic similarity between movies. Basically, the semantic similarity of movies can be measured by the semantic (conceptual) similarity of the *concepts* of the movies. In the literature, several semantic similarity measures were developed, including: (1) edge-based (path-length) similarities [13,15], (2) node-based similarities [12,14], and (3) FCA-based similarities [2].

5.1   Edge Based (Path Length) Similarities

Let C_1 and C_2 be two concepts in a concept lattice (or in a taxonomy or an is-a semantic net). A measure of the conceptual distance between C_1 and C_2 is given by the minimum number of edges separating C_1 and C_2 [13,15]. The measure for distance on the nodes could be a path metric, i.e. length of the shortest path between them. Let C_0 be the least (most specific) common superconcept (*lcs*) of the concepts C_1 and C_2 (Fig. 3). Let N_1 and N_2 be the number of edges (on a shortest path) from C_1 and C_2 to their *lcs*, respectively; then the distance between C_1 and C_2 is given by $d(C_1, C_2) = N_1 + N_2$. One can transform a distance metric into a similarity measure, as follows:

$$\mathbf{S}_p(C_1, C_2) = \frac{1}{1 + d(C_1, C_2)} = \frac{1}{1 + N_1 + N_2} \tag{1}$$

The problem with this measure is that, it makes no difference between similarities of node pairs located at different depths. To cope with this issue, the previous formula can be adjusted to account for the depth of the nodes within the lattice, as follows:

$$\mathbf{S}_{adj}(C_1, C_2) = \frac{1 + N_0}{1 + N_0 + N_1 + N_2} \tag{2}$$

where N_0 is the distance between the lcs C_0 and the root (top concept). Another adjusted formula is proposed by Wu and Palmer [16] as follows:

$$\mathbf{S}_{WP}(C_1, C_2) = \frac{2N_0}{2N_0 + N_1 + N_2} \tag{3}$$

5.2 Node Based (Information Content) Similarities

Resnik Similarity [14]. This similarity measure is based on the notion of information content. The information content of a concept is the logarithm of the probability of finding an instance of the concept.

$$\mathbf{S}_{Resnik}(C_1, C_2) = -\log P(C_0) \tag{4}$$

where C_0 is the least common superconcept (aka. lowest common subsumer) of the two concepts C_1 and C_2. In our case, the probability of a concept $C = (A, B)$ can be simply given as the fraction of the objects of that concept (its extent) to all the objects in the context (the set G): $P(C) = \frac{|A|}{|G|}$

Lin Similarity [12]. This similarity measure is based on Resnik's similarity, however it considers the information content of lowest common subsumer (*lcs*) and the two compared concepts. It is given by:

$$\mathbf{S}_{Lin}(C_1, C_2) = \frac{2 * \log P(C_0)}{\log P(C_1) + \log P(C_2)} \tag{5}$$

5.3 FCA-Based Similarities

Two similarity measures specific for FCA were proposed in [2]:

Weighted Concept Similarity . Given formal concepts $C_1 = (A_1, B_1)$, $C_2 = (A_2, B_2)$, the weighted concept similarity of C_1 and C_2 is

$$\mathbf{S}_S^w(C_1, C_2) = w.S(A_1, A_2) + (1 - w).S(B_1, B_2) \tag{6}$$

where $0 \leq w \leq 1$ and S is some set-based similarity measure, such as the Jaccard index or Sorensen coefficient.

Zero Induced Similarity. Formal concepts may be viewed as maximal sub-matrices full of ones in a formal context $\mathbb{K}$, and thus combining any two concepts $C_1 = (A_1, B_1)$ and $C_2 = (A_2, B_2)$ to form a larger sub-matrix $D = (A_1 \cup A_2, B_1 \cup B_2)$ must result in the introduction of zeros. The zeros induced by C_1 and C_2, denoted as $z(C_1, C_2)$, is the number of zeros enclosed by the sub-matrix induced by rows $(A_1 \cup A_2)$ and columns $(B_1 \cup B_2)$ in $\mathbb{K}$:

$$z(C_1, C_2) = \sum_{a \in A_1 \cup A_2} |(B_1 \cup B_2) \setminus a'|$$

The zeros-induced index of two concepts C_1 and C_2 is then given by:

$$\mathbf{S}_z = \frac{|A_1 \cup A_2|.|B_1 \cup B_2| - z(C_1, C_2)}{|A_1 \cup A_2|.|B_1 \cup B_2|} \tag{7}$$

5.4 Example

For example, let us consider the concept lattice example in Fig. 2, and let us measure the similarity between the movies *Batman* and *Jurassic Park*. We see that the *lcs* of these movies is the concept *Thriller*. We also can see that $N_1 = 2$, $N_2 = 1$, and $N_0 = 2$. Hence, $\mathbf{S}_p = \frac{1}{1+2+1} = 0.25$, $\mathbf{S}_{adj} = \frac{1+2}{1+2+2+1} = 0.5$, and $\mathbf{S}_{WP} = \frac{2*2}{2*2+2+1} = 0.57$.

Let us look at our example, and measure the similarity between the movies *Batman* and *Jurassic Park*. In this example, there are 7 movies: $|G| = 7$. The *lcs* of those movies is the concept *Thriller* which contains 4 movies, hence: $P(\text{Thriller}) = \frac{4}{7} = 0.57$. Then Resnik similarity is: $\mathbf{S}_{Resnik} = -\log P(\text{Thriller}) = 0.56$.

To find Lin similarity, we need also the probabilities of the compared concepts: $P(\text{Batman}) = \frac{1}{7}$, and $P(\text{Jurassic Park}) = \frac{2}{7}$.

$$\mathbf{S}_{Lin} = \frac{2 * \log P(\text{Thriller})}{\log P(\text{Batman}) + \log P(\text{Jurassic Park})} = \frac{2 * \log \frac{4}{7}}{\log \frac{1}{7} + \log \frac{2}{7}} = 0.35.$$

In our example, the concepts are: $C_1 = (\{\text{Batman}\}, \{\text{Crime, Action, Thriller}\})$, $C_2 = (\{\text{Jurassic Park, Independence Day}\}, \{\text{Action, Adventure, Thriller, Sci-Fi}\})$. Let $w = 0.5$, hence the weighted concept similarity is: $\mathbf{S}_{Jac}^{0.5}(C_1, C_2) = 0.2$ and $\mathbf{S}_{Sor}^{0.5}(C_1, C_2) = 0.29$.

To calculate the zero induced index, we draw the sub-context induced by the concepts C_1 and C_2, as shown in Table 3. The size of this sub-context is $3 \times 5 = 15$, and it introduces 4 zeros. Thus, $\mathbf{S}_z = \frac{15-4}{15} = 0.73$

Table 3. Sub-context induced by C_1 and C_2

		Crime	Action	Adventure	Thriller	Sci-Fi
C_1	Batman	×	×		×	
C_2	Jurassic Park		×	×	×	×
	Independence Day		×	×	×	×

6   Conclusion

In this paper, we have proposed to use Formal Concept Analysis in order to characterize movies and genres. We start be constructing a formal context, in which movies are the objects and the genres are the attributes. Since the size of the constructed formal context is large, we opt to clarify it, i.e., remove redundant objects. Then, using the formal context, formal concepts have been identified and organized in a concept lattice. A promising application of having a conceptual structure of movies and genres is the ability to measure semantic genre-based similarity among movies. We have presented several semantic similarity measures that were proposed in the literature. Those measures can be used as alternatives of traditional set-theory based measures (e.g., Jaccard) in many areas such as content-based recommender systems. However, an open question remains about the effectiveness of those measures and which one to choose. Answering this question requires a comparative study in the context of recommender systems, which will be the focus of our future work.

References

1. Alam, M., Buzmakov, A., Codocedo, V., Napoli, A.: Mining definitions from RDF annotations using formal concept analysis. In: 24th International Joint Conference on Artificial Intelligence, IJCAI, Buenos Aires, Argentina, pp. 823–829 (2015)
2. Alqadah, F., Bhatnagar, R.: Similarity measures in formal concept analysis. Ann. Math. Artif. Intell. **61**(3), 245–256 (2011)
3. Carpineto, C., Romano, G.: Using concept lattices for text retrieval and mining. In: Ganter, B., Stumme, G., Wille, R. (eds.) Formal Concept Analysis. LNCS (LNAI), vol. 3626, pp. 161–179. Springer, Heidelberg (2005). https://doi.org/10.1007/11528784_9
4. Ganter, B., Grigoriev, P.A., Kuznetsov, S.O., Samokhin, M.V.: Concept-based data mining with scaled labeled graphs. In: Wolff, K.E., Pfeiffer, H.D., Delugach, H.S. (eds.) ICCS-ConceptStruct 2004. LNCS (LNAI), vol. 3127, pp. 94–108. Springer, Heidelberg (2004). https://doi.org/10.1007/978-3-540-27769-9_6
5. Ganter, B., Wille, R.: Formal Concept Analysis. Springer, Heidelberg (1999). https://doi.org/10.1007/978-3-642-59830-2
6. Harper, F.M., Konstan, J.A.: The MovieLens datasets: history and context. ACM Trans. Interact. Intell. Syst. **5**(4), 19:1–19:19 (2015)
7. Hayward, S.: Cinema Studies: The Key Concepts. Routledge Key Guides, Taylor & Francis (2006)

8. Hwang, T.G., Park, C.S., Hong, J.H., Kim, S.K.: An algorithm for movie classification and recommendation using genre correlation. Multimedia Tools Appl. **75**(20), 12843–12858 (2016)
9. Ignatov, D.I.: Introduction to formal concept analysis and its applications in information retrieval and related fields. In: Braslavski, P., Karpov, N., Worring, M., Volkovich, Y., Ignatov, D.I. (eds.) RuSSIR 2014. CCIS, vol. 505, pp. 42–141. Springer, Cham (2015). https://doi.org/10.1007/978-3-319-25485-2_3
10. Kuznetsov, S.O.: Machine learning and formal concept analysis. In: Eklund, P. (ed.) ICFCA 2004. LNCS (LNAI), vol. 2961, pp. 287–312. Springer, Heidelberg (2004). https://doi.org/10.1007/978-3-540-24651-0_25
11. Kuznetsov, S.O.: Fitting pattern structures to knowledge discovery in big data. In: Cellier, P., Distel, F., Ganter, B. (eds.) ICFCA 2013. LNCS (LNAI), vol. 7880, pp. 254–266. Springer, Heidelberg (2013). https://doi.org/10.1007/978-3-642-38317-5_17
12. Lin, D.: An Information-Theoretic Definition of Similarity. In: In Proceedings of the 15th International Conference on Machine Learning, pp. 296–304 (1998)
13. Rada, R., Mili, H., Bicknell, E., Blettner, M.: Development and application of a metric on semantic nets. IEEE Trans. Syst. Man Cybern. **19**(1), 17–30 (1989)
14. Resnik, P.: Using Information Content to Evaluate Semantic Similarity in a Taxonomy. In: Proceedings of the 14th International Joint Conference on Artificial Intelligence, IJCAI 1995, vol. 1. pp. 448–453, San Francisco, CA, USA (1995)
15. Sologub, G.: On Measuring of similarity between tree nodes. In: Proceedings of Young Scientists Conference in Information Retrieval, pp. 63–71 (2011)
16. Wu, Z., Palmer, M.: Verbs Semantics and lexical selection. In: Proceedings of the 32nd Annual Meeting on Association for Computational Linguistics, pp. 133–138. ACL 1994, Association for Computational Linguistics, USA (1994)

Reasoning Models

Restricting the Maximum Number of Actions for Decision Support Under Uncertainty

Marcel Gehrke[1]📷, Tanya Braun[1]([✉])📷, and Simon Polovina[2]📷

[1] Institute of Information Systems, University of Lübeck, Lübeck, Germany
{gehrke,braun}@ifis.uni-luebeck.de
[2] Conceptual Structures Research Group, Sheffield Hallam University, Sheffield, UK
s.polovina@shu.ac.uk

Abstract. Standard approaches for decision support are computing a maximum expected utility or solving a partially observable Markov decision process. To the best of our knowledge, in both approaches, external restrictions are not accounted for. However, restrictions to actions often exists, for example in the form of limited resources. We demonstrate that restrictions to actions can lead to a combinatorial explosion if performed on a ground level, making ground inference intractable. Therefore, we extend a formalism that solves a lifted maximum expected utility problem to handle restricted actions. To test its relevance, we apply the new formalism to enterprise architecture analysis.

1 Introduction

Supporting decision making often involves suggesting from a pool of actions the action with the highest expected reward based on some reward function. Two standard approaches are solving a maximum expected utility (MEU) problem in a probabilistic model to find the action with the highest expected utility [19] or solving a partially observable Markov decision process (POMDP) [2,4] yielding a policy that maps belief states to actions. To the best of our knowledge, in both approaches, external restrictions are not accounted for. However, resources are not limitless, leading to restrictions on actions. Consider a small company with five employees and ten tasks to be performed. If each employee can only perform one task at a time, delegating all ten tasks is not possible. Hence, the number of possible actions (delegating a task) actually is restricted to five.

That inference is intractable in general [5] becomes noticeable if modelling all tasks and employees as propositional random variables (randvars) with the number of tasks and employees reasonably high. Further, with each task an own randvar, restricting the number of executable tasks is not straightforward. In a lifted model with lifted computations, however, inference is at most polynomial in domain sizes [20], leading to tractable inference for models with many tasks and employees. Additionally, in lifted decision support, actions are executed for

M. Alam et al. (Eds.): ICCS 2020, LNAI 12277, pp. 145–160, 2020.
https://doi.org/10.1007/978-3-030-57855-8_11

sets of indistinguishable individuals. Therefore, in this paper, we investigate how to restrict actions in lifted models to given numbers of individuals.

Specifically, we focus on solving MEU problems in parameterised probabilistic decision models (PDecMs) to support online decision support in contrast to the offline support provided by (relational) POMDPs. To this end, this paper contributes (i) a restricted version of PDecMs, which allows for specifying resources, overall as well as required per action, and restrictions on the number of times an action is executable, and (ii) an algorithm called ReLiA for restricted lifted assignments, which computes all possible lifted assignments in restricted PDecMs by building on the Ford-Fulkerson algorithm for computing a maximum flow in a network [8]. Given the assignments computed, one can solve the MEU problem in the underlying model. Using ReLiA leads to significantly fewer assignments to test for MEU in contrast to working with all permutations of assignments, lifted or ground. The contributions are accompanied by an ongoing case study to highlight an application. We end with an application of our formalism to enterprise architecture (EA) analysis.

2   Case Study Setup

In this section, we show how to support decision making with PDecMs. Along the way, we recapitulate parameterised probabilistic models (PMs), first introduced by Poole [21], and PDecMs, based on [9]. The case study involves a simple case of business process modelling with a pool of employees and a set of tasks, which need delegating in a way that as many tasks as possible are delegated while avoiding tasks being overdue. The following sections set up a fitting PDecM.

2.1   Parameterised Probabilistic Model

In PMs, parameterised randvars (PRVs) represent sets of indistinguishable randvars, with logical variables (logvars) as parameters. For the case study, we model tasks being done as a PRV using a randvar for done with a logvar for tasks. For the sake of simplicity, all tasks are equally important, making them indistinguishable. After defining PMs, we set up PRVs for the case study.

Definition 1 (PRV, parfactor, PM). *Let $\mathbf{R}$ be a set of randvar names, $\mathbf{L}$ a set of logvar names, Φ a set of factor names, and $\mathbf{D}$ a set of constants. All sets are finite. Each logvar L has a domain $\mathcal{D}(L) \subseteq \mathbf{D}$. A constraint is a tuple $(\mathcal{X}, C_{\mathbf{X}})$ of a sequence of logvars $\mathcal{X} = (X_1, \ldots, X_n)$ and a set $C_{\mathcal{X}} \subseteq \times_{i=1}^n \mathcal{D}(X_i)$. The symbol $\top$ for C marks that no restrictions apply, i.e., $C_{\mathcal{X}} = \times_{i=1}^n \mathcal{D}(X_i)$. A PRV $R(L_1, \ldots, L_n), n \geq 0$ is a construct of a randvar $R \in \mathbf{R}$ possibly combined with logvars $L_1, \ldots, L_n \in \mathbf{L}$. If $n = 0$, the PRV is parameterless and forms a propositional randvar. The term $\mathcal{R}(A)$ denotes the possible values (range) of a PRV A. An event $A = a$ denotes the occurrence of PRV A with range value $a \in \mathcal{R}(A)$. We denote a parametric factor (parfactor) g by $\phi(\mathcal{A})_{|C}$ with $\mathcal{A} = (A_1, \ldots, A_n)$ a sequence of PRVs, $\phi : \times_{i=1}^n \mathcal{R}(A_i) \mapsto \mathbb{R}^+$ a function with name $\phi \in \Phi$, and C a constraint on the logvars of $\mathcal{A}$. A PRV A or logvar L under* constraint C is given by $A_{|C}$ or $L_{|C}$, respectively. We may omit $|\top$ in $A_{|\top}$, $L_{|\top}$, or $\phi(\mathcal{A})_{|\top}$. A PM G is a set of parfactors $\{g_i\}_{i=1}^n$.

The term $rv(P)$ refers to the set of PRVs with their constraints in a parfactor or PM, $lv(P)$ to the logvars. The term $gr(P)$ denotes the set of all instances of P w.r.t. given constraints. An instance is an instantiation (grounding) of P, substituting the logvars in P with a set of constants from given constraints. If P is a constraint, $gr(P)$ refers to the second component $C_{\mathbf{X}}$. Given a parfactor $\phi(\mathcal{A})_{|C}$, ϕ is identical for the propositional randvars in $gr(\mathcal{A}_{|C})$.

Given $\mathbf{R} = \{Done, Overdue\}$, $\mathbf{L} = \{X\}$, and $\mathcal{D}(X) = \{x_1, \ldots, x_{100}\}$, we build boolean PRVs $Done(X)$ and $Overdue(X)$. With $C = ((X), \{(x_1), (x_2)\})$, $gr(Done(X)_{|C}) = \{Done(x_1), Done(x_2)\}$. The set of $gr(Done(X)_{|\top})$ also contains the instances $Done(x_3) \ldots Done(x_{100})$.

The semantics of a model is given by grounding and building a full joint distribution. In general, a query asks for a probability distribution of a randvar given the full joint of a model and fixed events as evidence. Answering a query then requires eliminating all randvars in G not occurring in the query.

Definition 2 (Semantics, query). *With Z as normalising constant, a model G represents the full joint distribution $P_G = \frac{1}{Z} \prod_{f \in gr(G)} f$. The term $P(Q|\mathbf{E})$ denotes a query in G with Q a grounded PRV and $\mathbf{E}$ a set of events.*

PMs allow for modelling relational aspects between objects including recurring patterns in these relations. PDecMs build on PMs, also containing actions and utilities to support decision making.

2.2   Parameterised Probabilistic Decision Model

For the case study, we need to encode in our model that overdue tasks lead to a punishment, i.e., negative utility, and done tasks lead to a reward, i.e., positive utility. To this end, we need to form a PDecM, which contains actions and utilities [9]. Actions are modelled using PRVs with the actions in its range. Utilities are modelled with PRVs as well, which are identical for groups of indistinguishable objects, leading to utility parfactors, defined as follows.

Definition 3 (PDecM). *Let Φ_u be a set of utility factor names. A parfactor with a utility PRV U as output is a utility parfactor $\mu(\mathcal{A})_{|C}$ where C is a constraint on $lv(\mathcal{A})$ and μ is given by $\mu : \times_{A \in \mathcal{A} \setminus \{U\}} \mathcal{R}(A) \mapsto \mathbb{R}$, with $\mu \in \Phi_u$. The output of μ is the value of U. A PDecM G is a PM with an additional set G_u of utility parfactors. The term $rv(G_u)$ refers to all probability PRVs in G_u. G_u represents the combination of all utilities $U_G = \sum_{v \in \times_{r \in rv(gr(G_u))} \mathcal{R}(r)} P_{G_u}(v)$.*

The semantics already shows how lifting can speed up performance: The calculations for each $f \in gr(g_u), g_u \in G^u$ are identical, allowing for rewriting summing over all groundings $f \in gr(g_u)$ into a product of $|gr(g_u)|$ and g_u.

For the case study, we introduce a boolean action PRV $Delegate(X)$ to delegate tasks and a parameterless utility PRV $Util$ to amass rewards and punishments. Figure 1 shows the model with $Delegate(X)$ and $Util$ in grey next to regular PRVs $Done(X)$ and $Overdue(X)$. Further, a utility parfactor g^u (crosses) and a regular parfactor g_0 are depicted, which connect $Done(X)$ and $Overdue(X)$ with $Delegate(X)$ and $Util$, respectively. The potentials in g^u encode that a task done on time gets a high positive utility, an overdue task done gets a small positive utility, an overdue task not done gets a high negative utility, and a task that is not done but also not overdue gets a small negative utility.

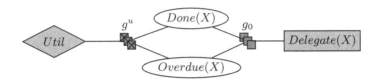

Fig. 1. Delegating tasks with action and utility nodes in grey

On such a PDecM, one can solve an MEU problem to determine the best actions, i.e., how to delegate tasks (without any restrictions). To define the MEU problem on a PDecM, we need to define expected utilities in a PDecM. The MEU problem asks for those action assignments that lead to the *maximum* expected utility, defined as follows.

Definition 4 (Expected utility, MEU). *Given a PDecM G, events $\mathbf{E}$, action assignments $\mathbf{a}$, the expected utility of G is defined by*

$$eu(\mathbf{E}, \mathbf{a}) = \sum_{v \in \times_{r \in rv(G)} \mathcal{R}(r)} P(v|\mathbf{E}, \mathbf{a}) \cdot U(v, \mathbf{E}, \mathbf{a}) \tag{1}$$

with $U(\mathbf{V})$ the utility of PRVs $\mathbf{V}$. Then, the MEU problem is given by

$$meu[G|\mathbf{E}] = (\arg\max_{\mathbf{a}} eu(\mathbf{E}, \mathbf{a}), \max_{\mathbf{a}} eu(\mathbf{E}, \mathbf{a})). \tag{2}$$

The inner product in Eq. (1) calculates a belief state $P(v|\mathbf{E}, \mathbf{a})$ and combines it with corresponding utilities $U(v, \mathbf{E}, \mathbf{a})$. By summing over the range of all PRVs of G, one obtains a scalar representing an expected utility. Equation (2) suggests a naive algorithm for solving an MEU problem, namely by iterating over all possible action assignments, solving Eq. (1) for each assignment. However, with lifting, the complexity of computing Eq. (2) is no longer exponential in the number of ground actions, enabling tractable inference in terms of domain sizes [20]. Instead of the domain sizes, the complexity is exponential in the number of groups forming due to evidence, which is usually very much lower than the number of constants in domains.

Assume that we observe whether a task is overdue. Observations are of the range of $Overdue(X)$ (boolean). Thus, X can be split into three groups, with observed values of $true$, of $false$, or no observation. For each group individually, $Delegate(X)$ can be set to either $true$ or $false$. Thus, there are 2^1 to 2^3 action assignments depending on evidence.

In Fig. 1, simply delegating all tasks leads to the highest expected utility. However, with limited resources or other more general restrictions, it might not be possible to perform all actions. E.g., employees can only perform one task at a time and there is not an unbounded number of employees. Such restrictions currently are not captured in PDecMs.

3   ReLiA: Restricting Lifted Action Assignments

In our case study, we have a pool of employees that can perform tasks, which so far have no effect on the model. Therefore, we introduce two types of restrictions. The first type restricts how often an action can be performed, i.e., an action can be performed at most five times. The second type restricts resources, e.g., an action can only be performed if sufficient resources are available. Within the boundaries of restrictions, ReLiA constructs possible action assignments. Solving the corresponding MEU problem only requires iterating over the assignments computed by ReLiA, saving unnecessary computations. Algorithm 1 shows an overview of the steps of ReLiA, which we present in the next sections.

3.1   Restricting Actions

To restrict actions, we need a way to specify resources required for an action and how often an action is executable. We first introduce resources to the model.

Definition 5 (Resources). *Let* **B** *be a set of resource names. Each resource B has assigned a number of available resources $v \in \mathbb{N}$, denoted by $B = v$.*

To restrict actions, we introduce action parfactors. An action parfactor specifies resources required and restrictions on executions for one action PRV.

Definition 6 (Action parfactors). *Let Θ be a set of* action *factor names. We denote an* action parfactor *g by $\theta(A)_{|C}$ with A an action PRV, $\theta : \mathcal{R}(A) \mapsto ((B, \mathbb{N}), \mathbb{N})$ a function with name $\theta \in \Theta$ and $B \in$ **B***, and C a constraint on the logvars of A. The first element of the tuple, $(B, \mathbb{N})$, denotes how many resources of B are required to set A to the corresponding range value for one grounding. The second element of the tuple determines how often the corresponding range value can be selected. The symbol $\perp$ indicates that no restrictions apply. A restricted PDecM G is a PDecM, which also contains a set of action parfactors G_a.*

Algorithm 1. ReLiA: Construct Lifted Action Assignments under Restrictions

  function ReLiA(Restricted model G)
      Resource graph $R \leftarrow$ ConstructResourceGraph(G)
      Assignments **A** $\leftarrow$ ObtainAssignments(R, $|G_a|$)
      return A   ▷ Input to an algorithm solving an MEU problem

---

Action parfactors are ignored during calculations for query answering since they do not form a part of a full joint. Given $\mathbf{B} = \{Employee\}$, we specify that there are 15 employees by setting $Employee = 15$. Further, we specify an action parfactor for our action PRV $Delegate(X)$. We specify that setting the action to true requires one employee with $(Employee, 1)$ and that the action can be set to true at most 20 times, i.e., $true \mapsto ((Employee, 1), 20)$ Setting the action to false does not require any resources and can be set to false as often as desired, leading to $\perp$ in both cases, i.e., $false \mapsto (\perp, \perp)$.

With the pool of employees incorporated, our restricted PDecM fully represents our initial setting. But, we still need a way to efficiently identify valid assignments to the action PRV, which we present next. Afterwards, we are able to iterate over these assignments to solve the corresponding MEU problem.

3.2 Computing All Action Assignments Given Restrictions

Our case study has 15 employees and 100 tasks. Assume that 10 tasks are overdue (evidence), which leads to splitting X into two groups, X' for the 90 tasks without evidence and X'' for the overdue tasks. A valid action assignment would be $Delegate(X'') = true$, requiring 10 employees, $Delegate(X') = true$ for 5 X' instances (5 employees), and $Delegate(X') = false$ for the remaining 85 instances. Another assignment is $Delegate(X'') = false$, $Delegate(X') = true$ for 15 X' instances, and $Delegate(X') = false$ for the remaining 75 instances. The assignments $Delegate(X'') = true$, $Delegate(X') = false$ as well as $Delegate(X'') = false$, $Delegate(X') = false$ do not use all resources available.

To construct such action assignments, we reformulate our problem as a max-flow problem [11] to benefit from the well-understood problem of computing a maximum flow in a network with capacities. To formulate our problem as a max-flow problem, we build a resource graph from our resource restrictions. Ford and Fulkerson [8] propose a well-known algorithm to solve the max-flow problem. However, we are not only interested in one set of paths that maximises the flow, but all assignments that maximise the flow. Thus, we present how ReLiA builds a resource graph and then identifies all flows.

Constructing a Resource Graph. The resource graph needs to account for the number of groundings, restrictions of how often an action is applicable, and resource restrictions. Algorithm 2 outlines how ReLiA constructs such a resource graph R with a model G as input. G is a restricted PDecM, which has its parfactors already split based on evidence. First, ReLiA adds a source node S and a target node T to R. Second, ReLiA goes through all action parfactors g_a to span R. For an action parfactor g_a, ReLiA adds a node $temp^i$ as a successor to S to R. Then, ReLiA assigns the number of groundings of g_a as capacity. By definition, the set of PRVs of each action parfactor contains exactly one action PRV. Next, ReLiA iterates over all range values of the action PRV A in g_a to account for the given restrictions specified in the action parfactor.

Algorithm 2. Constructing Resource Graph

---

function CONSTRUCTRESOURCEGRAPH(Restricted model G)
    Resource graph R with starting node S and target node T
    for $g_a \in G_a$ of G **do**
        Add node $temp^i$ and edge $S \longrightarrow temp^i$ to R
        Assign $|gr(g_a)|$ as capacity to $S \longrightarrow temp^i$
        Action PRV $A \leftarrow rv(g_a)$
        for $r \in \mathcal{R}(A)$ **do**
            if $A = r$ not a node in R **then**
                Add node $A = r$ to R
                Add node $temp^r$ and edge $A = r \longrightarrow temp^r$ to R
                Get $((B,n),m)$ from $\theta(A = r)$
                Assign m as capacity to $A = r \longrightarrow temp^r$
                if B not a node in R **then**
                    Add node B and edge $B \longrightarrow T$ to R
                    Assign v from resource restriction $B = v$ as capacity to R
                Add edge $temp^r \longrightarrow B$ to R
                Assign capacity ∞ to $temp^r \longrightarrow B$ and n
            Add edge $temp^i \longrightarrow A = r$ to R
            Assign capacity ∞ to $temp^i \longrightarrow A = r$
    return R

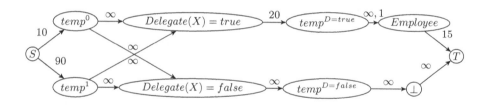

Fig. 2. Resource graph for our example

For each range value r, ReLiA checks if a node $A = r$ for the assignment of action r to action PRV A is already included in R. This check is included as evidence may split parfactors including action parfactors, leading to multiple parfactors regarding different instances of the same action PRV and therefore, $A = r$ may already be in R. However, the restrictions defined in the action parfactors still apply over all split action parfactors combined. If r is not included in R, ReLiA ensures that the restrictions of r are represented in R. To this end, ReLiA adds a node $A = r$ to R. Further, ReLiA adds a node $temp^r$ to R to be able to represent that a range value as well as a resource can be restricted while accounting for the fact that a resource can be used in multiple actions.

For the resource restriction, ReLiA obtains the name of the resource, B, the number of the resource used for executing that range value for one grounding, n, and the restriction of how often r can be selected, m. Then, ReLiA adds an edge from $A = r$ to $temp^r$ to R and assigns m as capacity to the edge.

Next, ReLiA checks if there already exists a node B corresponding to this resource in R. In case there is no node B, ReLiA adds a node B to R as well as an edge from B to T with the corresponding resource restriction v of the model, $B = v$, as capacity. Having B in the model, ReLiA adds an edge between $temp^r$ and B while storing how many resources selecting the range value requires, i.e., storing n. When calculating the maximum flow, ReLiA has to multiply all values arriving at $temp^r$ with n to obtain the resources used at B from r. After ReLiA has added the nodes and edges for the resource restrictions and resources, it adds an edge between $temp^i$ and $A = r$ to R without any capacity limitations to connect this path to S over $temp^i$. In the last step, after having iterated over all resources, range values, and actions parfactors, ReLiA returns R.

Figure 2 shows the corresponding resource graph for our case study. We can see that our tasks are split into 2 groups. The first group with 10 tasks that are overdue corresponds to $temp^0$ and the other group with 90 tasks, where we have no additional information, corresponds to $temp^1$. For both groups, we have the very same action PRV, leading to both $temp^0$ and $temp^1$ being connected to the same range values without any capacity restrictions. Overall, delegating a task can be done at most 20 times as shown on the edge between $Delegate(X) = true$ and $Temp^{D=true}$. Further, delegating a task requires 1 employee, evident at the edge between $Temp^{D=true}$ and $Employee$. Additionally, there are 15 employees as depicted on the edge between $Employee$ and T. For not assigning a task, no restrictions apply, which can be seen in the lower part of the network with the paths going over $Delegate(X) = false$.

Based on such a graph, ReLiA computes all action assignments within the boundaries of the restrictions, which is a max-flow problem on such a graph.

Calculating Assignments of Maximum Flow. To obtain all action assignments that lead to the maximum flow in a given resource graph, ReLiA has to iterate over all action PRVs and their corresponding range values. The rough idea is that for each action parfactor, ReLiA has to select paths from source to target. By combining all paths, ReLiA obtains valid action assignments. An assumption we make for ReLiA is that each action PRV always has an unrestricted default case. In the case study, the unrestricted default case in $Delegate(X) = false$, which has no further restrictions as denoted by the $\bot$ symbols.

Algorithm 3 outlines how ReLiA obtains assignments. Inputs are a resource graph R of a model G and the number num of action parfactors in G, i.e., $num = |G_a|$. First, ReLiA fills a list $\mathbf{n}$ of nodes to traverse with all $temp^i$ nodes, which correspond to action parfactors. Second, ReLiA calls a function named COMPILE with $\mathbf{n}$ and an empty list of paths, $\mathbf{p}$, to compute assignments.

In COMPILE, ReLiA gets the first node, $currentNode$, from $\mathbf{n}$ and computes all possible paths from S to T over $currentNode$ that assign an action to all instances of the action parfactor behind $currentNode$. The paths are constructed in a way that they always use as many instances as possible. For each path, ReLiA also has to obtain assignments for all other action parfactors. Therefore, ReLiA calls COMPILE again with the current path(s) and the remaining nodes

Algorithm 3. Obtaining All Assignments

---

function OBTAINASSIGNMENTS(Resource graph R, number of action parf. num)
    n empty list of nodes
    p empty list of paths
    $i := 0$
    for $i < num$ **do**
        $\mathbf{n} = \mathbf{n} + temp^i$
    return COMPILE($\mathbf{n}, \mathbf{p}$)

---

function COMPILE(Nodes to traverse **n**, current paths **p**)
    $currentNode :=$ pop **n**
    for each successor $A = r$ of $currentNode$ **do**
        $tempP :=$ path from S over $currentNode$ and r to T
        $\mathbf{p}' := tempP + \mathbf{p}$
        if $tempP$ uses all capacities of $currentNode$ **then**
            if n not empty **then**
                return COMPILE($\mathbf{n}, \mathbf{p}'$)
            else
                $a :=$ get all capacities and their assignments from $\mathbf{p}'$
                return a
        else
            for each possible completion to use all capacities of $currentNode$ **do**
                $\mathbf{p}' := \mathbf{p}' +$ completion path(s)
                if n not empty **then**
                    return COMPILE($\mathbf{n}, \mathbf{p}'$)
                else
                    $a :=$ get all capacities and their assignments from $\mathbf{p}'$
                    return a

---

to traverse. Last, when ReLiA has no more nodes to traverse, it obtains the assignments and the corresponding capacities by propagating the used capacities backwards from the target to the source. Overall, ReLiA roughly computes max^{num} action assignments, where max refers to the highest number of range values in any of the action PRVs and $num = |G_a|$ as above.

Let us explain Algorithm 3 in more detail by having a look at the resource graph in Fig. 2. ReLiA starts by adding $temp^0$ and $temp^1$ to **n**. Then, ReLiA calls the helper function COMPILE with **n** and an empty list of paths **p**. In COMPILE, $temp^0$ becomes $currentNode$. The capacity between S and $temp^0$ is 10. As $temp^0$ comes from the action parfactor with two values in the range of its action PRV, $temp^0$ has two assignments, $Delegate(X) = true$ and $Delegate(X) = false$, as successors. For the first assignment, $Delegate(X) = true$, ReLiA finds a path from S over $temp^0$ and $Delegate(X) = true$ to T. Thus, the path is added to $\mathbf{p}'$. That path is able to let all 10 instances of the capacity flow to T. Then, ReLiA again calls COMPILE.

This time, **n** only contains $temp^1$ and $\mathbf{p}'$ contains one path. Now, $temp^1$ becomes $currentNode$, which again has two assignments as successors, over which ReLiA iterates. For the first assignment, $Delegate(X) = true$, ReLiA finds a path from S over $temp^1$ and $Delegate(X) = true$ to T. Thus, the path is added to $\mathbf{p}'$, leading to two paths being in $\mathbf{p}'$. This newly added path does not send all 90 instances, but only 5 since 5 is the remaining capacity on the last edge going into T. The remaining 85 instances can be send from S over $temp^1$ and $Delegate(X) = false$ to T, which then is added to $\mathbf{p}'$. In case there would be other paths to use all instances, ReLiA would have to iterate over them. Having no more nodes to travers, ReLiA computes the assignment for the paths in $\mathbf{p}'$. Here, ReLiA outputs $Delegate(X) = true$ for the 10 overdue tasks, $Delegate(X) = true$ for 5 tasks, where we have no additional information, and $Delegate(X) = false$ for the remaining 85 tasks.

We now jump back to the point where ReLiA iterates over all successors of $temp^1$ with $\mathbf{p}'$ containing only the path from S over $temp^0$ and $Delegate(X) = true$ to T sending 10 instances. The node $temp^1$ has another assignment, namely $Delegate(X) = false$, as successor and ReLiA finds a path from S over $temp^1$ and $Delegate(X) = false$ to T. Hence, that path is added to $\mathbf{p}'$ in addition to the one path from $temp^0$ in $\mathbf{p}$. That path uses all 90 instances, leading to an assignment of $Delegate(X) = true$ for the 10 overdue tasks and $Delegate(X) = false$ for 90 tasks, where we have no additional information.

ReLiA also traverses the path for $Delegate(X) = false$ for $temp^0$, for which ReLiA again has to traverse all paths from $temp^1$ as it is still contained in $\mathbf{n}$ at this point. Finally, ReLiA returns four action assignments to test for MEU. In addition to the two assignments above, the third assignment set reads $Delegate(X) = false$ for the 10 overdue tasks, $Delegate(X) = true$ for 15 tasks, where we have no additional information, and $Delegate(X) = false$ for the remaining 75 tasks. The forth assignment set contains $Delegate(X) = false$ for the 10 overdue tasks and $Delegate(X) = false$ for the 90 tasks, where we have no additional information. Hence, ReLiA computes the desired four action assignments with corresponding capacities that obey all restrictions.

Before we discuss theoretical aspects of ReLiA, we consider related work of lifted inference and relational decision support.

3.3   Related Work

We take a look at inference under uncertainty in relational models as well as relational decision support.

First-order probabilistic inference leverages relational aspects. For models with known domain size, it exploits symmetries in a model by handling indistinguishable instances with representatives, known as lifting [21]. Poole [21] introduces parametric factor graphs as relational models and proposes lifted variable elimination (LVE) as an exact inference algorithm on relational models. Other lifted inference algorithms include (i) the lifted junction tree algorithm (LJT) [6], (ii) first-order knowledge compilation [7], (iii) probabilistic theorem proving [10], and (iv) lifted belief propagation [1],

Nath and Domingos [16] introduce Markov logic decision networks (MLDNs), which are relational models with action and utility nodes. Nath and Domingos calculate approximate solutions to an MEU problem in a MLDN, grounding the model [18]. Another approach of Nath and Domingos includes unnecessary groundings [17]. Apsel and Brafman [3] propose an exact lifted solution to the MEU problem based on [16]. Gehrke et al. [9] extend LJT to meuLJT to solve MEU problems in PDecMs exactly while also supporting marginal queries.

Additional research focuses on sequential decision making by investigating first-order (PO)MDPs [13,23,24], which use lifting techniques from de Salvo Braz, Amir, and Roth [22]. In contrast to first-order POMDPs, which are solved offline using policy iteration, we propose to support online decision making, i.e., by solving an MEU problem. In this paper, we introduce resources and enable restriction actions to bring PDecMs closer to real-world applications.

3.4   Discussion

In this section, we discuss the assumption we make about restrictions as well as how to compute an MEU with the possible actions.

Assumptions about Restrictions. An assumption we make is that each action parfactor has a default action, which is unrestricted. The implication of the assumption for ReLiA is that it has to iterate over all action parfactors one time. In case such an assumption would not hold, the difference would be that the order in which ReLiA iterates over the action parfactors could matter in the sense that a different iteration order could lead to other assignments for actions. Thus, without the assumption, ReLiA would need to iterate over each permutation of action parfactors to calculate the action assignments.

Extending our Case Study. An interesting extension to our case study is to introduce hard tasks as a new logvar name with a corresponding PRVs and action parfactor. Assume that delegating a hard tasks requires two employees for execution. Although our model then has two different action PRVs and the two corresponding action parfactors require the same resource, ReLiA computes valid assignments given the number of employees available. While constructing the resource graph, ReLiA identifies that both action parfactors require the same type of resource, even though they concern different action PRVs. Thus, there only is one node for employees in the resource graph. While computing the assignments, ReLiA ensures that the capacity gets multiplied with 2 when taking the edge between the nodes $temp^{DelegateHardTask(Y)}$ and $Employee$ in the corresponding resource graph. Hence, the required resources to perform an action are accounted for. Similar to our case study so far, with splits due to evidence, both action parfactors pointing to the same resource poses no problem to ReLiA.

To complete our case study, we briefly describe how to obtain the best action for the action assignments next.

Computing an MEU. Having the action assignments, any algorithm solving the lifted MEU problem, e.g., [3,9], can calculate best actions leading to the highest expected utility. The action assignments ReLiA computes are the actions to iterate over in Eq. (2). Thus, an algorithm solving the MEU problem does not have to generate (all) action assignments anymore. However, normally in a lifted MEU, a range value of an action is selected for each group of indistinguishable instances. The action assignments of ReLiA do not necessarily assign the same range value for all indistinguishable instances of a group as a result of the restrictions. In our case study, one assignment is $Delegate(X) = false$ for the 10 overdue tasks, $Delegate(X) = true$ for 15 tasks, where we have no additional information, and $Delegate(X) = false$ for the remaining 75 tasks. Thus, the tasks, for which we have no additional information, need to be split even further. As all instances are indistinguishable, it does not matter which instances are split off. Thus, an algorithm solving the MEU problem using the action assignments of ReLiA might need to split logvars before it can calculate the corresponding expected utility.

3.5   Theoretical Analysis

Let us now investigate the theoretical implications of ReLiA. Here, we focus on two points, namely whether always using the maximum capacity for paths to obtain assignments is reasonable as well as how ReLiA compares to calculating action assignments in a similar fashion for a ground model.

Fewest Possible Action Sets. ReLiA only obtains assignments with the highest possible capacity given the restrictions, e.g., $Delegate(X) = true$ for the 10 overdue tasks. In theory, ReLiA could also compute all other assignments, e.g., $Delegate(X) = true$ for 9 overdue tasks and $Delegate(X) = false$ for the one remaining overdue task, $Delegate(X) = true$ for 8 and $Delegate(X) = false$ for 2, and so on. The reason why ReLiA only obtains assignments with the highest capacity and not also all other possible assignment lies within the semantics of PDecMs. Computing an expected utility involves adding up all utilities at the end. Assuming that the two action range values map to different potentials and keeping in mind that the instances within a group are indistinguishable, one of the range values leads to a higher expected utility than the other, which is true for all instances of that group. Thus, we only need to check assigning all instances either the one value or the other. As a consequence, ReLiA only has to obtain assignments with the highest possible capacity. Preferably, ReLiA assigns all instances the same action but with restrictions, groups may be split further to stay within the boundaries of the restrictions. Hence, by only obtaining assignments with the highest capacity, ReLiA provides reasonable assignments and highly reduces the number of action assignments to reason over.

Comparison to the Ground Case. While computing action assignments, ReLiA uses the fact that instances are indistinguishable. Calculating such action assignments on a ground model, a corresponding algorithm could not exploit this fact. Without indistinguishable instances, such an algorithm would have to model actions for each instance. Each instance would be connected to the source with an edge having a capacity of 1. ReLiA iterates over all of these nodes and then their range values. As mentioned above, ReLiA roughly computes max^{num}, where num is the number of action parfactors after splitting. In a ground case the number of assignments would be max^{num}, where num is the number of groundings of action parfactors, which can be a huge number. In our example num would be 100, so even for boolean range values a ground algorithm would have to compute roughly 2^{100} action assignments. Hence, there is a combinatorial blow up as all permutations of actions would need to be tested. Further, while solving an MEU problem, there are many redundant calculations, which is infeasible for large enough numbers. Therefore, restricting resources and actions in a lifted case allows for a practical formalism.

4   Case Study: Enterprise Architecture Analysis

Johnson et al. [12] present an Enterprise Architecture (EA) analysis, extending propositional influence diagrams, which essentially are Bayesian networks with utility and action or decision nodes added. They do not consider the relational aspect, which blows up a propositional model if many components, processes, or employees are involved. Therefore, we can review EA analysis using PDecMs and consider what role ReLiA can play in this analysis. We take the case study in [12] and adapt it to the relational setting, which enables us to consider employees and work stations.

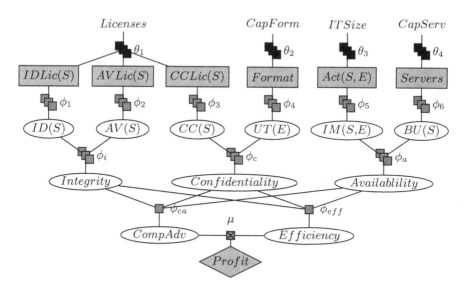

Fig. 3. A PDecM about IT security components (resources are represented as nodes without a border)

Figure 3 shows a PDecM for an EA scenario regarding IT security for a company where a decision maker has to set up an architecture for its IT security system. The model considers the following components of IT security as randvars: (i) intrusion detection applications (ID), (ii) anti-virus applications (AV), (iii) cryptographic control applications (CC), (iv) user training processes (UT), (v) incident management processes (IM), and (vi) back-up processes (BU). The randvars are parameterised with S for work stations and E for employees where appropriate. Regarding the applications, there are decisions to be made about the number of licenses to purchase, which may be limited. Regarding user training, the format of the training sessions is to be considered in terms of cost and number of people that can be trained at once. Regarding incident management, the number of people trained to handle incidents is limited. Regarding back-ups, the capacity of servers is limited. Overall, these components influence the integrity, confidentiality, and availability of a company, which in turn influence the competitive advantage as well as the efficiency emerging out of the decisions, which then influences the profit the company might make.

Given different scenarios for capacities, ReLiA computes the action assignments to consider for each scenario. Using these assignment sets, meuLJT solves the corresponding MEU problems for each scenario, yielding one MEU assignment set for each scenario. The decision maker then can compare the results and incorporate further external factors in their final decision.

5   Conclusion

We introduce restrictions to PDecMs as a representation for models to support decision making. Restrictions are crucial as not every action can be performed as often as desired as well as resources are not limitless. We presnt ReLiA to compute all possible lifted assignments in restricted PDecMs. ReLiA computes all required action assignments, which an algorithm that solves the MEU problem in a lifted way can iterate over to identify best actions given restrictions. Further, ReLiA significantly reduces the assignment space to iterate over, making explicit that calculating assignments under restrictions is only feasible in lifted models.

Future work includes investigating whether actions can be learnt online, as for example Morgenstern does for agents using a specific logic [15]. Another interesting path would be to look into the situation calculus [14] and investigate whether additional restrictions can be included for decision support without adding another layer of logic on top. Additionally, we look into applying the presented theory to business process modelling. Johnson et al. [12] enabled us to show the usefulness of the theory in EA analysis for extended influence diagrams, going beyond propositional probabilistic models. With many instances, a lifted approach such as the presented one appears to be indispensable.

References

1. Ahmadi, B., Kersting, K., Mladenov, M., Natarajan, S.: Exploiting symmetries for scaling loopy belief propagation and relational training. Mach. Learn. **92**(1), 91–132 (2013)

2. Aoki, M.: Optimal control of partially observable Markovian systems. J. Franklin Inst. **280**(5), 367–386 (1965)
3. Apsel, U., Brafman, R.I.: Extended lifted inference with joint formulas. In: Proceedings of the 27th Conference on Uncertainty in Artificial Intelligence, pp. 11–18. AUAI Press (2011)
4. Åström, K.J.: Optimal control of Markov processes with incomplete state information. J. Math. Anal. Appl. **10**(1), 174–205 (1965)
5. Boyen, X., Koller, D.: Tractable inference for complex stochastic processes. In: Proceedings of the Fourteenth Conference on Uncertainty in Artificial Intelligence. pp. 33–42. Morgan Kaufmann Publishers Inc. (1998)
6. Braun, T., Möller, R.: Lifted junction tree algorithm. In: Friedrich, G., Helmert, M., Wotawa, F. (eds.) KI 2016. LNCS (LNAI), vol. 9904, pp. 30–42. Springer, Cham (2016). https://doi.org/10.1007/978-3-319-46073-4_3
7. Van den Broeck, G., Taghipour, N., Meert, W., Davis, J., De Raedt, L.: Lifted probabilistic inference by first-order knowledge compilation. In: IJCAI11 Proceedings of the Twenty-Second International Joint Conference on Artificial Intelligence, pp. 2178–2185. AAAI Press/International Joint Conferences on Artificial Intelligence (2011)
8. Ford, L.R., Fulkerson, D.R.: Maximal flow through a network. Can. J. Math. **8**, 399–404 (1956)
9. Gehrke, M., Braun, T., Möller, R., Waschkau, A., Strumann, C., Steinhäuser, J.: Lifted maximum expected utility. In: Koch, F., et al. (eds.) AIH 2018. LNCS (LNAI), vol. 11326, pp. 131–141. Springer, Cham (2019). https://doi.org/10.1007/978-3-030-12738-1_10
10. Gogate, V., Domingos, P.M.: Probabilistic Theorem Proving. In: UAI 2011, Proceedings of the Twenty-Seventh Conference on Uncertainty in Artificial Intelligence, Barcelona, Spain, 14–17 July 2011, pp. 256–265. AUAI Press (2011)
11. Harris, T., Ross, F.: Fundamentals of a method for evaluating rail net capacities. Technical report, Rand Corp, Santa Monica, CA (1955)
12. Johnson, P., Lagerström, R., Närman, P., Simonsson, M.: Enterprise architecture analysis with extended influence diagrams. Inf. Syst. Front. **9**, 163–180 (2007)
13. Joshi, S., Kersting, K., Khardon, R.: Generalized first order decision diagrams for first order markov decision processes. In: IJCAI09 Proceedings of the 21st International Joint Conference on Artifical Intelligence, pp. 1916–1921. Morgan Kaufmann Publishers Inc. (2009)
14. McCarthy, J.: Situations, actions, and causal laws. Stanford Univ CA Dept of Computer Science, Technical report (1963)
15. Morgenstern, L.: Knowledge preconditions for actions and plans. In: Readings in Distributed Artificial Intelligence, pp. 192–199. Elsevier (1988)
16. Nath, A., Domingos, P.: A language for relational decision theory. In: International Workshop on Statistical Relational Learning (2009)
17. Nath, A., Domingos, P.: Efficient lifting for online probabilistic inference. In: Proceedings of the 6th AAAI Conference on Statistical Relational Artificial Intelligence, AAAIWS 2010-06, pp. 1193–1198. AAAI Press (2010)
18. Nath, A., Domingos, P.M.: Efficient belief propagation for utility maximization and repeated inference. In: AAAI10 Proceedings of the Twenty-Fourth AAAI Conference on Artificial Intelligence, pp. 1187–1192. AAAI Press (2010)
19. von Neumann, J., Morgenstern, O.: Theory of Games and Economic Behaviour. Princeton University Press, Princeton (1944)

20. Niepert, M., Van den Broeck, G.: Tractability through exchangeability: a new perspective on efficient probabilistic inference. In: AAAI14 Proceedings of the Twenty-Eighth AAAI Conference on Artificial Intelligence, pp. 2467–2475. AAAI Press (2014)
21. Poole, D.: First-order probabilistic inference. In: IJCAI03 Proceedings of the 18th International Joint Conference on Artificial Intelligence, pp. 985–991. Morgan Kaufmann Publishers Inc. (2003)
22. de Salvo Braz, R., Amir, E., Roth, D.: MPE and partial inversion in lifted probabilistic variable elimination. In: AAAI, pp. 1123–1130. AAAI Press (2006)
23. Sanner, S., Boutilier, C.: Approximate solution techniques for factored first-order MDPs. In: 17th International Conference on Automated Planning and Scheduling, pp. 288–295. AAAI Press (2007)
24. Sanner, S., Kersting, K.: Symbolic dynamic programming for first-order POMDPs. In: AAAI10 Proceedings of the Twenty-Fourth AAAI Conference on Artificial Intelligence, pp. 1140–1146. AAAI Press (2010)

Vocabulary-Based Method for Quantifying Controversy in Social Media

Juan Manuel Ortiz de Zarate[1,2](✉) [iD] and Esteban Feuerstein[1,2,3](✉) [iD]

[1] Departamento de Computación, FCEyN, Universidad de Buenos Aires,
Buenos Aires, Argentina
{jmoz,efeuerst}@dc.uba.ar
[2] Instituto de Ciencias de la Computación, Buenos Aires, Argentina
[3] Fundación Sadosky, Buenos Aires, Argentina

Abstract. Identifying controversial topics is not only interesting from a social point of view, it also enables the application of methods to avoid the information segregation, creating better discussion contexts and reaching agreements in the best cases. In this paper we develop a systematic method for controversy detection based primarily on the jargon used by the communities in social media. Our method dispenses with the use of domain-specific knowledge, is language-agnostic, efficient and easy to apply. We perform an extensive set of experiments across many languages, regions and contexts, taking controversial and non-controversial topics. We find that our vocabulary-based measure performs better than state of the art measures that are based only on the community graph structure. Moreover, we shows that it is possible to detect polarization through text analysis.

1 Introduction

Controversy is a phenomenon with a high impact at various levels. It has been broadly studied from the perspective of different disciplines, ranging from the seminal analysis of the conflicts within the members of a karate club [45] to political issues in modern times [9,30]. The irruption of digital social networks [14] gave raise to new ways of intentionally intervening on them for taking some advantage [7,38]. Moreover highly contrasting points of view in some groups tend to provoke conflicts that lead to attacks from one community to the other by harassing, "brigading", or "trolling" it [25]. The existing literature shows different issues that controversy brings up such as splitting of communities, biased information, hateful discussions and attacks between groups, generally proposing ways to solve them. For example, Kumar, Srijan, et al. [25] analyze many techniques to defend us from attacks in *Reddit*[1] while Stewart, et al. [38] insinuate that there was external interference in Twitter during the 2016 US presidential elections to benefit one candidate.

---

[1] https://www.reddit.com/.

© Springer Nature Switzerland AG 2020
M. Alam et al. (Eds.): ICCS 2020, LNAI 12277, pp. 161–176, 2020.
https://doi.org/10.1007/978-3-030-57855-8_12

Also, as shown in [24], detecting controversy could provide the basis to improve the *"news diet"* of readers, offering the possibility to connect users with different points of views by recommending them new content to read [31].

Other studies on "bridging echo chambers" [16] and the positive effects of inter-group dialogue [2,33] suggest that direct engagement could be effective for mitigating such conflicts. Moreover, a recent work [8] have found that small changes on social networks made by an administrator could have a big impact on the polarization of the discussion. Therefore, easily and automatically identifying controversial topics could allow us to quickly implement different strategies for preventing miss-information, fights and bias. *Quantifying* the controversy is even more powerful, as it allows us to establish controversy levels, and in particular to classify controversial and non-controversial topics by establishing a threshold score that separates the two types of topics. With this aim, we propose in this work a systematic, language-agnostic method to quantify controversy on social networks taking tweet's content as root input. Our main contribution is a new vocabulary-based method that works in any language and equates the performance of state-of-the-art structure-based methods. Besides, controversy quantification through vocabulary analysis opens several research avenues to analyze whether polarization is being created, maintained or augmented by the ways of talking of each community.

Having this in mind, and if we draw from the premise that when a discussion has a high controversy it is in general due to the presence of two principal communities fighting each other (or, conversely, that when there is no controversy there is just one principal community the members of which share a common point of view), we can measure the controversy by detecting if the discussion has one or two principal jargon in use. Our method is tested on Twitter datasets. This micro-blogging platform has been widely used to analyze discussions and polarization [30,35,40,42,44]. It is a natural choice for these kind of problems, as it represents one of the main fora for public debate in online social media [42], it is a common destination for affiliative expressions [20] and is often used to report and read news about current events [37]. An extra advantage of Twitter for this kind of studies is the availability of real-time data generated by millions of users. Other social media platforms offer similar data-sharing services, but few can match the amount of data and the accompanied documentation provided by Twitter. One last asset of Twitter for our work is given by *retweets*, whom typically indicate endorsement [4] and hence become a useful concept to model discussions as we can set "who is with who". However, our method has a general approach and it could be used a priori in any social network. In this work we report excellent results tested on Twitter but in future work we plan to test the method in other social networks.

Our paper is organized as follows. In Sect. 2, we review related work. Section 3 contains the detailed explanation of the pipeline we use for quantifying controversy of a topic, and each of its stages. In Sect. 4 we report the results of an extensive empirical evaluation of the proposed measure of controversy. Finally,

Sect. 5 is devoted to discuss possible improvements and directions for future work, as well as lessons learned.

2   Related Work

Many previous works are dedicated to quantifying the polarization observed in online social networks and social media [1,3,9,10,18,19]. The main characteristic of those works is that the measures proposed are based on the structural characteristics of the underlying graph. Among them, we highlight the work of Garimella et al. [18] that presents an extensive comparison of controversy measures, different graph-building approaches, and data sources, achieving the best performance of all.

In their research they propose different metrics to measure polarization on Twitter. Their techniques based on the structure of the endorsement graph can successfully detect whether a discussion (represented by a set of tweets), is controversial or not regardless of the context and most importantly, without the need of any domain expertise. [18] also considers two different methods to measure controversy based on the analysis of the posts contents, but both fail when used to create a measure of controversy.

Matakos et al. [29] develop a *polarization index*. Their measure captures the tendency of opinions to concentrate in network communities, creating echo-chambers. They obtain a good performance at identifying controversy by taking into account both the network structure and the existing opinions of users. With this aim, they model opinions as positive or negative with a real number between -1 and 1. Their performance is good but, although their method is opinion-based, it is not a text-related one. Other recent works [27,36,39] have shown that communities may express themselves with different terms or ways of speaking, or use different jargon, something that in turn can be detected with the use of text-related techniques.

In his thesis [22], Jang explains controversy via generating a summary of two conflicting stances that conform the controversy. This work shows that a sub-set of tweets could represent the two opposite positions in a polarized debate.

A good tool to *see* how communities interact is ForceAtlas2 [21], a force-directed layout widely used for visualization. This layout has been recently found to be very useful at visualizing community interactions [41], as this algorithm will draw groups with little communication between their members in different areas, whereas, if they have many interactions they will be drawn closer to each other. Therefore, whenever there is controversy the layout will show two well separated groups and will tend to show only one big community otherwise.

The method we propose to measure the controversy equates in accuracy the one developed by Garimella et al.[18] and improves considerably computing time and robustness with respect to the amount of data needed to effectively apply it. Our method is also a graph-based approach but it has its main focus on the vocabulary. We first train an NLP classifier that estimates opinion polarity of the main users, then we run label-propagation [46] on the endorsement graph to get the polarity of the whole network.

Finally, we establish the controversy score through a computation inspired in Dipole Moment, a measure used in physics to estimate electric polarity on a system.

In our experiments we use the same data-sets from other works [11,17,18] as well as other datasets that we collected by us using a similar criterion (described in Sect. 4).

3 Method

Our approach to measuring controversy is based on a systematic way of characterizing social media activity through content. We employ a pipeline with five stages, namely *graph building, community identification, model training, predicting* and *controversy measure*. The final output of the pipeline is a value that measures how controversial a topic is, with higher values corresponding to higher degrees of controversy. The method is based on analyzing posts content through Fasttext [23], a library for efficient learning of word representations and sentence classification developed by Facebook Research team. In short, our method works as follows: through Fasttext we train a language-agnostic model which can predict the community to which the users belong by their jargon. Then we take their predictions and compute a score based on the physic notion *Dipole Moment*[2] using a language approach to identify core or characteristic users and set the polarity through them. We provide a detailed description of each stage in the following.

3.1 Graph Building

This paragraph provides details about the approach used to build graphs from raw data. As we said in Sect. 1, we extract our discussions from Twitter. Our purpose is to build a conversation graph that represents activity related to a single topic of discussion -a debate about a specific event.

For each topic, we build a graph G where we assign a vertex to each user who contributes to it and we add a directed edge from node u to node v whenever user u retweets a tweet posted by v. Retweets typically indicate endorsement [4]: users who retweet signal endorsement of the opinion expressed in the original tweet by propagating it further. Retweets are not constrained to occur only between users who are connected in Twitter's social network, but users are allowed to retweet posts generated by any other user. As many other works in literature [5,7,15,26,30,38] we establish that one retweet among a pair of users is needed to define an edge between them.

---

[2] In physics, the electric dipole moment is a measure of the separation of positive and negative electrical charges within a system, that is, a measure of the system's overall polarity.

3.2 Community Identification

To identify a community's jargon we need to be very accurate at defining its members. If we, in our will of finding two principal communities, force the partition of the graph in that precise number of communities, we may be adding noise in the jargon of the principal communities that are fighting each other. Because of that, we cluster the graph using two popular algorithms: Walktrap [34] and Louvain [6]. Both are structure-based algorithms that have very good performance with respect to the Modularity Q measure[3]. These techniques do not detect a fixed number of clusters; their output depends on the Modularity Q optimization, resulting in less "noisy" communities. The main differences between the two methods, in what regards our work, are that Louvain is a much faster heuristic algorithm but produces clusters with worse Modularity Q. Therefore, in order to analyze the trade-off between computing time and quality we decide to test both methods. At this step we want to capture the tweets of the principal communities to create the model that could differentiate them. Therefore, we take the two communities identified by the cluster algorithm that have the maximum number of users, and use them for the following step of our method.

3.3 Model Training

After detecting the principal communities we create our training dataset to feed the model. To do that, we extract the tweets of each cluster, we sanitize them and we subject them to some transformations. First, we remove duplicate tweets -e.g. retweets without additional text. Second, we remove from the text user names, links, punctuation, tabs, leading and lagging blanks, general spaces and "RT" - the text that points that a tweet is in fact a retweet.

As shown in previous works, emojis[4] are correlated with sentiment [32]. Moreover, as we think that communities will express different sentiment during discussion, it is foreseeable that emojis will play an important role as separators of tweets that differentiate between the two sides. Accordingly, we decide to add them to the train-set by translating each emoji into a different word. For example, the emoji :) will be translated into *happy* and :(into *sad*. Relations between emojis and words are defined in the R library *textclean*[5].

Finally, we group tweets by user concatenating them in one string and labelling them with the user's community, namely with tags *C1* and *C2*, corresponding to the biggest and second biggest groups respectively. It is important to note that we take the same number of users of each community to prevent bias in the model. Thus, we use the number of users of the smallest principal community.

---

[3] $Q(G) = \sum_{C \in G}(e_c - a_c)$, where G is the graph, C each of its communities, e_c the fraction of internal edges and a_c the fraction of edges in the border.

[4] https://emojipedia.org/twitter/.

[5] https://cran.r-project.org/web/packages/textclean/textclean.pdf.

The train-set built that way is used to feed the model. As we said, we use Fasttext [23] for this training. To define the values of the hyper-parameters we use the findings of [43], where the best hyper-parameters to train word embedding models using Fasttext and Twitter data are found. We also change the default value of the hyper-parameter *epoch* to 20 instead of 5 because we want more convergence preventing as much as possible the variance between different training. These values could change in other contexts or social networks where we have more text per user or different discussion dynamics.

3.4   Predicting

The next stage consists of identifying the *characteristic users* of each side of the discussion. These are the users that better represent the jargon of each side. To do that, tweets of the users belonging to the largest connected component of the graph are sanitized and transformed exactly as in the Training step.

We decide to restrict to the largest connected component because in all cases it contains more than 90% of the nodes. The remaining 10% of the users don't participate in the discussion from a collective point of view but rather in an isolated way and this kind of intervention does not add interesting information to our approach. Then, we remove from this component users with degree smaller or equal to 2 (i.e. users that were retweeted by another user or retweeted other person less than three times in total). Their participation in the discussion is marginal, consequently they are not relevant wrt controversy as they add more noise than information at measuring time. This step could be adjusted differently in a different social network. We name this result component *root-graph*.

Finally, we classify the users. Considering that Fasttext returns for each classification both the predicted tag and the probability of the prediction, we classify each user of the resulting component by his sanitized tweets with our trained model, and take users that were tagged with a probability greater or equal than 0.9. These are the *characteristic users* that will be used in next step to compute the controversy measure.

3.5   Controversy Measure

This section describes the controversy measures used in this work. This computation is inspired in the measure presented by Morales et al. [30], and is based on the notion of dipole moment that has its origin in physics.

First, we assign to the *characteristic users* the probability returned by the model, negativizing the value if the predicted tag was *C2*. Therefore, these users are assigned values in the set $[-1, -0.9] \cup [0.9, 1]$. Then, we set values for the rest of the users of the *root-graph* by label-propagation [46] - an iterative algorithm to propagate values through a graph by node's neighbourhood.

Let n^+ and n^- be the number of vertices with positive and negative values respectively, V be the total number of vertices , and $\Delta A = \dfrac{|n^+ - n^-|}{|V|}$ the absolute difference of their normalized size. Moreover, let gc^+ (resp. gc^-) be the average value among vertices n^+ (resp. n^-) and set τ as half their absolute difference, $\tau = \dfrac{\mid gc^+ - gc^- \mid}{2}$. The dipole moment content controversy measure is defined as: $DMC = (1 - \Delta A)\tau$.

The rationale for this measure is that if the two sides are well separated, then label propagation will assign different extreme values to the two partitions, where users from one community will have values near to 1 and users from the other to -1, leading to higher values of the DMC measure. Note also that larger differences in the size of the two partitions (reflected in the value of ΔA) lead to smaller values for the measure, which takes values between zero and one.

4 Experiments

We run the above method over different discussions, with the following results.

4.1 Topic Definition

In the literature, a topic is often defined by a single hashtag. However, this might be too restrictive in many cases. Sometimes a discussion in a particular moment could not have a defined hashtag but it could be around a certain *keyword*, i.e. a word or expression that is not specifically a hashtag but it is widely used in the topic. For example during the Brazilian presidential elections in 2018 we captured the discussion by the mentions to the word *Bolsonaro*, that is the principal candidate's surname. In our approach, a topic is operationalized as a specific hashtag or *key word*. Thus, for each topic we retrieve all the tweets that contain one of its hashtags or the *keyword* and that are generated during the observation window. We also ensure that the selected topic is associated with a large enough volume of activity.

4.2 Datasets

In this section we detail the discussions we use to test our metric and how we determine the ground truth (i.e. whether the discussion is controversial or not). We use thirty different discussions that took place between March 2015 and June 2019, half of them with controversy and half without it. We considered discussions in four different languages: English, Portuguese, Spanish and French, occurring in five regions over the world: South and North America, Western Europe, Central and Southern Asia. We also studied these discussions taking first 140 characters and then 280 from each tweet to analyze the difference in performance and computing time wrt the length of the posts.

To define the amount of data needed to run our method we established that the Fasttext model has to predict at least one user of each community with a probability greater or equal than 0.9 during ten different trainings. If that is not the case, we are not able to use DMC method. This decision made us consider only a subset of the datasets used in [18], because due to the time elapsed since their work, many tweets had been deleted and consequently the volume of the data was not enough for our framework. To enlarge our experiment base we added new debates, more detailed information about each one is available in the code repository[6]. To select new discussions and to determine if they are controversial or not we looked for topics widely covered by mainstream media, and that have generated ample discussion, both online and offline. For non-controversy discussions we focused on "soft news" and entertainment, but also on events that, while being impactful and/or dramatic, did not generate large controversies. To validate that intuition, we manually checked a sample of tweets, being unable to identify any clear instance of controversy. On the other side, for controversial debates we focused on political events such as elections, corruption cases or justice decisions.

To furtherly establish the presence or absence of controversy in our datasets, we visualized the corresponding networks through ForceAtlas2 [21]. Figure 1a and b show an example of how non-controversial and controversial discussions look like respectively with ForceAtlas2 layout. As we can see in these figures, in a controversial discussion this layout tends to show two well separated groups while in a non-controversial one it tends to be only one big group.

To avoid potential overfitting, we use only twelve graphs as testbed during the development of the measures, half of them controversial (netanyahu, ukraine, @mauriciomacri 1–11 Jan, Kavanaugh 3 Oct, @mauriciomacri 11–18 Mar, Bolsonaro 27 Oct) and half non-controversial (sxsw, germanwings, onedirection, ultralive, nepal, mothersday). This procedure resembles a 40/60% train/test split in traditional machine learning applications.

Some of the discussions we consider refer to the same topics but in different periods of time. We needed to split them because our computing infrastructure does not allow us to compute such an enormous amount of data. However, being able to estimate controversy with only a subset of the discussion is an advantage, because discussions could take many days or months and we want to identify controversy as soon as possible, without the need of downloading the whole discussion. Moreover, for very long lasting discussions in social networks gathering the whole data would be impractical for any method.

4.3   Results

Training a Fasttext model is not a deterministic process, as different runs could yield different results even using the same training set in each one. To analyze if these differences are significant, we decided to compute 20 scores for each discussion. The standard deviations among these 20 scores were low in all cases, with mean 0.01 and maximum 0.05. Consequently, we decided to report in this paper the average between the 20 scores, in practice taking the average between 5 runs would be enough. Figure 2 reports the scores computed by our measure in each topic for the two clustering methods. The beanplot shows the estimated

---

[6] Code and networks used in this work are available here: http://github.com/jmanuoz/ Vocabulary-based-Method-for-Quantify-Controversy.

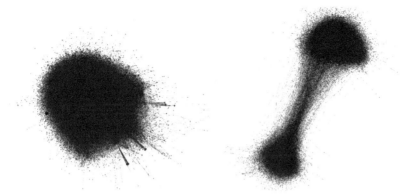

(a) ForceAtlas2 layout over the root graph of Halsey discussion

(b) ForceAtlas2 layout over the root graph of Kavanaugh discussion

Fig. 1. ForceAtlas2 layout over controversial and no-controversial discussions

probability density function for a measure computed on the topics, the individual observations are shown as small white lines in a one-dimensional scatter plot, and the median as a longer black line. The beanplot is divided into two groups, one for controversial topics (left/dark) and one for non-controversial ones (right/light). Hence, the black group shows the score distribution over controversial discussions and the white group over non-controversial ones. A larger separation of the two distributions indicates that the measure is better at capturing the characteristics of controversial topics, because a good separation allows to establish a threshold in the score that separates controversial and non-controversial discussions.

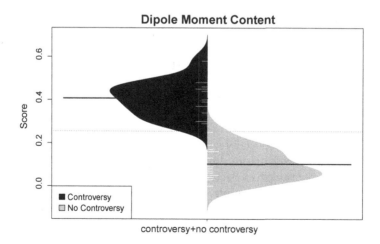

Fig. 2. Average controversy scores over 20 runs on datasets with 280 characters

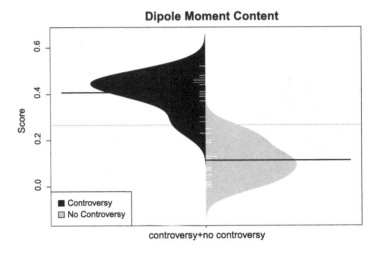

Fig. 3. Average controversy scores over 20 runs on datasets of 140 character per tweet

As we may see in the figure, the medians are well separated in both cases, with little overlapping. To better quantify this overlap we measure the sensitivity [28] of these predictions by measuring the area under the ROC curve (AUC ROC), obtaining a value of 0.98 for Walktrap clustering and 0.967 for Louvain (where 1 represents a perfect separation and 0.5 means that they are indistinguishable).

As Garimella et al. [18] have made their code public[7], we reproduced their best method *Randomwalk*[8] on our datasets and measured the AUC ROC, obtaining a score of 0.935. An interesting finding was that their method had a poor performance over their own datasets. This was due to the fact (already explained in Sect. 4) that it was not possible to retrieve the complete discussions, moreover, in no case could we restore more than 50% of the tweets. So we decided to remove these discussions and measure again the AUC ROC of this method, obtaining a 0.99 value. Our hypothesis is that the performance of that method was seriously hurt by the incompleteness of the data. We also tested our method on these datasets, obtaining a 0.99 AUC ROC with Walktrap and 0.989 with Louvain clustering.

We conclude that our method works better, as in practice both approaches show same performances -specially with Walktrap, but in presence of incomplete information our measure is more robust. The performance of Louvain is slightly worse but, as we mentioned in Sect. 3, this method is much faster. Therefore, we decided to compare the running time of our method with both clustering techniques and also with the *Randomwalk* algorithm. In Fig. 4 we can see the distribution of running times of all techniques through box plots. Both versions of our method are faster than *Randomwalk*, while Louvain is faster than Walktrap.

---

[7] https://github.com/gvrkiran/controversy-detection.
[8] This is a measure based on random walks over the graph structure.

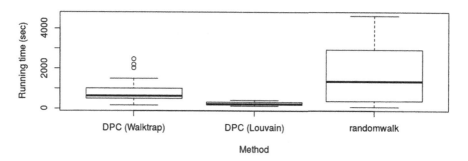

Fig. 4. Running time measures of our method with each cluster type and Randomwalk algorithm

We now analyze the impact of the length of the considered text in our method. Figure 3 depicts the results of similar experiment as Fig. 2, but considering only 140 characters per tweet. As we may see, here the overlapping is bigger, having an AUC of 0.88. As for the impact on computing time, in practice we observed a linear growth as a function of the size of the text. Previous results of [23] reported a complexity of $O(h\ log_2(k))^9$ at training and test tasks.

We measured the running times of the training and predicting phases (the two text-related phases of our method), the resulting times are reported in Fig. 5, which shows running time as a function of the text-size. We include also the best estimated function that approximate computing time as a function of text-set size. As it may be seen, time grows almost linearly, ranging from 30 s for a set of

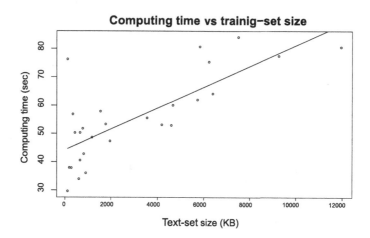

Fig. 5. Time text-related runs measures as a function of text-set size

---

[9] Where k is the number of classes and h the dimension of the text representation.

111 KB to 84 s for a set of 11941 KB[10]. Finally, we measured running times for the whole method over each dataset with 280 characters. Times were between 170 and 2467 s with a mean of 842, making it in practice a reasonable amount of time.

5   Discussions

The task we address in this work is certainly not an easy one, and our study has some limitations, which we discuss in this section. Our work leads us to some conclusions regarding the overall possibility of measuring controversy through text, and what aspects need to be considered to deepen our work.

5.1   Limitations

As our approach to controversy is similar to that of Garimella et al. [18], we share some of their limitations with respect to several aspects: *Evaluation* -difficulties to establish ground-truth, *Multisided controversies* -controversy with more than two sides, *Choice of data* - manually pick topics, and *Overfitting* - small set of experiments.

Although we have more discussions, it is still a small set from a statistical point of view. Apart from that, our language-based approach has other limitations which we mention in the following, together with their solutions or mitigation.

Data-Size. Training an NLP model that can predict tags with a probability greater or equal than 0.9 requires significant amount of text, therefore our method works only for "big" discussions. Most interesting controversies are those that have consequence at a society level, in general big enough for our method.

Multi-language Discussions. When multiple languages are participating in a discussion it is common that users tend to retweet more tweets in their own language, creating sub-communities. In this cases our model will tend to predict higher controversy scores. This is the case for example of #germanwings, where users tweet in English, German and Spanish and it has the highest score in no-controversial topics. However, the polarization that we tackle in this work is normally part of a society cell (a nation, a city, etc.), and thus developed in just one language. We think that limiting the effectiveness of our analysis to single-language discussions is not a serious limitation.

Twitter Only. Our findings are based on datasets coming from Twitter. While this is certainly a limitation, Twitter is one of the main venues for online public discussion, and one of the few for which data is available. Hence, Twitter is a natural choice. However, Twitter's characteristic limit of 280 characters per message (140 till short time ago) is an intrinsic limitation of that network. We

---

[10] We compare polynomial models of degree 1 to 5 and logmodel, linear model has the lowest RMSE error training with 10-fold cross-validation.

think that in other social networks as Facebook or Reddit our method will work even better, as having more text per user could redound on a better NLP model as we verified comparing the results with 140 and 280 characters per post.

5.2   Conclusions

In this article, we introduced the first large-scale systematic method for quantifying controversy in social media through content. We have shown that this method works on Spanish, English, French and Portuguese, it is context-agnostic and does not require the intervention of a domain expert.

We have compared its performance with state-of-the-art structure-based controversy measures showing that it has the same performance while being more robust. We also have shown that more text implies better performance without significantly increasing computing time, therefore, the method could be used in other contexts such as other social networks like Reddit or Facebook. We plan to test it in those network as future work.

Training the model is not an expensive task since Fasttext has a good performance at this. However, the best performance for detecting principal communities is obtained by Walktrap. The complexity of that algorithm is $O(mn^2)$[34], where m and n are the number of edges and vertices respectively. This makes this method rather expensive to compute on big networks. Nevertheless, we have shown that with Louvain the method still obtains a very similar AUC ROC (0.99 with Walktrap and 0.989 with Louvain). With incomplete information its performance gets worse but it is still good (0.96) and better than previous state of the art.

This work opens several avenues for future research. One is identifying what words, semantics/concepts or language expressions make differ one community from the other. There are various ways to do this, for instance through the word-embbedings that Fasttext returns after training [23]. Also we could use interpretability techniques on machine learning models [13]. Finally, we could try other techniques for measuring controversy through text, using another NLP model as pre-trained neural network BERT [12] or, in a completely different approach measuring the dispersion index of the discussions word-embbedings [36]. We are currently starting to follow this direction.

References

1. Akoglu, L.: Quantifying political polarity based on bipartite opinion networks. In: Eighth International AAAI Conference on Weblogs and Social Media (2014)
2. Allport, G.W., Clark, K., Pettigrew, T.: The nature of prejudice (1954)
3. Amelkin, V., Bogdanov, P., Singh, A.K.: A distance measure for the analysis of polar opinion dynamics in social networks. In: 2017 IEEE 33rd International Conference on Data Engineering (ICDE), pp. 159–162. IEEE (2017)
4. Bessi, A., Caldarelli, G., Del Vicario, M., Scala, A., Quattrociocchi, W.: Social determinants of content selection in the age of (Mis)Information. In: Aiello, L.M., McFarland, D. (eds.) SocInfo 2014. LNCS, vol. 8851, pp. 259–268. Springer, Cham (2014). https://doi.org/10.1007/978-3-319-13734-6_18

5. Bild, D.R., Liu, Y., Dick, R.P., Mao, Z.M., Wallach, D.S.: Aggregate characterization of user behavior in twitter and analysis of the retweet graph. ACM Trans. Internet Technol. (TOIT) **15**(1), 4 (2015)
6. Blondel, V.D., Guillaume, J.L., Lambiotte, R., Lefebvre, E.: Fast unfolding of communities in large networks. J. Stat. Mech: Theory Exp. **2008**(10), P10008 (2008)
7. Calvo, E.: Anatomía política de twitter en argentina. Tuiteando# Nisman. Buenos Aires: Capital Intelectual (2015)
8. Chitra, U., Musco, C.: Analyzing the impact of filter bubbles on social network polarization. In: Proceedings of the 13th International Conference on Web Search and Data Mining, pp. 115–123 (2020)
9. Conover, M.D., Ratkiewicz, J., Francisco, M., Gonçalves, B., Menczer, F., Flammini, A.: Political polarization on twitter. In: Fifth International AAAI Conference on Weblogs and Social Media (2011)
10. Dandekar, P., Goel, A., Lee, D.T.: Biased assimilation, homophily, and the dynamics of polarization. Proc. Natl. Acad. Sci. **110**(15), 5791–5796 (2013)
11. Darwish, K.: Quantifying polarization on twitter: the kavanaugh nomination. In: International Conference on Social Informatics, pp. 188–201. Springer (2019)
12. Devlin, J., Chang, M.W., Lee, K., Toutanova, K.: Bert: pre-training of deep bidirectional transformers for language understanding. arXiv preprint arXiv:1810.04805
13. Doshi-Velez, F., Kim, B.: Towards a rigorous science of interpretable machine learning. arXiv preprint arXiv:1702.08608 (2017)
14. Easley, D., Kleinberg, J., et al.: Networks, Crowds and Markets, vol. 8. Cambridge University Press, Cambridge (2010)
15. Feng, W., Wang, J.: Retweet or not?: personalized tweet re-ranking. In: Proceedings of the Sixth ACM International Conference on Web Search and Data Mining, pp. 577–586. ACM (2013)
16. Garimella, K., De Francisci Morales, G., Gionis, A., Mathioudakis, M.: Reducing controversy by connecting opposing views. In: Proceedings of the Tenth ACM International Conference on Web Search and Data Mining, pp. 81–90. ACM (2017)
17. Garimella, K., Mathioudakis, M., Morales, G.D.F., Gionis, A.: Exploring controversy in twitter. In: Proceedings of the 19th ACM Conference on Computer Supported Cooperative Work and Social Computing Companion, pp. 33–36. ACM (2016)
18. Garimella, K., Morales, G.D.F., Gionis, A., Mathioudakis, M.: Quantifying controversy on social media. ACM Trans. Soc. Comput. **1**(1), 3 (2018)
19. Guerra, P.C., Meira Jr, W., Cardie, C., Kleinberg, R.: A measure of polarization on social media networks based on community boundaries. In: Seventh International AAAI Conference on Weblogs and Social Media (2013)
20. Hong, S.: Online news on twitter: newspapers' social media adoption and their online readership. Inf. Econ. Policy **24**(1), 69–74 (2012)
21. Jacomy, M., Venturini, T., Heymann, S., Bastian, M.: Forceatlas2, a continuous graph layout algorithm for handy network visualization designed for the gephi software. PLoS ONE **9**(6), e98679 (2014)
22. Jang, M.: Probabilistic Models for Identifying and Explaining Controversy (2019)
23. Joulin, A., Grave, E., Bojanowski, P., Mikolov, T.: Bag of tricks for efficient text classification. arXiv preprint arXiv:1607.01759 (2016)
24. Kulshrestha, J., Zafar, M.B., Noboa, L.E., Gummadi, K.P., Ghosh, S.: Characterizing information diets of social media users. In: Ninth International AAAI Conference on Web and Social Media (2015)

25. Kumar, S., Hamilton, W.L., Leskovec, J., Jurafsky, D.: Community interaction and conflict on the web. In: Proceedings of the 2018 World Wide Web Conference on World Wide Web, pp. 933–943. International World Wide Web Conferences Steering Committee (2018)
26. Kupavskii, A., et al.: Prediction of retweet cascade size over time. In: Proceedings of the 21st ACM International Conference on Information and Knowledge Management, pp. 2335–2338. ACM (2012)
27. Lahoti, P., Garimella, K., Gionis, A.: Joint non-negative matrix factorization for learning ideological leaning on twitter. In: Proceedings of the Eleventh ACM International Conference on Web Search and Data Mining, pp. 351–359. ACM (2018)
28. Macmillan, N.A., Creelman, C.D.: Detection Theory: A User's Guide. Psychology press (2004)
29. Matakos, A., Terzi, E., Tsaparas, P.: Measuring and moderating opinion polarization in social networks. Data Min. Knowl. Discovery 31(5), 1480–1505 (2017). https://doi.org/10.1007/s10618-017-0527-9
30. Morales, A., Borondo, J., Losada, J.C., Benito, R.M.: Measuring political polarization: twitter shows the two sides of venezuela. Chaos Interdiscipl. J. Nonlinear Sci. 25(3), 033114 (2015)
31. Munson, S.A., Lee, S.Y., Resnick, P.: Encouraging reading of diverse political viewpoints with a browser widget. In: Seventh International AAAI Conference on Weblogs and Social Media (2013)
32. Novak, P.K., Smailović, J., Sluban, B., Mozetič, I.: Sentiment of emojis. PLoS ONE 10(12), e0144296 (2015)
33. Pettigrew, T.F., Tropp, L.R.: Does intergroup contact reduce prejudice? recent meta-analytic findings. In: Reducing Prejudice and Discrimination, pp. 103–124. Psychology Press (2013)
34. Pons, P., Latapy, M.: Computing communities in large networks using random walks. In: Yolum, I., Güngör, T., Gürgen, F., Özturan, C. (eds.) ISCIS 2005. LNCS, vol. 3733, pp. 284–293. Springer, Heidelberg (2005). https://doi.org/10.1007/11569596_31
35. Rajadesingan, A., Liu, H.: Identifying users with opposing opinions in twitter debates. In: Kennedy, W.G., Agarwal, N., Yang, S.J. (eds.) SBP 2014. LNCS, vol. 8393, pp. 153–160. Springer, Cham (2014). https://doi.org/10.1007/978-3-319-05579-4_19
36. Ramponi, G., Brambilla, M., Ceri, S., Daniel, F., Di Giovanni, M.: Vocabulary-based community detection and characterization (2019)
37. Shearer, E., Gottfried, J.: News use across social media platforms 2017. Pew Res. Center 7 (2017)
38. Stewart, L.G., Arif, A., Starbird, K.: Examining trolls and polarization with a retweet network. In: Proceedings ACM WSDM, Workshop on Misinformation and Misbehavior Mining on the Web (2018)
39. Tran, T., Ostendorf, M.: Characterizing the language of online communities and its relation to community reception. arXiv preprint arXiv:1609.04779 (2016)
40. Trilling, D.: Two different debates? investigating the relationship between a political debate on tv and simultaneous comments on twitter. Social science computer review 33(3), 259–276 (2015)
41. Venturini, T., Jacomy, M., Jensen, P.: What do we see when we look at networks. an introduction to visual network analysis and force-directed layouts. An introduction to visual network analysis and force-directed layouts, 26 April 2019
42. Weller, K., Bruns, A., Burgess, J., Mahrt, M., Puschmann, C.: Twitter and society, vol. 89. Peter Lang (2014)

43. Yang, X., Macdonald, C., Ounis, I.: Using word embeddings in twitter election classification. Inf. Retrieval J. **21**(2–3), 183–207 (2018)
44. Yardi, S., Boyd, D.: Dynamic debates: an analysis of group polarization over time on twitter. Bull. Sci. Technol. Soc. **30**(5), 316–327 (2010)
45. Zachary, W.W.: An information flow model for conflict and fission in small groups. J. Anthropol. Res. **33**(4), 452–473 (1977)
46. Zhur, X., Ghahramanirh, Z.: Learning from labeled and unlabeled data with label propagation (2002)

Multi-label Learning with a Cone-Based Geometric Model

Mena Leemhuis[1]([✉]) [ID], Özgür L. Özçep[1] [ID], and Diedrich Wolter[2] [ID]

[1] University of Lübeck, Lübeck, Germany
mena.leemhuis@student.uni-luebeck.de, oezcep@ifis.uni-luebeck.de
[2] University of Bamberg, Bamberg, Germany
diedrich.wolter@uni-bamberg.de

Abstract. Recent approaches for knowledge-graph embeddings aim at connecting quantitative data structures used in machine learning to the qualitative structures of logics. Such embeddings are of a hybrid nature, they are data models that also exhibit conceptual structures inherent to logics. One motivation to investigate embeddings is to design conceptually adequate machine learning (ML) algorithms. This paper investigates a new approach to embedding ontologies into geometric models that interpret concepts by closed convex cones. As a proof of concept this cone-based embedding was implemented in a ML algorithm for weak supervised multi-label learning. The system was tested with the gene ontology and showed a performance similar to comparable approaches, but with the advantage of exhibiting the conceptual structure underlying the data.

Keywords: Concept learning · Knowledge graph embedding · Multi-label learning

1 Introduction

Recent approaches to knowledge-graph embeddings [12] aim at linking quantitative data structures used in machine learning (ML), such as (low-dimensional) Euclidean spaces, to the qualitative structures of logics. Conceptual structures of logics like that of first-order logic (FOL) are characterized by the respective domain of models considered, specific individuals, as well as the relations and functions defined. By restricting the language of FOL, several specialized logics can be defined, each giving rise to a certain repertoire of structures that can be expressed. In this work we consider a subclass of description logics (DL) [2] that is particularly suited to the representation of concept structures. Therefore, DL presents an ideal candidate when investigating the link between data models and structures of logics. Once a link between a specific embedding and a specific logic has been established, embeddings induce logic structures in the quantitative domain, say Euclidean space.

Embeddings present a promising approach to the development of concept-level machine learning. Assume a knowledge graph is given, i.e., triples stating

© Springer Nature Switzerland AG 2020
M. Alam et al. (Eds.): ICCS 2020, LNAI 12277, pp. 177–185, 2020.
https://doi.org/10.1007/978-3-030-57855-8_13

relations between objects, then specific concept definitions learned by means of ML techniques get enhanced by the structure of the knowledge graph. Put differently, one obtains a grounding of abstract entities mentioned in the knowledge graph that respects the relational structure of that graph. Pushing the idea even further, one may even consider embedding to go beyond capturing single knowledge graphs, but to represent whole ontologies—as is the case for the convex region based geometric models of [6].

In this paper we consider geometric models based on convex cones as possible groundings of concepts. One reason for considering convex entities is their adequacy from a linguistic-cognitive point of view to model natural concepts, as has been argued by Gärdenfors in his book on conceptual spaces [4]. We are motivated to consider cones as they enable us to define negation (using polarity [9]) which pushes forward the expressivity of structures exhibited by embeddings. We note that Gärdenfors [4, p. 202] considered the representation of negation (and quantification) as particularly difficult. Most importantly, for this paper, convex regions are computationally attractive as efficient methods from the area of convex optimization [3] become available to realizing ML algorithms.

The contribution of this paper is to show how cone-based geometric models can be used for the important ML task of (weak) supervised multi-label learning [5], while retaining the conceptual structures defined by an ontology. We present a cone-based semantics for DL ontologies defined in the language of propositional $\mathcal{ALC}$ [2]. Based on this semantics we propose a new ML method for acquiring an embedding. This paper concentrates on the application of the cone-based embedding to Machine Learning. The theoretical basis of the cone-based approach like characterizing the link of cone models to models in the sense of logics is not in the scope of this paper. For these aspects we refer the reader to our [8] which considers full $\mathcal{ALC}$ (not just propositional $\mathcal{ALC}$).

Multi-label problems are problems in which each entity has to be attached one or more labels. They may be regarded as a generalization of the ML task of classification, which assigns exactly one label to each object. The multi-labeling problem is considered to be a hard ML task [5], but is particularly important for mastering non-trivial conceptual structures: every entity may be a member of several conceptual classes.

There are several types of weak supervised learning problems. We concentrate on handling inexact data, i.e., the training data set may include labels that are not fine-grained [13]. This represents a typical case of how humans would label an entity: we may claim a lion to be a carnivore, but omit class labels such as mammal or animal. A particular feature of our cone models is their ability to express partial knowledge: elements are not required to be labeled with respect to every class. In case of the lion the ML method may thus refrain from assigning a class label like "can swim" or its negation "cannot swim", if neither evidence is given in the training data. By linking a given ontology to the ML model by means of an embedding it is guaranteed that the result, i.e., the grounding of entities, conforms to the ontology. Coming back to the example of animals, we would be able to guarantee that no animal will be labeled herbivore if it is known to eat other animals.

In this paper we consider a medical scenario based on the gene ontology [1] that could for example be used to make disease predictions. The ML method described in this paper demonstrates that learning with cone-based models is competitive to related approaches for multi-label learning [11]. Above all, we are able to demonstrate that a given ontology can be exploited and leads to better results in learning.

Parts of this work were published in the proceedings of a student conference held at the University of Lübeck [7].

2 Preliminaries

The family of description logics is a family of variable-free fragments of FOL that are designed, in particular, for the representation of ontologies. Hence, DLs provide a good balance of expressivity and computational feasibility. They can be classified by the set of concept-constructors offered. Any DL vocabulary contains a set of constants N_c, a set of concept names N_C and role names (corresponding to binary relations). We consider here the propositional part of the logic $\mathcal{ALC}$ [2]. The set of Boolean $\mathcal{ALC}$ concepts C is defined according to the following context-free grammar:

$$C \rightarrow A \mid \perp \mid \top \mid C \sqcup C \mid C \sqcap C \mid \neg C, \tag{1}$$

with atomic concepts $A \in N_C$ and an arbitrary concepts C. An $\mathcal{ALC}$ interpretation $(\Delta, \cdot^{\mathcal{I}})$ consists of the domain Δ (the space of possible elements) and an interpretation function $\cdot^{\mathcal{I}}$ mapping constants to elements in Δ and concept names to subsets of Δ. The semantics of arbitrary concepts is given in Table 1.

Table 1. Syntax and semantics for Boolean $\mathcal{ALC}$ for an interpretation $\mathcal{I}$

Name	Syntax	Semantics
Top	$\top$	$\Delta^{\mathcal{I}}$
Bottom	$\perp$	$\emptyset$
Conjunction	$C \sqcap D$	$C^{\mathcal{I}} \cap D^{\mathcal{I}}$
Disjunction	$C \sqcup D$	$C^{\mathcal{I}} \cup D^{\mathcal{I}}$
Negation	$\neg C$	$\Delta^{\mathcal{I}} \setminus C^{\mathcal{I}}$

An ontology $\mathcal{O}$ is a pair $(\mathcal{T}, \mathcal{A})$. The terminological-box ($\mathcal{T}$-box) $\mathcal{T}$ contains general concept inclusions of the form $C \sqsubseteq D$ stating that C is a subconcept of D, for arbitrary concepts C and D. The assertional-box ($\mathcal{A}$-box) $\mathcal{A}$ consists of facts of the form $C(a)$, $a \in N_c$, which says that a is in the extension of C.

3 Geometric Models

In our cone-based models, Boolean $\mathcal{ALC}$ ontologies are embedded into geometric models of a Euclidean vector space with a linear product $\langle \cdot, \cdot \rangle$ that measures the similarity of vectors (representation of objects) by the cosine. The geometric model $\mathcal{I}$ represents the $\mathcal{T}$-box axioms in a geometric way and is region-based, that means in particular, when $A^{\mathcal{I}} \sqsubseteq B^{\mathcal{I}}$, then A is a subspace of B in the model. The main idea is to split the vector space into convex regions. To preserve the convexity under disjunction and negation, a special convex structure—namely an axis-aligned cone (al-cone)—is used.

Definition 1. *An al-cone is a special case of a closed convex cone. An al-cone in the n-dimensional space is of the form*

$$(X_1, ..., X_n) \text{ where each } X_i \in \{\mathbb{R}, \mathbb{R}_+, \mathbb{R}_-, \{0\}\}. \tag{2}$$

The negation of arbitrary cones X (and in particular of an al-cone), is defined by its polar cone [9] X°, which is the set of all vectors leading to a negative or zero similarity with all vectors in X.

$$X^\circ = \{v \in \mathbb{R}^n | \forall w \in X : \langle v, w \rangle \leq 0\}. \tag{3}$$

For better readability, subsequently $\mathbb{R}, \mathbb{R}_+, \mathbb{R}_-, \{0\}$ are replaced by $u, +, -, 0$.

Every concept of an ontology is assigned to an al-cone as defined in (2) with respect to the $\mathcal{T}$-box axioms. An operation on an al-cone assignment of a concept is executed dimension-wise. So, e.g., the intersection of $(+, -)$ and $(+, +)$ reduces to considering the intersection of the first components $+$ and $+$ (giving $+$) and the intersection of the second components $-$ and $+$, giving 0. The constants are placed in a region were the corresponding $\mathcal{A}$-box axioms are valid. Special cases are the top concept $\top$, represented as $\{u\}^n$ which thus covers the whole space and the bottom concept $\bot$, which is represented as the point of origin $\{0\}^n$.

A special feature of this geometric model is its ability to model partial knowledge. It is not obligatory that an element is an instance of a concept or of its negation, its assignment can also be unknown. When representing negation with polarity, any point neither contained in an al-cone A nor its polar cone A° represents an entity for which class membership of the class A is unknown.

Figure 1 is an example of a geometric model for an empty $\mathcal{T}$-box and two concepts A and B. The $\mathcal{A}$-box consists of $B(a_1), B(a_2)$ and $\neg A(a_2)$. The element a_1 is in a region where it is neither in A nor in $\neg A$.

The geometric model for a given $\mathcal{T}$-box is constructed based on the set K of all possible fully specified concepts k in the ontology. A concept is fully specified when it contains every atomic concept or its negation. The geometric model has the dimension $d = \left\lceil \frac{|K|}{2} \right\rceil$. No conjunction between fully specified concepts is possible, so every k is placed on one half-axis. The al-cone for each atomic concept can be determined by constructing the union of all k in which it appears positively. The corresponding negative concept can be found by negating the

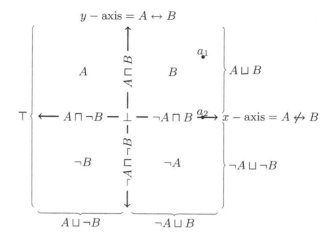

Fig. 1. Example of a geometric model

positive concept. With an empty $\mathcal{T}$-box with n concepts this results in 2^n fully specified concepts and thereby in a geometric model with $d = 2^{n-1}$ dimensions.

With a non-empty $\mathcal{T}$-box the number of possible k decreases, but it is still exponential in the most cases. The construction of the model is similar to the empty case (using the Lindenbaum-Tarski algebra induced by the $\mathcal{T}$-box).

For example the construction of the geometric model with an empty $\mathcal{T}$-Box is conducted as follows: The fully specified concepts are $\{A, B\}, \{A, \neg B\}, \{\neg A, B\}$, and $\{\neg A, \neg B\}$. The geometric representation of each of this concepts is placed on an individual half axis. Thus the geometric representation $\Psi(\cdot)$ is

$$\Psi(\{A, B\}) = (0, +) \tag{4}$$
$$\Psi(\{A, \neg B\}) = (-, 0) \tag{5}$$
$$\Psi(\{\neg A, B\}) = (+, 0) \tag{6}$$
$$\Psi(\{\neg A, \neg B\}) = (0, -). \tag{7}$$

The representations of the other concepts are unions of the representations of the fully specified concepts and thus the resulting model is the one shown in Fig. 1.

4 Multi-label Classification with a Geometric Model

The geometric model can be used in combination with the $\mathcal{A}$-box axioms given by the training data to train a classifier. To this end, every element x of the training data is mapped to a subspace of the vector space by creating a code vector $cv(x)$ with $cv(x) = \{+, -, 0, u\}^d$. In this way an element is not represented by an individual point in space but by an al-cone. In every al-cone there could be several individuals. Thus the training elements are embedded into the geometric model, and therefore into the ontology space. The main idea is to use the knowledge incorporated in the geometric model to train a classifier for each dimension of the geometric model.

For each dimension of the code-vectors a classifier is trained separately to divide the code-vectors in classes determined by their entry in this dimension, because elements with the same region in one dimension should have some shared attributes. For each dimension $1 \le i \le d$ all elements are separated into classes as follows:

$$X_{pos,i} = \{x \mid cv(x)_i = +\} \tag{8}$$
$$X_{neg,i} = \{x \mid cv(x)_i = -\} \tag{9}$$
$$X_{zero,i} = \{x \mid cv(x)_i = 0\} \tag{10}$$

A code-vector with an u at dimension i is ignored.

Training of the classifier is done as follows: For each dimension i the separation of $X_{pos,i}$, $X_{neg,i}$, and $X_{zero,i}$ is computed as follows. When only one of the three classes in dimension i is used, then training of the classifier is not possible and all elements are assigned to the existing class. When in one dimension there are only two of the three labels chosen, then a binary classifier is trained and the third class is ignored. For three existing classes two classifiers are trained, one separating $+$ from the rest, one separating $-$ from the rest. This is explained in more detail at the end of this chapter.

For classification the classification result for the test element is determined for each dimension separately. The results of every dimension are concatenated and produce a code-vector (an al-cone) for the test element. This code vector is then placed in the geometric model. An element e is said to belong to a concept C if the code-vector of e is covered by the code-vector of C.

Our approach is used for weak supervised learning. In the weak supervised learning scenario, some labels are given, but they can be incomplete or inaccurate and it is possible that not all labels are determinable for a given element. In particular, an individual which is not labeled with a specific concept could be contained in it or its negation.

Each entry in code-vectors shows information about its properties. Our aim is to find a separation of 0 vs. $+$ vs. $-$. So why should this be possible?

First we note that an element whose code-vector is u in dimension i is ignored in this dimension because it does not represent a single piece of information. In a geometric model, every operation can be executed per dimension. By definition, in each dimension, 0 is covered by $+$ and $-$. So $+$ and $-$ are not disjoint. This means that their separability depends on the training data and is not necessarily given. Individuals which are labeled as $+$ (or $-$) could be in fact 0, but never $-$ (or $+$). But when a code vector is 0 in the specific dimension, then it stays 0 even after gaining new knowledge. This property is used for the separation task.

One option for training this separation for all three classes existing is to train two classifiers. The first one separates $+$ from the rest, the second one separates $-$ from the rest. Of course there are some $+$ ($-$) which are not fully classified and thus wrongly appear in an area which is in fact 0. By increasing the misclassification cost for a 0 this error is mitigated. The classifier is interpreted as + only when one classifier is + and the second 0 and analogue for −. In the other cases it is classified as 0.

It follows that even the elements which are incompletely classified and thus have a + or − which in fact is a 0 give information because the probability for their appearance is higher close to their actual region.

5 Experiments

Data. The method can be used for any ontology expressed in Boolean $\mathcal{ALC}$. Here the Gene Ontology (GO) [1] is used. It does not contain negation or union and is hence a directed acyclic graph. The relations of GO have not been considered. The data set for the experiments is that of Saccharomyces cerevisiae [10]. First the concepts of the training elements are extended in the way that all ancestor concepts of the given concepts are contained. Then every concept without enough elements representing it was deleted to facilitate the training process. The number of concepts was reduced to eight and for every element the most specific concepts were determined. With these concept labels the training and testing was conducted.

Implementation. For classification a support vector machine with a polynomial kernel is used, because it is an established method for handling bioinformatic datasets like the one used. For the test of the method the assumption is used that not having a positive label means that it could be contained or not.

For comparison purposes we implemented the approach of Wan and Xu [11]. The approach presented in [11] does not use ontology information. It is based on a variant of the 1-vs-1-classifier. Any two concepts are compared to each other in a ternary way. A separation of elements of concept A, of concept B, and of concept $A \sqcap B$ is learned for all concepts A, B. Via a voting-scheme and a threshold the concepts of an element are obtained. This approach is used for comparison because of its high similarity to the presented approach. Its main difference is that the ontology information is not used. In this way the advantage of using this information is investigated. For better comparability—instead of the Tri-class SVM as used in their approach—we use in our implementation the SVM-architecture presented above.

Results and Discussion. Classification of the test set using a six-fold cross validation results in similar performance measures for the presented and the comparison approach (see Table 2).

An advantage of the presented approach is that it can only have ontological correct results, while the other approach can result in contradictions. In every dimension more training elements and thus more information than in normal 1-vs-1 can be used, because not only elements with the same concept, but also with some similar attributes are used in the same class for training.

The similarity in the results of both approaches is caused by the simple structure of GO, which incorporates no negation or disjunction. Only subsumption needs to be considered. Without negated elements or negated concept inclusions there is no knowledge about concept exclusions and therefore the space of possible concepts per element cannot be restricted. Another reason could be the choice of the binary classifier, which could perhaps improve the generalization quality.

The presented approach has improvement potential w.r.t. the error tolerance. Concepts at the bottom of the tree have only a small al-cone where the elements could be placed. This means, that even a small misclassification in one dimension could prevent the correct classification. One possible solution is to incorporate knowledge of the certainty of the classification for each dimension. For a test element an uncertain result in a dimension could be changed to 0 to reduce its influence.

In a second experiment our method was tested with an empty $\mathcal{T}$-box. This resulted in an accuracy near to zero and demonstrates the usefulness of the ontology information for training. Without this information the knowledge about dependencies of elements cannot be used and elements which have similar attributes can not be separated from elements without similar attributes. With an empty $\mathcal{T}$-box impossible separations are tried to be learned as well. Therefore classifying a test element results in a code-vector not containing any information and thus no assigned concept. This shows that the approach can actually use the knowledge represented in the ontology.

Table 2. Results for the presented method and the approach of Wan and Xu [11]

	Accuracy	Precision	Recall
This approach	0.185 ± 0.03	0.190 ± 0.02	0.164 ± 0.03
Wan, Xu [11]	0.197 ± 0.03	0.199 ± 0.03	0.278 ± 0.08

6   Conclusion

The paper presented a proof-of-concept implementation of an algorithm for weak multi-label learning that relies on a geometric model of a Boolean $\mathcal{ALC}$ ontology. As the test results showed, having a geometric model of a non-empty $\mathcal{T}$-box leads to useful information that can be exploited for multi-labeling.

The tests were conducted for an ontology over a very weak logic (not even containing negation) to show its general applicability for weak supervised learning, but our approach is applicable for general Boolean $\mathcal{ALC}$-ontologies—whereas an approach such as that of [11] can not be used because it can not incorporate ontological knowledge. We expect to get even better results for ontologies that allow for full negation (and disjunction) because of the higher amount of ontological information contained.

Future work concerns incorporating a method for dimension reduction in order to reduce the exponential size (w.r.t. the number of atoms in the Boolean algebra of concepts induced by the $\mathcal{T}$-box) of the geometric model. Moreover, we plan to improve the approach by using a different classifier for the dimensions instead of the ternary SVM: the idea is to consider certainty of the answer for each dimension and to improve the dimension-wise separation quality.

References

1. Ashburner, M., et al.: Gene ontology: tool for the unification of biology. Nat. Genet. **25**(1), 25 (2000). https://doi.org/10.1038/75556
2. Baader, F., Calvanese, D., McGuinness, D., Nardi, D., Patel-Schneider, P.F. (eds.): The Description Logic Handbook: Theory, Implementation, and Applications. Cambridge University Press, Cambridge (2003)
3. Boyd, S., Vandenberghe, L.: Convex Optimization. Cambridge University Press, Cambridge (2004)
4. Gärdenfors, P.: Conceptual Spaces: The Geometry of Thought. The MIT Press, Cambridge (2000)
5. Gibaja, E., Ventura, S.: Multilabel learning: a review of the state of the art and ongoing research. Wiley Interdisc. Rev. Data Min. Knowl. Discovery **4**, 411–444 (2014)
6. Gutiérrez-Basulto, V., Schockaert, S.: From knowledge graph embedding to ontology embedding? an analysis of the compatibility between vector space representations and rules. In: Thielscher, M., Toni, F., Wolter, F. (eds.) Principles of Knowledge Representation and Reasoning: Proceedings of the Sixteenth International Conference, KR 2018, Tempe, Arizona, 30 October–2 November 2018, pp. 379–388. AAAI Press (2018)
7. Leemhuis, M., Özçep, Ö.: Multi-label learning with a cone based geometric model. In: Proceedings of the Student Conference 2020. Infinite Science Publishing (2020)
8. Özçep, Ö.L., Leemhuis, M., Wolter, D.: Cone semantics for logics with negation. In: Proceedings of the Twenty-Ninth International Joint Conference on Artificial Intelligence, IJCAI-20 (2020). (To appear)
9. Rockafellar, R.T.: Convex Analysis. Princeton University Press, Princeton (1997)
10. Vens, C., Struyf, J., Schietgat, L., Džeroski, S., Blockeel, H.: Decision trees for hierarchical multi-label classification. Mach. Learn. **73**(2), 185 (2008). https://doi.org/10.1007/s10994-008-5077-3
11. Wan, S.P., Xu, J.H.: A multi-label classification algorithm based on triple class support vector machine. In: 2007 International Conference on Wavelet Analysis and Pattern Recognition, vol. 4, pp. 1447–1452, November 2007. https://doi.org/10.1109/ICWAPR.2007.4421677
12. Wang, Q., Mao, Z., Wang, B., Guo, L.: Knowledge graph embedding: a survey of approaches and applications. IEEE Trans. Knowl. Data Eng. **29**(12), 2724–2743 (2017). https://doi.org/10.1109/TKDE.2017.2754499
13. Zhou, Z.H.: A brief introduction to weakly supervised learning. Nat. Sci. Rev. **5**(1), 44–53 (2017). https://doi.org/10.1093/nsr/nwx106

Conceptual Reasoning for Generating Automated Psychotherapeutic Responses

Graham Mann[✉] ⃝, Beena Kishore ⃝, and Pyara Dhillon ⃝

Murdoch University, 90 South Street, Murdoch, WA 6150, Australia
{g.mann,b.kishore,p.dhillon}@murdoch.edu.au

Abstract. The need for software applications that can assist with mental disorders has never been greater. Individuals suffering from mental illnesses often avoid consultation with a psychotherapist, because they do not realize the need, or because they cannot or will not face the social and economic consequences, which can be severe. Between ideal treatment by a human therapist and self-help websites lies the possibility of a helpful interaction with a language-using computer. A practical model of empathic response planning for sentence generation in a forthcoming automated psychotherapist is described here. The model combines emotional state tracking, contextual information from the patient's history and continuously updated therapeutic goals to form suitable conceptual graphs that may then be realized as suitable textual sentences.

Keywords: Natural language generation · Conceptual graphs · Model-based reasoning

1 Introduction

Many parts of the world now face a serious mental health care treatment gap, especially in low to middle income countries, and non-urban areas in high income countries [1]. The reasons are complex, but much of the shortage is caused by a lack of available skilled psychiatric professionals, and a failure of engagement by patients for economic or social stigma reasons [2]. A review of evidence shows that there are good reasons to think computerized therapy may be one effective approach to overcoming these difficulties [3]. While we do not imagine that these would be equivalent to consultation with skilled human psychiatrists, even existing mental health care apps can play a role and would often be better than nothing. In the case of "talking" therapies – those relying primarily on psychiatric interviews - software can today carry out natural conversations with a patient, simulating the role of the therapist. This paper deals with the formation and expression of appropriate responses to be used by an automated therapist during a consultation. It is a conceptual graph (CG) based language theory realized as a computer model of language generation.

Current trends in conversational systems tend to favour machine learning (ML) approaches, typically employing neural networks (NN), but we believe that these are not ideal in this application, for the following reasons. First, the knowledge and executable

© Springer Nature Switzerland AG 2020
M. Alam et al. (Eds.): ICCS 2020, LNAI 12277, pp. 186–194, 2020.
https://doi.org/10.1007/978-3-030-57855-8_14

skills of a machine learning system are typically opaque, lack auditability and so lack trust [4]. This is a serious drawback in medical applications. Knowledge and skills in conceptual graph (CG) based systems are as a rule much more human-readable and subject to logical reasoning that can readily be comprehended and verified. Second, NN-based or statistical ML approaches (with the possible exception of Bayesian learners) cannot easily incorporate high level, *a priori* knowledge into their processing [5]. This disadvantages learners in domains where such high-level knowledge is available or must be policy. But by virtue of their standardized knowledge representation, CG systems can freely mix prior knowledge incoming data relatively easily. Third, ML language systems are typically very data-hungry, and while large corpuses of language knowledge are now available, using these is computationally expensive. By contrast, model-based CG systems can, with some labour, be made to work with a relatively small amount of domain-specific language knowledge and with little or no learning.

In the rest of this paper, Sect. 2 proposes a linguistic model that integrates tracked emotional states, patient's utterances and background information on the patient with pragmatic cues from a control executive to generate a suitable response in conceptual form. Section 3 then describes our experimental implementation, consisting of heuristic Lisp functions to fetch instances of the above informative content from diverse sources, and calling on conceptual functions to bring these together to form CGs that can be realised as linear texts. The whole process is controlled by an expert system implementing psychotherapeutic rules. Finally, Sect. 4 concludes with some current challenges of this approach and its prospects for further development.

2 Sources Informing the Generation of Responses

2.1 Tracking of Patient's Expressed Emotions

It is difficult to imagine a successful psychotherapist who is not concerned with the emotional state of the patient. Even behaviourist therapies that emphasise overt actions in response to stimuli over mental state today include emotions as a recognised behavioural response, if not an important internal state determining them [e.g. 6]. The evidence is clear that the patient's emotional state is important for treatment needs to be closely monitored [7]. This state must be dealt with properly to maintain patients a comfortable place, while at the same time empathizing, noting the significance of the emotion and helping the patient to find meaning from it. Much emotional information can be obtained by monitoring a speaker's tone of voice, facial expression or other body language. Today's mobile devices, with their microphones and cameras could hope to read these forms of expression, but since our larger system is working with text alone it may not depend on non-verbal cues.

According to the survey conducted by Calvo and D'Mello [8] on models of affect, early approaches to detect emotional words in text include lexical analysis of the text to recognize words that are imminent of the affective states [9] or specific semantic analyses of the text based on an affect model [10]. Another approach is to construct affective models from large corpora of world knowledge and apply these models [e.g. 11]. The current work adapts Smith & Ellsworth's six-dimensional model [12] to make a system that can better grasp the subtleties of patient affect. Their chosen modal values on the principle component states for 15 distinguished emotional states are shown in Table 1.

One way that emotional tracking can be used is for the appropriate application of sympathy. We define a "safe region" in the 6D affective space. The therapist should be able to continue the therapy as long as the patient's tracked emotional state is within the safe region. A single point in the 6D affective space was chosen as the "most distressed" emotional state (we used {1.10 1.3 1.15 1.0 −1.15 2.0}). The simplest model of a safe region is outside a hypersphere of fixed radius centered on this point. The process is then reduced to finding the Euclidian distance between the current emotional state and the above-defined distressed center:

$$\Delta\Omega = \sqrt{(P_i - P_j)^2 + (E_i - E_j)^2 + (C_i - C_j)^2 + (A_i - A_j)^2 + (R_i - R_j)^2 + (O_i - O_j)^2}$$

Table 1. Mean locations of labelled emotional points in the range [−1.5, +1.5] as compiled in Smith & Ellsworth's study.

Emotion	P	R	C	A	E	O
Happiness	−1.46	0.09	−0.46	0.15	−0.33	−0.21
Sadness	0.87	−0.36	0	−0.21	−0.14	1.15
Anger	0.85	−0.94	−0.29	0.12	0.53	−0.96
Boredom	0.34	−0.19	−0.35	−1.27	−1.19	0.12
Challenge	−0.37	0.44	−0.01	0.52	1.19	−0.2
Hope	−0.5	0.15	0.46	0.31	−0.18	0.35
Fear	0.44	−0.17	0.73	0.03	0.63	0.59
Interest	−1.05	−0.13	−0.07	0.7	−0.07	0.41
Contempt	0.89	−0.5	−0.12	0.08	−0.07	−0.63
Disgust	0.38	−0.5	−0.39	−0.96	0.06	−0.19
Frustration	0.88	−0.37	−0.08	0.6	0.48	0.22
Surprise	−1.35	−0.97	0.73	0.4	−0.66	0.15
Pride	−1.25	0.81	−0.32	0.02	−0.31	−0.46
Shame	0.73	1.31	0.21	−0.11	0.07	−0.07
Guilt	0.6	1.31	−0.15	−0.36	0	−0.29

If the calculated distance is greater than an arbitrarily-defined tolerance threshold (radius), the patient's current emotional state is considered safe. The calculated $\Delta\Omega$ of an emotional state {1.15 0.09 1.3 0.15 −0.33 −0.21} from the above-defined distress point would be 1.70. For an arbitrary tolerance radius of 2.5 units from the distress point, the patient's tracked emotive state would not be in the safe region. Further work on a better model of the actual "shape of distress" might improve the heuristic's ability to pick a highly appropriate response for any given emotional state.

2.2 Conceptual Analysis of Patient's Utterances

Study of a reference corpus of 118 talking therapy interviews [13], reveals that these patient utterances can be long and rambling, often incoherent and quite difficult for a person, much less a machine, to comprehend. While we have a conceptual parser, SAVVY, capable of converting real, non-grammatical paragraphs into meaning-preserving CGs [14], it was not developed for use in this domain. Though possible in principle, for the present work we do not intend to improve it to the point of creating meaningful conceptual representations for most of the utterances observed in our corpus. Conceptual parsers depend on an ontology in the form of a hierarchy of concepts, a set of relations and a set of actors. Manually creating representations of all the terms used in those interviews for SAVVY would be a very difficult and time-consuming task. (This most serious of drawbacks for conceptual knowledge-based systems is now being addressed in automated ontology-building machines [e.g. 15, 16]). Our focus in this study is the *generation* of language.

Yet this kind of psychotherapy is essentially conversational, so we must allow the conceptual representations of patient utterances to be an input even to test response formation. Therefore, SAVVY will be adapted to accept selected patient utterances of interest. In some cases, to keep the project manageable, we hand-write plausible input CGs to avoid diverting too much time and energy away from our generation pipeline.

2.3 Using Context to Inform the Planning Process

In regular clinical practice, the first step for a new patient is an admitting (or triage) interview, that can capture important biographical details, a presenting complaint, background histories, and perhaps an initial diagnosis. Because we wish our model of language generation to account for existing, contextual information, we will not actively model this initial interview, but rather only subsequent interviews that have access to this previously gathered background. A set of background topics that should be sought during an admitting interview is described by Morrison [17]. Our current model draws 12 topics from this source and adds three extra topics specific to our clinical model.

2.4 Executive Control

An executive based on a theory about how therapy should be done is needed for overall control. At each conversational turn, the executive should recommend the best "pragmatic move" for the response generation process. This allows selection and instantiation of appropriate high-level conceptual templates that form the therapist's utterances to support, guide, query, inform or sympathize with the patient as appropriate during the treatment process. Our executive is based on the brief therapy of Hoyt [18] and the solution-based therapy of Shoham et al. [19]. As recommended by Hoyt, the focus is on negotiating treatment practices, not diagnostic classification. However, in this experiment a working diagnosis might become available as a result of the therapy or be input as background knowledge.

For a natural interviewing style, the executive must allow its goal-seeking behaviour to be interrupted by certain imperatives imposed by conversational conventions and good clinical practice. If the patient asks a question, this deserves some kind of answer. If the patient wishes to express some attitude or feeling about some point, that should usually be entertained immediately. If the patient's estimated emotional state falls into distress, it is important that the treatment model is suspended until the patient can be comforted and settled. Similarly, if rapport with the patient is lost (the quality of the patient's responses deteriorates), special steps must be taken to recover this before anything else can be done. We call these *forced* responses, to distinguish them from less obligatory pragmatic moves, which in our model are driven by key goals in the therapy.

In most cases, a conceptual structure representing a suitable therapist's response can be formed by unifying pragmatically-selected schemata with content-bearing information from the other sources. This process is to be handled by heuristic rules that must be sufficiently general to keep the number needed as low as possible. In a few cases, a single standardized expressive form can be accessed without the need for unification.

3   Implementation Details

3.1   Collection of Emotional State, Patient Utterances and Background Knowledge

To track emotions, we are experimenting with computationally cheap heuristics that can distinguish the patient's current emotional states directly from the text (Fig. 1), though this has the disadvantage that it does not model cognitive aspects of emotion. For example, a patient would be talking about his or her current emotional reaction if there is a cluster of words in an utterance that includes, within a window of n words, one or more members of the word bag {I, I'm, me, myself}, optionally one of {feel, think, consider, say} AND at least one emotion cue such as {hate, love, enjoy, relax...etc.}. Additional rules have to be implemented to account for negation and to check for past tense such as {was, did, suffixes such as 'ed'}. The 15 emotional states were annotated with synonyms retrieved from WordNet-Affect [20]. A short list of common generic non-emotional words such as {the, then, who, when... etc.} is also provided (excluded_list).

```
Function DetectEmotion (text)
 {For each word in a text
   {If the word is in one of the 15 annotated lists
      {If the emotion belongs to the patient and not past tense
         {emotion_list ← push the 6D value of identified state
         }}}
   {If #(emotion_list) > 1
       emotional_state ← mean(emotion_list)}
    Else {emotional_state ← emotion_list}
 return emotional_state  }
```

Fig. 1. Pseudocode for the heuristic function detecting the emotional state in the utterance

To bring patient's conversational utterances into the picture, a text-to-CG parser is required. But even if it was feasible to construct complete representations for every utterance made by a patient, this would not be desirable, because from analysis of the corpus, surprisingly few such representations would actually have useful implications for treatment, at least within our simplified model. Therefore whatever method we use to parse patient input into CGs can afford to be selective about the outputs it forms, using top-down influences to prefer those interpretations that are likely to lead to useful content. Our conceptual parser, SAVVY, can do this because it assembles composite CGs out of prepared conceptual components that are already pre-selected for the domain of use to which they will be put. This means that the composite graphs are strongly weighted toward semantic structures of implicit value, leaving utterances that result in disjoint or useless component parts not able to aggregate at all. For example, if the patient says

I'm scared that one day, he'll just stab me
SAVVY is able to assemble the conceptual graph

```
[FEAR] –
        (expr) -> [PERSON:Patient]
        (attr) -> [NEGATIVE]
        (caus) ->[ (futr) -> [SITUATION: [PERSON] < - (agnt) <- [PTRANS] -
                                (ptnt) -> [PERSON: Patient] - - - - - - - - - - - - - - - - -¡
                                (rslt) -> [PHARM] -> (expr ) -> [PERSON:Patient] - -!
                                (inst) -> [BLADE]
                                (ptim) -> [DAY:@1] ]
```

only because the lexicon had definitions of useful subgraphs for "scared", "stab" etc. which, because they would likely represent harm to someone, are considered important inclusions. Not every act or even every emotion is so provided for.

A simple database currently provides background knowledge for our experiments. Each entry in the knowledgebase is a history list of zero or more CGs, indexed by both a patient identifier and one of the 15 background topics (Sect. 2.3) such as suicide_attempts, willingness_to_change and chief_complaint. Entries may be added, deleted or modified during processing, so the database can be used as a working memory to update and maintain therapeutic reasoning over sessions. Initially these entries are provided manually to represent information from the pre-existing admitting interview, but these can be updated, edited or deleted by the automated therapist. Automatic entries are vetted by domain-specific heuristic filters focussed on the topic of interest, so that only relevant CGs can be pushed onto the appropriate lists. Our experience suggests that it is not difficult to write these provided high-level conceptual functions, based on the canonical operators, are available to find and test specific sections of the graphs.

3.2 Expert System for Executive Control

Psychiatric expertise is represented by a clinical Expert System Therapist (EST), based on TMYCIN [21]. This shell is populated with rules from the above-mentioned treatment theories. Consultation of the system is performed at each conversational turn, informed by the current state of variables from the inputs. Backward-chaining inference maintains internal state variables and recommends the best "pragmatic move" and" therapist's target" for the response generation process. These parameters allow the selection and instantiation of appropriate high-level template graphs that form the therapist's utterances to support, guide, query, inform or sympathize at that moment. In some simple cases, canned responses are issued to bypass the language pipeline and reduce processing demands.

3.3 Response Generation

Responses CGs are generated based on the three input sources and two variables from the therapeutic process (Fig. 2). The heuristic first checks the patient's emotional state. If this is outside the distressed region (Sect. 2), an expressive form CG is created by first maximally joining generalised CG templates for the pragmatic move (e.g. query) and the content recommended for the current therapeutic goal (e.g. establish_complaint). This is then instantiated with background information. If the patient's emotional state is inside the distressed region, the EST will recommend a pragmatic move of sympathy and the heuristic will force the use of a sympathy template for its expressive form. The constructed CG is subsequently passed to a realization heuristic, SentenceRealization()which in turn expresses the CG as a grammatically correct sentence using YAG (Yet Another Generator) [22].

```
Function GenerateSentence (emotional_state, patient_CG, background_info, pragmatic_move, therapeutic_goal) {
    If the emotional_state is not in distressed region {
        pragmatic_move_CG ← retrieve the template for this pragmatic move
        therapeutic_goal_CG ← retrieve the CG for this therapeutic goal, elaborated from patient_CG
        expressive_form_CG ← maximal_join (pragmatic_move_CG, therapeutic_goal_CG)
        constructed_CG ← instantiate_background (expressive_form_CG, background_info)
        SentenceRealization (constructed_CG, pragmatic_move)}}
    else {
    SentenceRealization (sympathy_CG, pragmatic_move)}
```

Fig. 2. Pseudocode for the heuristic function creating the expressive form.

YAG is a template-based syntactic realization system, which comes with a set of core grammar templates that can be used to generate noun phrases, verbs, prepositional phrases, and other clauses. We are developing a further set of custom templates using those core grammar templates with optional syntactic constraints. The heuristic function *SentenceRealization*()(Fig. 3) loops through the constructed CG and creates a list of attribute-value pairs, based on grammatical/semantic roles.

```
Function SentenceRealization (constructed_CG, pragmatic_move)
{For each concept in a CG
    {knowledge_list ← push attribute-value pair onto knowledge_list}
Retrieve template based on the pragmatic move and the constructed_CG
For each slot in the template
    {Override the slot default value with the value from knowledge_list}
Realize the template using the command surface-1 of YAG.}
```

Fig. 3. Pseudocode for realizing the expressive form as text.

4 Conclusion

This generation component is still in development, so no systematic evaluation has yet been conducted. Some components have been coded and unit tested. Getting the heuristics of the system to interact smoothly with each other is a challenge; that is to be expected in this modelling approach. We are concerned about the number of templates that may be required, particularly at the surface expression level. If they become too difficult or too many to create, the method might become infeasible. The heuristic tests are not difficult to write, but are, of course, imperfect compared to algorithms. Also, we have not fully tested the emotion tracking on real patient texts so far.

Our planned evaluation has two parts. First, a systematic "glass-box" analysis will discover the strengths and limitations of the generation component, particularly with respect to the amount of prior knowledge that needs to be provided and the generality of the techniques. Second, the "suitability", "naturalness" and "empathy" of the response generation for human use will be tested, using a series of ersatz patient interview scenarios to avoid the ethical complications of testing on real patients. The scenarios will provide human judges (expert psychotherapists or, more likely, students in training to be psychotherapists) with information about an ongoing therapeutic intervention. Example patient utterances and the actual responses generated by the system will also be provided as transcripts. The judges will then rate these transcripts on those variables using their own knowledge of therapy.

Finally, we reiterate that if hand-built conceptual representations can be practically built up using existing methods, the effort will be worthwhile if the systems are then more transparent and auditable than NN or statistical ML system and thus, more trustworthy.

References

1. Jack, H.E., Myers, B., Regenauer, K.S., Magidson, J.F.: Mutual capacity building to reduce the behavioral health treatment gap globally. Adm. Policy Mental Health Mental Health Serv. Res. **47**(4), 497–500 (2019). https://doi.org/10.1007/s10488-019-00999-y
2. Meltzer, H.E., et al.: The reluctance to seek treatment for neurotic disorders. Int. Rev. Psychiatry **15**(2), 123–128 (2003)
3. Fairburn, C.G., Patel, V.H.: The impact of digital technology on psychological treatments and their dissemination. Behav. Res. Therapy **88**, 19–25 (2017)
4. Marcus, G.: Deep learning: a critical appraisal. arXiv preprint arXiv:1801.00631 (2018)
5. Pearl, J.: Theoretical impediments to machine learning with seven sparks from the causal revolution. arXiv preprint arXiv:1801.04016 (2018)
6. Ellis, A.: Rational-emotive therapy. Big Sur Recordings, CA, USA, pp. 32–44 (1973)
7. Greenberg, L.S., Paivio, S.C.: Working with Emotions in Psychotherapy, vol. 13. Guilford Press, New York (2003)
8. Calvo, R.A., D'Mello, S.: Affect detection: an interdisciplinary review of models, methods, and their applications. IEEE Trans. Affect. Comput. **1**, 18–37 (2010)
9. Hancock, J.T., Landrigan, C., Silver, C.: Expressing emotion in text-based communication. In: Proceedings of the SIGCHI Conference on Human Factors in Computing Systems, pp. 929–932. Association for Computing Machinery (2007)
10. Gill, A.J., French, R.M., Gergle, D., Oberlander, J.: Identifying emotional characteristics from short blog texts. In: 30th Annual Conference of the Cognitive Science Society, Washington, DC, pp. 2237–2242. Cognitive Science Society (2008)

11. Breck, E., Choi, Y., Cardie, C.: Identifying expressions of opinion in context. In: IJCAI, vol. 7, pp. 2683–2688, January 2007
12. Smith, C.A., Ellsworth, P.C.: Attitudes and social cognition. J. Pers. Soc. Psychol. **48**(4), 813–838 (1985)
13. McNally, A., et al.: Counseling and Psychotherapy Transcripts, Volume II. Alexander Street Press, Alexandria (2014)
14. Mann, G.A.: Control of a navigating rational agent by natural language. Unpublished Ph.D. thesis, University of New South Wales, Sydney, Australia (1996). https://manualzz.com/doc/42762943/control-of-a-navigating-rational-agent-by-natural-language
15. Paola, P.V., et al.: Evaluation of OntoLearn, a methodology for automatic learning of domain ontologies. In: Ontology Learning from Text: Methods, Evaluation and Applications, vol. 123, p. 92 (2005)
16. Leuzzi, F., Ferilli, S., Rotella, F.: ConNeKTion: a tool for handling conceptual graphs automatically extracted from text. In: Catarci, T., Ferro, N., Poggi, A. (eds.) IRCDL 2013. CCIS, vol. 385, pp. 93–104. Springer, Heidelberg (2014). https://doi.org/10.1007/978-3-642-54347-0_11
17. Morrison, J.: The First Interview: A Guide for Clinicians. Guilford Press, New York (1993)
18. Hoyt, M.F.: The temporal structure of therapy. In: O'Donohue, W.E., et al. (ed.) Clinical Strategies for Becoming a Master Psychotherapist, pp. 113–127. Elsevier (2006)
19. Shoham, V., Rohrbaugh, M., Patterson, J.: Problem-and solution-focused couple therapies: the MRI and Milwaukee models. In: Jacobson, N.S., Gurman, A.S. (eds.) Clinical Handbook of Couple Therapy, pp. 142–163. Guilford Press, New York (1995)
20. Strapparava, C., Valitutti, A.: WordNet-affect: an affective extension of WordNet. In: 4th International Conference on Language Resources and Evaluation, pp. 1083–1086 (2004)
21. Novak, G.: TMYCIN expert system tool. Technical Report AI87–52, Computer Science Department, University of Texas at Austin (1987). http://www.cs.utexas.edu/ftp/AI-Lab/tech-reports/UT-AI-TR-87-52.pdf. Accessed 5 Feb 2018
22. Channarukul, S., McRoy, S.W., Ali, S.S.: Enriching partially-specified representations for text realization using an attribute grammar. In: Proceedings of the 1st International Conference on NLG, Mitzpe Ramon, Israel, vol. 14, pp. 163–170. Association for Computational Linguistics (2000)

Benchmarking Inference Algorithms for Probabilistic Relational Models

Tristan Potten(ORCID) and Tanya Braun$^{(\boxtimes)}$(ORCID)

Institute for Information Systems, University of Lübeck, Lübeck, Germany
`tristan.potten@student.uni-luebeck.de`, `braun@ifis.uni-luebeck.de`

Abstract. In the absence of benchmark datasets for inference algorithms in probabilistic relational models, we propose an extendable benchmarking suite named `ComPI` that contains modules for automatic model generation, model translation, and inference benchmarking. The functionality of `ComPI` is demonstrated in a case study investigating both average runtimes and accuracy for multiple openly available algorithm implementations. Relatively frequent execution failures along with issues regarding, e.g., numerical representations of probabilities, show the need for more robust and efficient implementations for real-world applications.

Keywords: StaRAI · Lifted inference · Probabilistic inference

1 Introduction

At the heart of many machine learning algorithms lie large probabilistic models that use random variables (randvars) to describe behaviour or structure hidden in data. After a surge in effective machine learning algorithms, efficient algorithms for inference come into focus to make use of the models learned or to optimise machine learning algorithms further [5]. This need has lead to advances in probabilistic relational modelling for artificial intelligence (also called statistical relational AI, StaRAI for short). Probabilistic relational models combine the fields of reasoning under uncertainty and modelling incorporating relations and objects in the vein of first-order logic. Handling sets of indistinguishable objects using representatives enables tractable inference [8] w.r.t. the number of objects.

Very few datasets exist as a common baseline for comparing different approaches beyond models of limited size (e.g., epidemic [11], workshops [7], smokers [18]). Therefore, we present an extendable benchmarking suite named `ComPI` (Compare Probabilistic Inference) that allows for benchmarking implementations of inference algorithms. The suite consists of (1) an automatic generator for models and queries, (2) a translation tool for providing the generated models in the format needed for the implementations under test, and (3) a measurement module that batch-executes implementations for the generated models and collects information on runtimes and inference results.

In the following, we begin with a formal definition of the problem that the benchmarked inference algorithms solve. Afterwards, we present the functions of the modules of `ComPI`. Lastly, we present a case study carried out with `ComPI`.

© Springer Nature Switzerland AG 2020
M. Alam et al. (Eds.): ICCS 2020, LNAI 12277, pp. 195–203, 2020.
https://doi.org/10.1007/978-3-030-57855-8_15

2   Inference in Probabilistic Relational Models

The algorithms considered in `ComPI` solve query answering problems on a model that defines a full joint probability distribution. In this section, we formally define a model and the query answering problem in such models. Additionally, we give intuitions about how query answering algorithms solve these problems.

2.1   Parameterised Models

Parameterised models consist of parametric factors (parfactors). A parfactor describes a function, mapping argument values to real values (potentials). Parameterised randvars (PRVs) constitute arguments of parfactors. A PRV is a randvar parameterised with logical variables (logvars) to compactly represent sets of randvars [9]. Definitions are based on [13].

Definition 1. *Let $\mathbf{R}$ be a set of randvar names, $\mathbf{L}$ a set of logvar names, Φ a set of factor names, and $\mathbf{D}$ a set of constants (universe). All sets are finite. Each logvar L has a domain $\mathcal{D}(L) \subseteq \mathbf{D}$. A constraint is a tuple $(\mathcal{X}, C_{\mathbf{X}})$ of a sequence of logvars $\mathcal{X} = (X_1, \ldots, X_n)$ and a set $C_{\mathcal{X}} \subseteq \times_{i=1}^n \mathcal{D}(X_i)$. The symbol $\top$ for C marks that no restrictions apply, i.e., $C_{\mathcal{X}} = \times_{i=1}^n \mathcal{D}(X_i)$. A PRV $R(L_1, \ldots, L_n), n \geq 0$ is a syntactical construct of a randvar $R \in \mathbf{R}$ possibly combined with logvars $L_1, \ldots, L_n \in \mathbf{L}$. If $n = 0$, the PRV is parameterless and constitutes a propositional randvar. The term $\mathcal{R}(A)$ denotes the possible values (range) of a PRV A. An event $A = a$ denotes the occurrence of PRV A with range value $a \in \mathcal{R}(A)$. We denote a parfactor g by $\phi(\mathcal{A})_{|C}$ with $\mathcal{A} = (A_1, \ldots, A_n)$ a sequence of PRVs, $\phi : \times_{i=1}^n \mathcal{R}(A_i) \mapsto \mathbb{R}^+$ a function with name $\phi \in \Phi$, and C a constraint on the logvars of $\mathcal{A}$. A set of parfactors forms a model $G := \{g_i\}_{i=1}^n$.*

The term $gr(P)$ denotes the set of all instances of P w.r.t. given constraints. An instance is a grounding, substituting the logvars in P with constants from given constraints. The *semantics* of a model G is given by grounding and building a full joint distribution P_G. Query answering refers to computing probability distributions, which boils down to computing marginals on P_G. Lifted algorithms seek to avoid grounding and building P_G. A formal definition follows.

Definition 2. *With Z as normalising constant, a model G represents the full joint distribution $P_G = \frac{1}{Z} \prod_{f \in gr(G)} f$. The term $P(Q|\mathbf{E})$ denotes a query in G with Q a grounded PRV and $\mathbf{E}$ a set of events. The query answering problem refers to solving a query w.r.t. P_G.*

2.2   Exact Lifted Inference Algorithms

The very first lifted algorithm is lifted variable elimination (LVE) [9], which has been further refined [2,7,11,13]. LVE takes a model G and answers a query $P(Q|\mathbf{E})$ by absorbing evidence $\mathbf{E}$ and eliminating all remaining PRVs except Q from G (cf. [13] for further details). With a new query, LVE restarts with the original model. Therefore, further research concentrates on efficiently solving

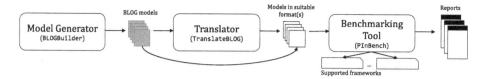

Fig. 1. Modules `ComPI`. The arrows indicate the direction of the flow of created models. The arrow bypassing the translator module indicates that no translation is needed for frameworks working on BLOG models.

multiple query answering problems on a given model, often by building a helper structure based on a model, yielding algorithms such as (i) the lifted junction tree algorithm (LJT) [1], (ii) first-order knowledge compilation (FOKC) [17,18], or (iii) probabilistic theorem proving (PTP) [3]. LJT solves the above defined query answering problem while FOKC and PTP actually solve a weighted first order model counting (WFOMC) problem to answer a query $P(Q|\mathbf{E})$.

For all algorithms mentioned, implementations are freely available (see Sect. 3.3). LVE and LJT work with models as defined above. The other algorithms usually use a different modelling formalism, namely Markov logic networks (MLNs) [10]. One can transform parameterised models to MLNs and vice versa [16]. Next, we present `ComPI`.

3 The Benchmarking Suite `ComPI`

`ComPI` allows for collecting runtimes and inference results from implementations given automatically generated models. Figure 1 shows a schematic description of `ComPI` consisting of three main parts, (i) a *model generator* `BLOGBuilder` that allows the automatic creation of multiple models (in the BLOG grammar [6]) following different generation strategies, (ii) a *translator* `TranslateBLOG` for translation from the BLOG format to correct input format for individual frameworks (if necessary), and (iii) a *benchmarking tool* `PInBench` for collection of runtimes and inference results, summarized in multiple reports.

The modules can be accessed at https://github.com/tristndev/ComPI. Below, we briefly highlight each module.

3.1 Model Generation

The goal is to generate models as given in Definition 1, generating logvar/randvar names and domain sizes, combining logvars and randvars as well as forming parfactors with random potentials. The input to `BLOGBuilder` is a model creation specification, which selects a model creation and augmentation strategy, which describe how models are created possibly based on a previous model.

Running `BLOGBuilder` creates a number of models as well as a number of reports and logs that describe specific characteristics of the created models. The output format of the models is BLOG. Additionally, `BLOGBuilder` generates reports describing the model creation process and highlighting possible deviations from the model creation specification. The module can be extended with additional model creation and augmentation strategies.

3.2   Model Translation

The task is to translate models from the baseline BLOG format into equivalent models of those different formats required for the frameworks in `PInBench`. Accordingly, `TranslateBLOG` takes a number of model files in the BLOG format as input. It subsequently translates the parsed models into different formats of model specifications. As of now, the generation of the following output types is possible: (i) Markov logic networks (MLNs) [10], (ii) dynamic MLNs [4], and (iii) dynamic BLOG files. `TranslateBLOG` is easily extendable as new output formats can be added by specifying and implementing corresponding translation rules and syntactic grammar to create valid outputs.

3.3   Benchmarking

The final module in `ComPI` is `PInBench` (Probabilistic Inference Benchmarking), which serves to batch process the previously created model files, run inferences, and collect data on these runs. `PInBench` can be interpreted as a control unit that coordinates the running of an external implementation which it continuously and sequentially supplies with the available model files. The following implementations in conjunction with the corresponding input formats are supported:

- GC-FOVE[1] with propositional variable elimination and LVE,
- WFOMC[2] with FOKC,
- Alchemy[3] with PTP and sampling-based alternatives, and
- the junction tree algorithm[4] in both its propositional and lifted form.

We also developed a dynamic version of `PInBench`, named `DPInBench`, for dynamic models, i.e., models with a sequence of state, which could refer to passage of time. Currently, the implementations of UUMLN, short for University of Ulm Markov Logic Networks[5] and the Lifted Dynamic Junction Tree (LDJT)[6] as well as their input formats are supported. The data collected by `PInBench` is stored in multiple reports, e.g., giving an overview on the inference success per file and query (queries on big, complex models might fail) or summarizing the run times and resulting inference probabilities.

Implementations not yet supported can easily be added by wrapping each in an executable file and specifying calls needed for execution. Additionally, parsing logics for generated outputs need to be implemented to extract information.

---

[1] dtai.cs.kuleuven.be/software/gcfove (accessed 16 Apr. 2020).
[2] dtai.cs.kuleuven.be/software/wfomc (accessed 16 Apr. 2020).
[3] alchemy.cs.washington.edu/ (accessed 16 Apr. 2020).
[4] ifis.uni-luebeck.de/index.php?id=518#c1216 (accessed 16 Apr. 2020).
[5] uni-ulm.de/en/in/ki/inst/alumni/thomas-geier/ (accessed 16 Apr. 2020).
[6] ifis.uni-luebeck.de/index.php?id=483 (accessed 16 Apr. 2020).

4   Case Study

To demonstrate the process of benchmarking different implementations using ComPI, we present an exemplary case study. Within the case study, the process consists of model generation with BLOGBuilder, model translation with TranslateBLOG, and benchmarking of inference runs with PInBench. All implementations currently supported by ComPI are included here. We do not consider sampling-based algorithms implemented in Alchemy as performance highly depends on the parameter setting for sampling, which requires an analysis of its own and is therefore not part of this case study.

4.1   Model Generation

Model generation starts with creating base models given a set of specified parameters (number of logvars/randvars/parfactors, domain sizes). Subsequently, these base models are augmented according to one of the following strategies:

- **Strategy A** - *Parallel Factor Augmentation*: The previous model is cloned and each parfactor extended by one additionally created PRV with randomly chosen existing logvars.
- **Strategy B** - *Increment By Model*: The base model is duplicated (renaming names) and appended to the current. A random randvar from the duplicate is connected with a random randvar of the current model via a new parfactor.

The strategies are set up to increase complexity based on LVE. Strategy A increases the so-called tree width (see, e.g., [12] for details). Strategy B increases the model size, while keeping the tree width close to constant.

It is non-trivial to generate series of models that increase in complexity without failing executions. Overall, we intend the generation of "balanced" models with moderately connected factors to allow all methods to demonstrate their individual strengths and weaknesses while maintaining manageable runtimes. Creating multiple base models with random influences (e.g., regarding relations between model objects) leads to multiple candidate model series, which allows for selecting one series that leads to runs with the least amount of errors. We tested multiple parameter settings for both strategies to generate candidate series. The specific numbers for parameters are random but small to generate models of limited size, ensuring that the tested programs successfully finish running them. We vary the domain sizes while keeping the number of logvars small for the models to be liftable from a theoretical point of view.[7] More precisely, the settings given by the Cartesian product of the following parameters have been evaluated for generating base models for each strategy:

- **Strategy A**: domain_size $\in \{10, 100, 1000\}$, #logvar $\in \{2\}$, #randvar $\in \{3, 4, 5\}$, #factor = #randvar $- 1$, max_randvar_args $= 2$. Augmentation in 16 steps.

---

[7] Models with a maximum of two logvars per parfactor are guaranteed to have inference runs without any groundings during its calculations [14,15].

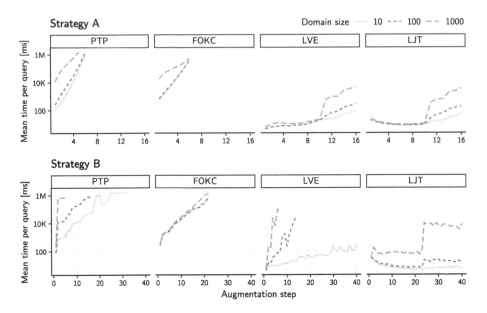

Fig. 2. Mean inference times per query (with logarithmic y-axis).

– **Strategy B**: domain_size ∈ {10, 100, 1000}, #logvar ∈ {1}, #randvar ∈ {2}, #factor ∈ {1}. Further restrictions: max_randvar_occurrences = 4, max_randvar_args = 2, max_factor_args = 2. Augmentation in 40 steps.

In each model file, one query is created per randvar. Model generation was executed in three independent runs to obtain multiple candidate models due to the included factors of randomness. The randomness may also lead to model series of potentially varying complexity. Preliminary test runs have led to the selection of the model series investigated below.

4.2   Evaluation Results

We analyse the given frameworks regarding two aspects: Firstly, runtimes of inference and secondly, inference accuracy.

Runtimes. Figure 2 shows runtimes, displaying the relation between augmentation steps, domain sizes, and mean query answering times for PTP, FOKC, LVE and LJT. The two propositional algorithms supported are not shown in the plots as both presented very steep increases along with failures on early augmentation steps for bigger domain sizes (as expected without lifting).

Regarding *Strategy A*, the mean time per query increases for bigger domain sizes for all frameworks. PTP and FOKC have a similar early increase and fail on the models after augmentation steps 6 and 7, respectively. They are the only implementations working with MLNs as input. As the original models have random potentials for each argument value combination in each parfactor, the translated MLNs do not have any local symmetries, which these algorithms would be able to exploit. Generating models with many local symmetries, e.g., only two different potentials per whole parfactor, may lead to better results for FOKC and PTP, with the remaining algorithms taking longer. Another possible explanation may (of course) also be that there are bugs in implementations or employed heuristics may be improvable. One could actually use ComPI to test an implementation with random inputs for bugs or better heuristics. The lifted algorithms LJT and LVE have steeper increases for high augmentation steps and the biggest domain size. The reason lies in so-called count-conversions that have a higher complexity than normal elimination operations and become necessary starting with augmentation step 11.

   A Technical Note on Count Conversions: A count-conversion is a more involved concept of lifted inference where a logical variable is counted to remove it from the list of logical variables [13]. A count-conversion involves reformulating the parfactor, which enlarges it. A PRV is replaced by a so called counted PRV (CRV), which has histograms as range values. Consider a Boolean PRV $R(X)$ with three possible X values, then a CRV $\#_X[R(X)]$ has the range values $[0, 3]$, $[1, 2]$, $[2, 1]$ and $[3, 0]$, which denote that given a histogram $[n_1, n_2]$, n_1 ground instances of $R(X)$ have the value *true* and n_2 instances the value *false*. Given the range size r of the PRV and the domain size n of the logical variable that gets counted, the new CRV has $\binom{n+r-1}{n-1}$ range values, which lies in $O(r^n)$ [12]. In the case study, we use boolean PRVs, so $r = 2$. If n is small, the blow up by a count conversion is easily manageable. However, with large n, the blow up leads to a noticeable increase in runtimes, which is the reason why the increase in runtimes with step 11, at which point count conversion become necessary, is more noticeable with larger domain sizes.

   Given *Strategy B*, the collected times display less extreme increases over the augmentation steps compared to Strategy A. PTP and FOKC exhibit similar behaviour compared to Strategy A. Again, changing domain sizes has little effect on FOKC. LVE only manages to finish models with small domain sizes as the models become too large overall. LJT is able to finish the models even for larger augmentation steps. The reason is that runtimes of LJT mainly depend on the tree width, i.e., the models of Strategy B have roughly the same complexity during query answering for LJT. The jump between augmentation step 23 and 24 again can be explained by more count conversions occurring.

Inference Accuracy. Investigating the actual inference results presents an alternative approach to analysing collected data. Since the tested implementations all perform exact inference, we expect the implementations to obtain the same results on equivalent files and queries. Looking at accuracy allows for identifying bugs. If adding implementations of approximate inference algorithms to ComPI, one could compare accuracy of approximate inference against exact results. Figure 3 shows a comparison of probabilities queried for one (smaller) model generated for this case study. In this case, the implementations under

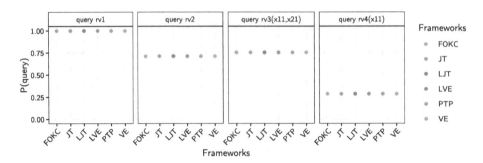

Fig. 3. Comparison of inference results between different frameworks.

investigation calculated identical results for all shown queries. However, examining models created at later augmentation steps reveals that increased model complexities lead to errors in the outputted probabilities or even to no interpretable values at all. The latter case is caused by flaws in the numerical representations: NaN values occur when potentials get so small that they become 0 if represented as a float. When normalising a distribution, the normalising constant is a sum over 0, leading to dividing 0 by 0, which results in a NaN.

5   Conclusion

We present ComPI, a benchmarking suite for comparing various probabilistic inference implementations. ComPI consists of extendable tools for automatic model generation, model translation, and inference benchmarking. A case study demonstrates the simplicity of comparative analyses carried out with ComPI. Similar analyses are needed in the evaluation of future novel algorithms in the field of probabilistic inference. The extensibility of ComPI has the potential to reduce the efforts for these evaluations.

For the tested implementations, it becomes evident that there is still a need to provide bulletproof implementations. Occurring issues range from high memory consumption to the lack of robustness regarding heuristics used by the algorithms, exact numerical representations of probabilities, or reliable handling of errors. Future work will need to address these points.

References

1. Braun, T., Möller, R.: Preventing groundings and handling evidence in the lifted junction tree algorithm. In: Kern-Isberner, G., Fürnkranz, J., Thimm, M. (eds.) KI 2017. LNCS (LNAI), vol. 10505, pp. 85–98. Springer, Cham (2017). https://doi.org/10.1007/978-3-319-67190-1_7
2. Braun, T., Möller, R.: Parameterised queries and lifted query answering. In: IJCAI 2018 Proceedings of the 27th International Joint Conference on AI, pp. 4980–4986. IJCAI Organization (2018)

3. Gogate, V., Domingos, P.: Probabilistic theorem proving. In: UAI 2011 Proceedings of the 27th Conference on Uncertainty in AI, pp. 256–265. AUAI Press (2011)
4. Kersting, K., Ahmadi, B., Natarajan, S.: Counting belief propagation. In: UAI 2009 Proceedings of the 25th Conference on Uncertainty in AI, pp. 277–284. AUAI Press (2009)
5. LeCun, Y.: Learning World Models: the Next Step Towards AI. Invited Talk at IJCAI-ECAI 2018 (2018). https://www.youtube.com/watch?v=U2mhZ9E8Fk8. Accessed 19 Nov 2018
6. Milch, B., Marthi, B., Russell, S., Sontag, D., Long, D.L., Kolobov, A.: BLOG: probabilistic models with unknown objects. In: IJCAI 2005 Proceedings of the 19rd International Joint Conference on AI, pp. 1352–1359. IJCAI Organization (2005)
7. Milch, B., Zettelmoyer, L.S., Kersting, K., Haimes, M., Kaelbling, L.P.: Lifted probabilistic inference with counting formulas. In: AAAI 2008 Proceedings of the 23rd AAAI Conference on AI, pp. 1062–1068. AAAI Press (2008)
8. Niepert, M., Van den Broeck, G.: Tractability through exchangeability: a new perspective on efficient probabilistic inference. In: AAAI 2014 Proceedings of the 28th AAAI Conference on AI, pp. 2467–2475. AAAI Press (2014)
9. Poole, D.: First-order probabilistic inference. In: IJCAI 2003 Proceedings of the 18th International Joint Conference on AI, pp. 985–991. IJCAI Organization (2003)
10. Richardson, M., Domingos, P.: Markov logic networks. Mach. Learn. **62**(1–2), 107–136 (2006). https://doi.org/10.1007/s10994-006-5833-1
11. de Salvo Braz, R., Amir, E., Roth, D.: Lifted first-order probabilistic inference. In: IJCAI 2005 Proceedings of the 19th International Joint Conference on AI, pp. 1319–1325. IJCAI Organization (2005)
12. Taghipour, N., Davis, J., Blockeel, H.: First-order decomposition trees. In: NIPS 2013 Advances in Neural Information Processing Systems, vol. 26, pp. 1052–1060. Curran Associates, Inc. (2013)
13. Taghipour, N., Fierens, D., Davis, J., Blockeel, H.: Lifted variable elimination: decoupling the operators from the constraint language. J. Artif. Intell. Res. **47**(1), 393–439 (2013)
14. Taghipour, N., Fierens, D., Van den Broeck, G., Davis, J., Blockeel, H.: Completeness results for lifted variable elimination. In: AISTATS 2013 Proceedings of the 16th International Conference on AI and Statistics, pp. 572–580. AAAI Press (2013)
15. Van den Broeck, G.: On the completeness of first-order knowledge compilation for lifted probabilistic inference. In: NIPS 2011 Advances in Neural Information Processing Systems, vol. 24, pp. 1386–1394. Curran Associates, Inc. (2011)
16. Van den Broeck, G.: Lifted inference and learning in statistical relational models. Ph.D. thesis, KU Leuven (2013)
17. Van den Broeck, G., Davis, J.: Conditioning in first-order knowledge compilation and lifted probabilistic inference. In: AAAI 2012 Proceedings of the 26th AAAI Conference on AI, pp. 1961–1967. AAAI Press (2012)
18. Van den Broeck, G., Taghipour, N., Meert, W., Davis, J., De Raedt, L.: Lifted probabilistic inference by first-order knowledge compilation. In: IJCAI 2011 Proceedings of the 22nd International Joint Conference on AI, pp. 2178–2185. IJCAI Organization (2011)

Analyzing Psychological Similarity Spaces for Shapes

Lucas Bechberger[1][(✉)] [iD] and Margit Scheibel[2]

[1] Institute of Cognitive Science, Osnabrück University, Osnabrück, Germany
lbechberger@uos.de
[2] Institute for Language and Information Science,
Heinrich-Heine-Universität Düsseldorf, Düsseldorf, Germany
scheibel@uni-duesseldorf.de

1 Background and Motivation

The cognitive framework of conceptual spaces [3] proposes to represent concepts and properties such as APPLE and ROUND as convex regions in perception-based similarity spaces. By doing so, the framework can provide a grounding for the nodes of a semantic network. In order to use this framework in practice, one needs to know the structure of the underlying similarity space. In our study, we focus on the domain of shapes. We analyze similarity spaces of varying dimensionality which are based on human similarity ratings and seek to identify directions in these spaces which correspond to shape features from the psychological literature. The analysis scripts used in our study are available at https://github.com/lbechberger/LearningPsychologicalSpaces.

Our psychological account of shapes can provide constraints and inspirations for AI approaches. For example, distances in the shape similarity spaces can give valuable information about visual similarity which can complement other measures of similarity (such as distances in a conceptual graph). Moreover, the interpretable directions in the similarity space provide means for verbalizing this information (e.g., by noting that tools are more elongated than electrical appliances). Furthermore, the shape spaces can be used in bottom-up procedures for constructing new categories, e.g., by applying clustering algorithms. Finally, membership in a category can be determined based on whether or not an item lies inside the convex hull of a given category.

2 Data Collection

We used 60 standardized black-and-white line drawings of common objects (six visually consistent and six visually variable categories with five objects each) for our experiments (see Fig. 1 for an example from each category). We collected 15 shape similarity ratings for all pairwise combinations of the images in a web-based survey with 62 participants. Image pairs were presented one after another on the screen (in random order) and subjects were asked to judge the respective

© Springer Nature Switzerland AG 2020
M. Alam et al. (Eds.): ICCS 2020, LNAI 12277, pp. 204–207, 2020.
https://doi.org/10.1007/978-3-030-57855-8_16

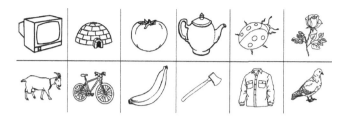

Fig. 1. Example stimuli for which various perceptual judgments were collected.

similarity on a Likert scale ranging from 1 (totally dissimilar) to 5 (very similar). The distribution of within-category similarities showed that the internal shape similarity was higher for visually consistent categories ($M = 4.18$) than for visually variable categories ($M = 2.56$; $p < .001$). For further processing, the shape similarity ratings were aggregated into a global matrix of dissimilarities by taking the mean over the individual responses and by inverting the scale (i.e., $dissimilarity(x, y) = 5 - similarity(x, y)$).

In the psychological literature, different types of perceptual features are discussed as determining the perception of complex objects, among others the line shape (LINES) and the global shape structure (FORM) [1]. We collected values for all images with respect to these two features in two experimental setups.

In a first line of experiments, we collected image-specific ratings which are based on *attentive (att)* image perception. We collected 9 ratings per image in a web-based survey with 27 participants. Groups of four images were presented one after another on the screen (in random order) together with a continuous scale representing the respective feature (LINES: absolutely straight to strongly curved; FORM: elongated to blob-like). Subjects were asked to arrange the images on the respective scale such that the position of each image in the final configuration reflected their value on the respective feature scale. The resulting values were aggregated for each image by using the median.

In a second line of experiments, we collected image-specific feature values which are based on *pre-attentive (pre-att)* image perception. This was done in two laboratory studies with 18 participants each. In both studies, the images were presented individually for 50 ms on the screen; immediately before and after the image a pattern mask was shown for 50 ms in order to prevent conscious perception of the image. Subjects were asked to decide per button press as fast as possible which value of the respective feature pertained to the critical image mostly (LINES study: straight or curved; FORM study: elongated or blob-like). The binary values (in total 18 per image for each feature) were transformed into graded values (percentage of curved and blob-like responses, respectively).

A comparison of the two types of feature values revealed a strong correlation between the judgements based on attentive and pre-attentive shape perception ($r_s = 0.83$ for LINES and $r_s = 0.85$ for FORM). In both cases, the 15 images with the highest and lowest values were used as positive and negative examples for the respective feature.

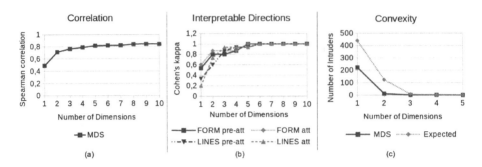

Fig. 2. Results of our analysis of the similarity spaces.

3 Analysis

We used the SMACOF algorithm [4] for performing nonmetric multidimensional scaling (MDS) on the dissimilarity matrix. Given a desired number n of dimensions, MDS represents each stimulus as a point in an n-dimensional space and arranges these points in such a way that their pairwise distances correlate well with the pairwise dissimilarities of the stimuli they represent. The SMACOF algorithm uses an iterative process of matrix multiplications to minimize the remaining difference between distances and dissimilarities.

A good similarity space should be able to reflect the psychological dissimilarities accurately. Figure 2a shows the Spearman correlation of dissimilarities and distances as a function of the number of dimensions. As we can see, a one-dimensional space is not sufficient for an accurate representation of the dissimilarities. We can furthermore observe that using more than five dimensions does not considerably improve the correlation to the dissimilarities. As a baseline, we have also computed the distances between the pixels of various downscaled versions of the images. These pixel-based distances reached only a Spearman correlation of $r_s = 0.40$ to the dissimilarities, indicating that shape similarity cannot easily be determined based on raw pixel information.

The framework of conceptual spaces assumes that the similarity spaces are based on interpretable dimensions. As distances between points are invariant under rotations, the axes of the coordinate system from the MDS solution might however not coincide with interpretable features. In order to identify interpretable directions in the similarity spaces, we trained a linear support vector machine to separate positive from negative examples for each of the psychological features. The normal vector of the separating hyperplane points from negative to positive examples and can therefore be interpreted as the direction representing this feature [2]. Figure 2b shows the quality of this separation (measured with Cohen's kappa) as a function of the number of dimensions. While a one-dimensional space again gives poor results, increasing the number of dimensions of the similarity space improves the evaluation metric. Six dimensions are always sufficient for perfect classification. Moreover, it seems like the feature FORM is found slightly earlier than LINES. Finally, we do not observe considerable differences between pre-attentive and attentive ratings.

The framework of conceptual spaces furthermore proposes that conceptual regions in the similarity space should be convex and non-overlapping. We have therefore constructed the convex hull for each of the categories from our data set. We then estimated the overlap between these conceptual regions by counting for each convex hull the number of intruder items from other categories. Figure 2c plots the overall number of these intruders as a function of the number of dimensions. As we can see, the number of intruders one would expect for randomly arranged points drops very fast with more dimensions and becomes zero in a five-dimensional space. However, the point arrangements found by MDS produce clearly less overlap between the conceptual regions than this random baseline. Overall, it seems that conceptual regions tend to be convex in our similarity spaces.

4   Discussion and Conclusions

In our study, we found that similarity spaces with two to five dimensions seem to be good candidates for representing shapes: A single dimension does not seem to be sufficient while more than five dimensions do not improve the quality of the space. The shape features postulated in the literature were indeed detectable as interpretable directions in these similarity spaces. In order to understand the similarity space for shapes even better, additional features from the literature (such as ORIENTATION) will be investigated.

The main limitations of our results are twofold: Firstly, we only consider two-dimensional line drawings in our study. Our results are therefore not directly applicable to three-dimensional real world objects. Secondly, the similarity spaces obtained through MDS can only be used for a fixed set of stimuli. In future work, we aim to train an artificial neural network on mapping also novel images to points in the shape similarity spaces (cf. [5]).

References

1. Biederman, I.: Recognition-by-components: a theory of human image understanding. Psychol. Rev. **94**(2), 115–147 (1987)
2. Derrac, J., Schockaert, S.: Inducing semantic relations from conceptual spaces: a data-driven approach to plausible reasoning. Artif. Intell. **228**, 66–94 (2015). https://doi.org/10.1016/j.artint.2015.07.002
3. Gärdenfors, P.: Conceptual Spaces: The Geometry of Thought. MIT Press, Cambridge (2000)
4. de Leeuw, J.: Recent Development in Statistics, Chap. Applications of Convex Analysis to Multidimensional Scaling, pp. 133–146. North Holland Publishing, Amsterdam (1977)
5. Sanders, C.A., Nosofsky, R.M.: Using deep-learning representations of complex natural stimuli as input to psychological models of classification. In: Proceedings of the 2018 Conference of the Cognitive Science Society, Madison (2018)

Author Index

Printed in the United States
By Bookmasters